STEALING HOME

How Artificial Intelligence Is
Hijacking the American Dream

James M. Nelson

BRC PUBLISHING HOUSE
SEATTLE, WA

For our grandchildren

TABLE OF

CONTENTS:

PREFACE

For forty years, I worked in the US banking system, spending much of my career financing what we now call main street America. I underwrote and managed billions of dollars in commercial loans, which means that I approved thousands of loan requests. Each of those requests was required to provide copies of their personal financial information.

During my career, banking changed from state and local banks to the international banking system we have today. Those of us in commercial banking had to adjust to changes in economic policies and political agendas that we could see negatively impacted America. We were firsthand witnesses to the human cost of those policies.

In early 2017 I was reading an older edition of *Forbes* magazine when the topic of wealth transference caught my attention. According to the article, the lowest 95 percent had transferred $2.5 billion every day *for more than twelve years* to the top 5 percent.

I grew up in poverty, but my children did not. Like many of you, I kept my head down, worked hard, and believed the life I was handing our next generation was going to be better than my own. However, this was not the case. It's always a struggle.

My children now have their own children, and I watch them living hectic lifestyles, working long and tiring jobs just to keep up with their bills. Their generation pays, in some cases, over 50% of their combined wages for housing, and many struggles with medical bills.

Even though I sacrificed so that my children would grow up in a middle-class family, they are nonetheless working harder than I did at their ages. The concept of what life will be like for my grandchildren is at times unimaginable.

In 2011, I completed my last assignment of cleaning up a failing bank, and I decided to shift to a new career as an independent loan broker providing financing for real estate projects, including large multifamily projects. Through that, I came to the realization that the financial industry had made subtle yet massive changes that had occurred overnight and right under my nose. The economic indicators were screaming that something was wrong; balance in the housing markets had become erratically unstable.

The conundrum of income inequality as it relates to the housing markets kept me awake at night. Therefore, at the close of 2017, I took a sabbatical and started on a research journey into the modern housing market, which led me to discover how the wealthy were taking that $2.5 billion every day—and why our children have been so affected.

In 1962 a relatively unknown author named Rachel Carson published a book called *Silent Spring*, a blistering documentary of the dangers of certain toxic pesticides and chemicals. Her research proved that the large chemical companies of the day had lied to the American public and in fact, put American people in extreme danger and caused untold numbers of deaths.

Rachel Carson cast a pebble into a pond, and it created a tsunami of changes for America. Her book led to the establishment of the EPA and other equally essential safety regulations. May our pebble be so lucky.

CHAPTER 1

IN THE BEGINNING: HUD'S HISTORY AND IMPORTANCE

SINCE 1934, FEDERAL Home Loan programs have impacted millions of lives and, until recently, almost always for the better. In fact, during the 1999 National Housing Conference when Fannie Mae surveyed a large group of urban scholars about the ten most important influences on the economic well-being of postwar America, the Housing Act of 1949 appears twice. There is little doubt that the act, which was "enacted to help eradicate slums and promote redevelopment programs and community development," had a profound effect on American cities.[1]

Today, however, cities are once again in trouble. Even after adjusting for inflation, the median rent payment rose 61 percent between 1960 and 2016. Conversely, median renter income grew only 5 percent during the same time period.[2] It comes as no surprise, then, that according to the National Low Income Housing Coalition, America has a crippling shortage of about seven million affordable rental units available to low-income renters or the severely rent-burdened.[3]

Low-income housing is simply vanishing from the marketplace. Since 1990, nationwide, more than 2.5 million apartments with rents lower than $800 per month have been upgraded into high-end condos or converted into hotels or offices.[4] Rents have been skyrocketing in metropolitan cities. Seattle, for instance, is up 53 percent from 2012. Forty-three percent of Americans—nearly 51 million households—can no longer afford the cost of housing. As a consequence, the homeless population is skyrocketing as well, up 47 percent from 2012.[5] At least ten cities on the West Coast have declared states of emergency in recent years.[6]

Yet in 2019, there was more government-backed housing debt than at any other point in US history, according to data from the Urban Institute. Fannie Mae, Freddie Mac, and the Federal Housing Administration (FHA) underwrite almost $7 trillion in mortgage-related debt, 33 percent more than before the 2008 housing crisis.[7] Why? How can there be such a shortage of affordable housing when the debt levels at the Department of Housing and Urban Development (HUD) are at all-time highs?

In short, we have an oversupply of multifamily units (apartments, condos, etc.) at the higher end of the market range (rents above $2,000 monthly), yielding vacancies nearing 10 percent. At the same time, we have a severe undersupply of affordable homes. Who is driving the housing markets? Who is making the decisions? Furthermore, who is responsible for this affordable housing crisis, and why isn't something being done about it?

Policy changes are at least partly to blame for this deplorable situation. Since the Nixon administration, HUD has been marked by a diminished federal leadership role and an effort to engage the "free (for-profit) market" in the production of low-income housing.[8] Unfortunately, since this significant change in policy, income inequality skyrocketed and is posing a substantial threat to our way of life and especially to that of the middle class. In fact, today, billionaires grow $2.5 billion wealthier every day, and those at the top enjoy a rigged system. In 2019, the richest of the rich held as large a wealth share as they did in the late 1920s before the great financial crashes. Worldwide, 2,200 billionaires took 95 percent of total income gains and maintained assets that grew 300 percent over ten years, reaching $9.1 trillion in 2018.[9] In stark contrast, 43 percent of households in the United States do not earn enough to afford a monthly budget that includes housing.

To understand how we arrived at this staggering income inequality once again, we need to acknowledge and trace the part played by the housing industry, and HUD specifically.[10] Housing markets affect everyone, and access to affordable housing undergirds our way of life.

THE HOME AND THE AMERICAN WAY OF LIFE

Home has always been a gathering spot, a sanctuary that provides safety, belonging, identity, and private space, among other things. Good health centers on having homes that are safe and free from physical hazards. We all need a place we can call home, where we can feel safe and comfortable—a place from which we leave each morning and to which we return each evening. Regardless of what place we call home, the very word strikes a deep feeling inside each of us.

When we create a space that meets our needs and expresses who we are, our lives improve. In contrast, substandard and unsatisfactory housing leads to health problems such as chronic diseases and injuries and can have harmful effects on childhood development.

Abraham Maslow, the psychologist who developed a theory of psychological health known as Maslow's hierarchy of needs,[11] argued that life satisfaction hinges on fulfilling essential basic human needs in order of priority. Housing was critical in Maslow's theory, necessary to meet the primary physiological need for warmth and rest. Whether one prefers to reside in a family-friendly suburb or a modern high-rise in the heart of the city, everyone needs a space to call home.

Location, location, location. This familiar Realtor catchphrase implies that homes can experience significant increases or decreases in value due to their location alone. The social and economic advantages in particular communities can influence health and well-being by providing access to employment opportunities and public resources, including adequate transportation, a police force that works for everybody, and access to good schools. A strong sense of community—based on trust among people within neighborhoods—has also been associated with improved health.

Our housing markets made America great. When it comes to financing the homes of our dreams, no other country offers the consumer such a buffet of options—veritable smorgasbord of prices, styles, and yes, locations. The thirty-year fixed-rate mortgage was revolutionary in its design, with its long-term amortization made possible by the government guaranteeing that loan. Taxpayers guarantee each other's mortgages, with some strings attached. However, this hasn't always been the case; in fact, the lending policies and terms used to be quite different.

1934, THE FIRST MEETING ON PUBLIC HOUSING

In January 1934, the head of the Consumers' Counsel, Frederic C. Howe, spoke at what would become the first Washington Conference on Public Housing. The task of the members was to establish a plan to provide affordable housing and clean up the slums that were breeding grounds for crime and disease during the Great Depression. This group would develop numerous housing acts and set the framework for the Department of Housing and Urban Development (HUD) we know and enjoy today. He began his speech by sharing the following story:

> Two thousand years ago, in Rome, the fire department was a private enterprise. It was owned and operated by Croesus [Crassus], the richest of the Romans. When a fire broke out, Croesus [Crassus] rushed to the fire with his [workers] to extinguish it, but nothing was done until the house owner appeared. Then there was bargaining over how much the owner would pay to have the fire put out. Ferrero, the Italian historian, tells about how it was done. At first, the price was reasonable. As time went on, however, Croesus charged what the traffic would bear. In the end, the price for extinguishing the fire was fixed at such a high point that the [home]owner accepted a small sum and turned over the property to the fire department. Neighbor-

ing house owners whose property was in danger were
also called by Croesus. They, too, were asked to pay
to see that their property was not destroyed. They, too,
paid all that the traffic would bear. Now, the net result
of this process was that Croesus became the biggest
landlord in the City of Rome. He took possession of
a great part of the city. It is hinted by the historian
that the [workers] of Croesus's started fires in order
that their master might put them out. In any event, in
a short time, he became rich and powerful enough to
be Rome's greatest money lender and to divide [unite]
the Roman world into the [F]irst [T]riumvirate [an
alliance of three men holding great political power].[12]

The point Howe makes about the need for government
oversight of business practices and intervention, especially
in the housing market, is salient. He goes on to argue that
"private capital," whose primary interest is in turning a
profit, "will not supply enough homes for persons of small
means."

1937, ROOSEVELT'S NEW DEAL

As part of Roosevelt's New Deal, Congress passed the landmark Housing Act of 1937, which set up the permanent
program that still exists today, now known as the Housing
Act of 1949. It is best remembered for its declaration that
every American deserves a "decent home and a safe living
environment."[13]

However, no sooner were the New Deal programs in place
following Roosevelt's momentous first one hundred days in

office than former president Herbert Hoover launched his offensive. The Hoover Coalition—initially called the American Liberty League—formed in 1934 in opposition to the New Deal. The League consisted of Republicans, Democrats, and business leaders who opposed the federal New Deal recovery programs. The group was unorganized yet vocal and included congressional representatives known as the Conservative Coalition. (This coalition initiated a conservative alliance that ultimately showed up to back Nixon in the 1968 presidential campaign.) The coalition's stated goal was "to defend the Constitution and defend the rights and religious liberties guaranteed by that Constitution."[14]

Since the beginning, there has been significant conflict regarding how the housing market should work. The fundamental basis of the opposing sides comes down to just who gets to control the housing markets: government (public utility) or the free market system (private utility).

Since the 1933 inception of the Home Owners' Loan Corporation (HOLC) under Roosevelt, there have been three wide-ranging areas of concern that have directed government actions in the housing industry, all three arising from the acknowledgment that government has (1) an obligation to preserve and encourage economic stability, (2) a public responsibility to help provide for the indigent, and (3) a growing interest in how the country's communities develop.[15]

In the early 1970s, attacks against government "interference" in industry and free trade began on a grand scale and included lobbying. This group of lobbyists included the National Association of Realtors (NAR), the US Chamber of Commerce, and wealthy plutocrats. Over the years they have been working diligently to undo the various aspects of the New Deal, including ending government involvement in the housing markets.[16]

From the outset, their attacks were emboldened by a labor pool trained in skills readily adapted for propaganda. Many of their lobbyists came from the Committee on Public Information (CPI), created in 1918 under the Wilson administration.[17]

The CPI trained tens of thousands of Americans in the arts and sciences as well as in propaganda and psychological warfare. After the war, many went into either advertising or military espionage. They would reassemble during World War II under Roosevelt, and their knowledge of propaganda would be mobilized on a scale never before witnessed. The methods of persuasion could be, and were, also turned to a variety of other uses, including lobbying.

But first, let's look at what led to this epic confrontation between the progressive New Dealers and those following the Hoover Doctrine. How does a New Dealer differ from a follower of Hoover? For the answer, we need to review our forgotten-yet-critical history that even today frames and impacts our housing markets.

During the 1920s, the wealthy industrial elites who controlled Congress handpicked a Supreme Court that maintained strongly pro-business, anti-labor positions. The outcome of a landmark court case (*Lochner v. New York*) in which labor unions unsuccessfully sued for a sixty-hour workweek gave rise to what became known as the Lochner era Supreme Court. Over decades this Court embodied outright judicial hostility toward labor and the working class. They struck down state-adopted economic regulations and passed numerous laws in defense of laissez-faire policies. If the wealthy elites decided any legislation infringed upon their rights to economic sovereignty or hindered their ability to make unfettered private contracts, they called upon the Supreme Court to overturn it.[18] This concept of government eventually became linked to the concept of "originalism."

ORIGINALISM

Originalism is a theory that asserts that the Constitution of the United States can only be interpreted based on the original understanding of the authors or the people at the time it was ratified. This concept views the Constitution as stable from the time of enactment, and the meaning of its contents changeable only by the steps set out in Article Five.[19]

During the late 1930s, the Republican Party had virtually collapsed after the Great Depression, having been blamed for the crisis and the lack of an effective response in the aftermath of the stock market crash and ensuing bank failures. Hoover helped to rally the party by organizing a new breed of Republican known as the Young Republicans. Hoover would spend decades rebuilding the GOP by establishing Young Republican Clubs on college campuses across the nation, including at Yale and the University of Chicago.[20]

The Hoover Doctrine was founded on the importance of unfettered access to wealth (with no regulations), and the trickle-down theory of economics. Ever since, followers of Hoover have sought to put the power of the government into the hands of the wealthy: corporations, monopolies, oligarchs, and the moneyed elite. This has been the battle since the Great Depression, when Hoover's plan to fix the economy was to invest tax dollars through partnerships with corporate America (special interests); Roosevelt's New Deal plan was to invest in and build the economy from the ground up, through the people.[21]

FHA: HOME OWNERS' LOAN CORPORATION ACT (HOLC)

Before the New Deal, the older mortgage system was based on down payments as high as 50 percent and terms as short as three to five years, which would lead to massive defaults.[22] During the Depression, the average value of homes fell some 40 percent, and the default rate jumped to about 50 percent of all households that had mortgages.[23] The American attitude against government intervention fundamentally shifted as vast numbers of people were thrown into the streets. Losses or cuts in employment, combined with the loss of their homes, caused hundreds of thousands of middle-class families to experience their first real taste of poverty.

HOLC 1933 (finalized in the 1949 Housing Act) provided mortgage assistance to struggling homeowners or would-be homeowners. In the beginning (1933), HOLC estimated that the homeowner should not pay more than 20 percent of their income toward housing. They compared the percentage to area median income (AMI), which at the time was $1,480 (annual), as a means of calculating what constituted rent burdening.[24] HOLC helped homeowners with mortgages currently in default by providing them with money or by refinancing their mortgages.

Within two years, HOLC had refinanced nearly 20 percent of all urban households in the nation. Ultimately, more than 800,000 people repaid their HOLC loans, and many repaid them early. By the HOLC's final year in 1936, it had provided just over a million new mortgages and had lent out approximately $350 billion ($750 billion today).[25]

HUD: ITS EVOLUTION AND MISSION

Deteriorating conditions in cities was another New Deal concern. Direct federal involvement in physically shaping cities was unknown before 1949. The Housing Act changed that. No longer was slum removal solely a local matter. The federal government now funded and managed city-building projects. Despite some continuing controversy, one of the Act's legacies is the fact that most Americans now accept the idea that the federal government has a legitimate role in local housing and development issues.[26] Thus the ground-work was laid for establishing HUD, a cabinet-level government agency tasked with developing policies and regulations for housing and urban development.

HOUSING FOR VETERANS POST-WORLD WAR II

The next stepping stones toward HUD came as a series of acts addressing needs in the aftermath of World War II. Wartime resettlement of the labor force to urban centers, combined with the increased marriage rates of the postwar years, led to a severe housing shortage following the war. Federal legislation to aid in this objective included the Servicemen's Readjustment Act (1944), the Veterans' Emer-

gency Housing Act (1946), the Price Control Extension
Act (1946), and the Housing and Rent Act of 1947. Post-
1945 suburbia was created by HOLC's, and later the FHA's,
low-down-payment, long-term, fully amortizing, fixed-rate
mortgages issued by federally chartered institutions. The
FHA created the financial instrument that would help raise
American homeownership from 44 percent in 1940 to the
near-record 66 percent it is today.[27]

As can be seen in this brief overview, the general trend
has been toward broad participation by the federal government in housing, which started during the Depression
and extended to a dominant position in post–World War
II years.[28]

This trend proved to be beneficial to the American public,
and HUD was officially established in September 1965 when
Lyndon B. Johnson signed the Department of Housing and
Urban Development Act into law. HUD's purpose, as outlined in its current mission statement, is "to create strong,
sustainable, inclusive communities and quality affordable
homes for all. HUD is working to strengthen the housing
market to bolster the economy and protect consumers,
meet the need for quality, affordable rental homes, utilize
housing as a platform for improving quality of life, [and]
build inclusive and sustainable communities free from discrimination."[29] The Housing Act of 1949 allows the federal
government to assist in normalizing the housing market,
saying "private enterprise shall be encouraged to serve as
it can."[30]

Is HUD as a government agency living up to its mission
statement? We look into this question in Chapter 3.

HISTORY OF HOUSING DISCRIMINATION

Housing shortages once again became a pressing concern, and in 1968 Congress found "that the supply of the Nation's housing was not increasing rapidly enough to meet the national housing goal, established in the Housing Act of 1949." To achieve that goal, Congress established a production schedule "within the next decade of the construction or rehabilitation of 26 million housing units, 6 million of these for low and moderate-income families," and enacted a further set of programs to assist in meeting the production schedule for low- and moderate-income families.[31]

However, the battle between the New Dealers and Hooverites would lead to negative consequences within the housing markets, as seen, for instance, in the proliferation of ghettos. Ghettos didn't just happen by accident. They developed as a direct result of specifically racist government programs, of economic and labor factors that harshly deprived black workers, and perhaps most distressing, of actual racial violence that made it impractical for blacks to live in other neighborhoods.[32]

Another major contributor was the discriminatory business practices of Realtors. For example, countless local Realtor associations would block anyone who wasn't a white male from becoming a member (and gaining access to MLS listings and other essential resources) as a standard way of doing business. Frequently their bylaws clearly stated that blacks, women, Jews, and other specifically excluded groups were not approved to join. Banned from joining traditional Realtor organizations in their communities, black real estate brokers formed their own boards to help their professional interests.

Meanwhile, NAR (National Association of Realtors) opposed fair housing legislation nationally during the 1950s and 1960s, and even after the passage of the Fair Housing Act, many local boards continued to prevent or discourage black real estate brokers from becoming Realtor members.[33]

As for financing, lenders would use redlining, the practice of denying a creditworthy applicant a loan for housing in a particular neighborhood even though the applicant may otherwise be eligible for the loan. The term refers to the presumed practice of mortgage lenders of drawing red lines around portions of a map to indicate areas or neighborhoods in which they do not want to make loans. Another behind-the-scenes maneuver was racial steering—deliberately guiding loan applicants or potential purchasers toward or away from certain types of loans or geographic areas because of race.[34]

Such seemingly minor discriminatory practices have had significant consequences. In his widely praised book *Segregation by Design*, Richard Rothstein, Distinguished Fellow of the Economic Policy Institute, attests, "This enormous difference in (wealth) is almost entirely attributable to federal housing policy implemented through the 20th century."[35]

In 2004, the high point of homeownership, nearly half of all African American families owned a home, according to census data. That record figure was still one-third less than housing rates for whites. However, since 2017, that number has fallen to 43 percent.[36] These numbers matter because, in the United States, purchasing a home is fundamental to a sense of stability and self-worth, the basis of achieving the American Dream. Forty-two percent of the net worth of all households consists of equity in their homes—their single largest asset. When HOLC made it possible for most Americans to fund the acquisition of their own home, it fundamentally paved the way for millions of Americans to start their own wealth-building.

Unfortunately, that did not include families of non-white Americans who were targeted by discriminatory practices in real estate markets. In 1995, the median white family had over eight times the net worth of the median black family. The gap is even more significant for Latinos: the median white household had over twelve times the wealth of the median Latino family.[37]

This is not all the fault of Realtor associations or NAR by any means. HUD itself fell victim to political pressures. After he became president, Richard Nixon chose George Romney to be his HUD Secretary. Romney, who sincerely lamented "the widening economic gulf between the races, which left many whites residing in comfortable suburbs while poor blacks endured a harsh life in urban slums," was determined "to move blacks from cities into suburbs." It was reported that Romney and other "HUD officials had construed the Fair Housing Act very broadly, as a mandate for integration." In fact, Romney's general counsel, David O. Maxwell, wrote that "HUD had an obligation to consider the extent to which its every action will, in fact, open up new, non-segregated housing opportunities that will contribute to decreasing the effects of past housing discrimination."[38]

This push toward desegregation in housing did not sit well with all the electorate. Nixon's supporters in the South and in white Northern suburbs took their complaints directly to the president. Nixon intervened immediately, and on February 2, 1972, he froze all HUD programs.[39]

Not surprisingly, efforts to curtail housing discrimination have rarely borne fruit. In 2015, Nikole Hannah-Jones reported in ProPublica that HUD's most extensive application of grants to needy communities had delivered $137 billion to more than 1,200 communities since 1974. To qualify for the funds, cities were required to identify obstacles to fair housing, keep records of their findings to overcome them, and certify that they did not discriminate. Yet Hannah-Jones could find only two occasions since Romney's time in which the department followed through on withholding money from communities for violating the Fair Housing Act. In several instances, records show, HUD sent grants to communities even *after* they'd been found by courts to have promoted segregated housing or been sued by the US Department of Justice.[40]

HOW FINANCING AFFORDABLE HOUSING WORKS: P3S AND HCVS

Today, most HUD programs are structurally public-private partnerships (P3s) or have some public-private aspects. The nation's foremost low-income tenant assistance subsidy, housing choice vouchers (HCVs), can be viewed as a grand P3: each voucher involves a contract between a local public housing authority (PHA) and a private entity.

All presidents from Nixon through George H. W. Bush used public-private partnerships (P3s) to devolve housing programs to local control, introducing voucher assistance and making it permanent. Under Presidents Bill Clinton through Barack Obama, HUD relied on P3s as a key policy tool to promote mixed-finance affordable housing and place-based development.[41]

In Chapter 2, we will look more closely into public-private partnerships, including the Multifamily Tax Exemption program (MFTE), one such P3 program that requires property owners to set aside 20 percent of their units for affordable housing. In exchange, the property is exempted from most real estate taxes. However, the underlying question remains: Who really benefits from these partnerships?

WHY WE NEED AFFORDABLE HOUSING

Frederic Howe's riveting story at the first Washington Conference on Public Housing about the Roman Crassus, who acquired his lucrative real estate holdings by setting fires to homes, comes to mind. In his speech, Howe went on to share the beginning framework of what would become HUD's mission statement—its Federalist papers, if you will: "We want, and we must have, attractive low-cost housing for those in the lower-income groups. The need for proper low-cost housing is not confined to the cities. But we do have a right to require that every child born into the world shall have an equal opportunity under the law with every other child. Every child is entitled to protection from the influence of vice and crime and physical degeneration."[42]

Is Howe's story of Crassus relevant today? Are our lower-income citizens protected from the unscrupulous machinations of the wealthy and powerful? Howe's concern was right on target. Government oversight of business practices and intervention, especially in the housing market, is absolutely necessary. As he noted in 1934, "private capital," whose primary interest is in turning a profit, "will not supply enough homes for persons of small means."

The same questions Howe raised nearly a century ago apply today: Does every child born into this country have an equal opportunity under the law with every other child? Are all of our children equally protected from "the influence of vice and crime and physical degeneration"? Does every one of our children have a safe place to lay his or her head?

Consider the following facts:

HOMELESSNESS: The homeless population in larger metro areas soared 47 percent between 2012 and 2017, and in Seattle, Washington, it increased by 16 percent in 2018 alone.[43]

Imagine a single mother from an impoverished background who had to rush her ill daughter to the hospital. With hospital bills mounting, she cannot make her rent payment. She works long hours at Walmart, earning less than fourteen dollars per hour. Her only hope of improving her life is through public housing, but there is a four-year waiting list. "Please," she pleads with her landlord, "I'll try to work a second job for payment. Just don't throw my children into the streets. Don't burn down their chance to live in a home." At least ten cities on the West Coast have declared states of emergency in recent years. And children are twice as likely to be homeless as adults.[44]

SKYROCKETING HOUSING COSTS: Growth in wages has been nonexistent, yet housing costs have skyrocketed, threatening to destabilize affordable housing all across America. From

2012 to 2017, one-bedroom-apartment rents soared 53 percent, according to Dupre + Scott Apartment Advisors.[45]

Imagine a single young man from an impoverished background who has worked his way through college but acquired significant student loan debt along the way. Even after graduating with honors, he works long hours at Amazon, making less than twenty dollars per hour. Now with student debt bills mounting, he cannot keep up on rent payments. "Please," he pleads with his landlord, "I just need two extra weeks to make the rent payment. Please don't throw me into the streets. I have nowhere to go."

In Washington, tenants can be evicted for missing one monthly payment by only four days—in Seattle, 45 percent of eviction filings were for missing rent for one month or less.[46]

"Please," they plead. "Don't burn down my chance to live in a home."

STEALING HOME

Thus far, we have explored the complex and often controversial legacy of the 1949 act that shaped the postwar housing and urban-policy landscape. We have further noted how the changes under President Nixon in the 1970s effectively shifted the burden of affordable housing back to the for-profit housing markets. This book will go on to answer whether there is a correlation between the Nixon policy changes and the ballooning income inequality in our housing markets. It also shows how the use of Artificial Intelligence (AI) technology is a factor in the rapidly escalating rental rates in metropolitan markets and the mounting homelessness that we see in these same markets.

In fact, the primary subject of this book is the implementation and control of Artificial Intelligence–driven technology in the multifamily housing markets, and how the technology interacts with tenants and the world at large. The housing markets affect everyone, and the American housing market is at imminent risk of failure. Artificial Intelligence–driven technology is a game changer. It has disrupted each and every industry it has entered, including mega-industries like Amazon and Netflix, to name just two.

Currently, property managers use a common operating platform: the RealPage platform. We will break down the four primary categories of solutions the platform offers and explore how the RealPage platform—particularly its database, Experian RentBureau—allows property managers and property owners to drive efficiency and execution by sharing and accessing massive amounts of data to prescreen renters, collect unpaid debt, and maximize their return on investment (ROI). The software also includes a lease transaction–driven platform that provides complete transparency (in real time) into current rents and rental survey data sourced from over 13 million apartment units (active leases) in over four hundred markets across the country—and that's just the beginning.[47]

The multifamily real estate market is a $12 trillion industry,[48] and the capability for property managers to make better-quality AI data–driven decisions can save time and earn vast sums of wealth. What is this technology, and what are technology developers promising in exchange for the billions of dollars property managers are investing in it?

Originally this book was written as a four-study review of the multifamily housing markets, each study focusing on one part of the four stages of the life cycle of properties. Currently, such a review does not exist, as most studies only include a single segment of the four-stage whole. The sum of the four studies provided here offers a clearer picture of what was and still is happening in the markets and the industry, and how various segments interact to create our current affordable-housing crises.

FIGURE 1.

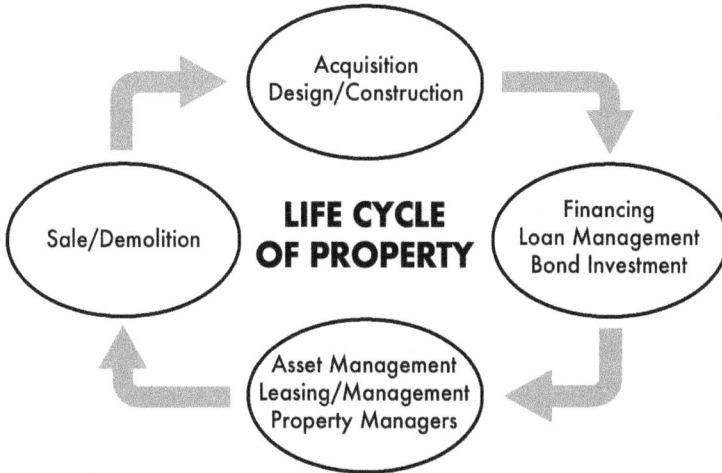

LIFE CYCLE OF PROPERTY

Acquisition
Design/Construction

Financing
Loan Management
Bond Investment

Asset Management
Leasing/Management
Property Managers

Sale/Demolition

The research brings to light the new multifamily housing market that now exists; most people are unaware of the extensive yet subtle dramatic changes that have occurred over the past few years.

The first study sets out to answer four questions about housing markets.

- First, to determine the type and nature of property managers, the role they perform, and how they impact the housing markets.

- Second, to discover and understand the Artificial Intelligence–driven (AI) technology they are currently using.

- Third, to ascertain what the developers of those technologies promise to deliver to significantly improve the bottom line—the return on investment (ROI).

- Fourth, to determine the consequences to tenants of utilizing the technology in the marketplace. Simply put, what about the children?

In the following chapters, we will consider the following questions: How has the technology been implemented, who controls the technology, and how has it impacted the tenants compared to the property owners' ever-increasing profitability, especially given the fact that the property managers are now organized as vertical trusts? (According to the Federal Trade Commission, most vertical trusts are illegal.)

The second study's objective was to determine whether HUD and, more specifically, the Enterprises, are administering their underwriting programs for loans following HUD regulations, policies, and procedures. Additionally, the study examines whether HUD is fulfilling its mission statement for affordable housing.

The study also discusses how the secondary markets work, and it then takes a closer look at what is happening today in the housing markets. Do we see a repeat of HUD's role in another pending economic crash, or has HUD been tamed? What is behind those loans and offsetting bonds?

How solid are they? The 2008 Great Recession saw nearly 30 percent of multifamily commercial mortgage-backed securities (CMBS) loans end in default, and the entire multifamily housing sector suffered catastrophic losses.

Nevertheless, today's rental incomes continue to show an ever-increasing profit margin based on rental rate increases. Perhaps the more important question to ask is, are those ever-rising rental rates sustainable? I have examined some of those multifamily loans and report on the findings.

The third study looks at the Consumer Financial Protection Bureau (CFPB). Who are they, what is their purpose, and why are they essential to the American taxpayer and consumer? It further investigates the story line of the Trump administration's role in the destruction of the CFPB—in a case currently before the US Supreme Court at the time of this writing, which has the intent to destroy the only regulator between AI technology and the consumer.

The fourth study centers on the current status of HUD and the Government Sponsored Enterprises (GSEs)—Fannie Mae and Freddie Mac—and the drive to privatize them. HUD is acquiring the same AI technology (RealPage) that property managers utilize in the multifamily housing markets. The study includes HUD's decision to change the disparate impact rule, a move that fair housing advocates claim is part of the Trump administration's effort to "gut" federal protections against housing discrimination. Do they intend to grant authorization to third-party providers to allow the discrimination to be hidden within the algorithms of the technology? Also of great importance are the 425 records wherein the Office of Inspector General (OIG) weighs in about what is currently happening at the Enterprises, and this administration's rush to privatize them.

The fundamental findings of these four studies indicate that the greatest threat America faces today lies within who gets to control the AI technology, not only in the marketplace but in the housing markets as well. Put simply, the fight now is over the future control of the technology and who will benefit, corporate America or the American taxpayers. Will it be the free market, for-profit business interests, or can people claim their rights as citizens to utilize the public utility at a fair price, one which benefits the consumer? We've witnessed what corporate America will do when faced with financial decisions; they always engineer ever more creative ways to bilk the consumers, generally at the expense of the taxpayers.

CONFLICTS OF INTEREST

In conclusion, allow me to make one final observation. A conflict of interest arises when a business or person becomes untrustworthy as a result of a clash between personal or self-serving interests and the interests of those by whom the person has been entrusted with a position of authority and prescribed duties or responsibilities. Such a conflict occurs when a business or person has a vested interest, such as money, position, knowledge, connections, or reputation, that puts into question whether their actions, judgment, and/or decision-making can truly be unbiased.[49]

A conflict of interest can also occur when a person must satisfy two different individuals or groups whose objectives are at odds with each other. In most situations, serving one individual or group will injure the other. So those of us who wish to be ethical people must deliberately avoid situations where we benefit ourselves by being untrustworthy to others.

Conflicts of interest have plagued our government since its inception. What would happen to the consumers should the AI technology be controlled by a large financial group with strong ties inside the government? Conflicts of interest. It has happened before (as outlined in the 1934 Pecora report, detailed in Chapter 5). Chapter 8 delves into the conflicts of interest associated with the implementation of the AI technology in the GSEs (Government Sponsored Enterprises) and traces the chain of command leading to the Shadow Group, my label for those hidden entities in charge of implementing the technology in the housing markets. This book will further detail whether a correlation exists between the use of AI technology, the skyrocketing rental rates in metropolitan markets, and the ballooning homelessness in these same markets. Then we will discover if there is a correlation between the Trump administration's role in the destruction of the CFPB—the only regulator between AI technology and the consumer—and their drive to privatize the Enterprises (Fannie Mae and Freddie Mac).

One last note on the method. While working as a federal bank examiner, I used the principle of Occam's razor, which gives precedence to simplicity, positing that when competing theories exist, the simplest explanation is usually correct.

CHAPTER 2

BLESSED ARE THE CHILDREN

ACCORDING TO THE National Low Income Housing Coalition, America has a crippling shortage of about seven million affordable rental units available to low-income renters or the severely rent-burdened.[1] Low-income housing is simply vanishing from the marketplace. Since 1990, more than 2.5 million apartments nationwide with rents lower than $800 per month have been upgraded into high-end condos or converted into hotels or offices.[2]

Growth in wages has been nonexistent, yet housing costs have skyrocketed, threatening to destabilize affordable housing all across America. In San Francisco, any available, reasonably priced housing quickly disappears. "It's not just techies fighting over $5,000 apartments," says Matt Schwartz, chief executive officer of the nonprofit California Housing Partnership. "The competition at the bottom end is fierce."[3] Top housing officials report that between 1987 and 2015, the number of very low-income renters grew by 6 million.[4]

Furthermore, as of early 2019, there were 8.5 million mobile homes in America, nearly 10 percent of the housing market.[5] Historically, the Mobile Home Community (MHC)

(also known as "parks") was a reliable source of affordable housing, especially in rural America. But that was then,
and this is now.

In 2016, Havenpark Capital, a Utah-based real estate
investment firm, acquired mobile home parks in the Iowa
City and Des Moines metro areas and began planned rent
increases. Rents at Golfview Mobile Home Park increased
by 58 percent, and rents at Midwest Country Estates
increased by 69 percent,[6] indications of a new trend in the
mobile home industry.

According to the United Way ALICE Project, nearly 51
million households—43 percent of households in the United
States—cannot afford housing in their monthly budgets.
This includes the 34.7 million families that the United
Way dubs "ALICE"—Asset Limited, Income Constrained,
Employed. This group accounts for 66 percent of the labor
force in the US, and makes less than twenty dollars per hour,
much less than what they need "to survive in the modern
economy," the study noted.[7]

In a 2017 poll highlighting the number of people living
in poverty, nearly 44 percent of respondents said they could
not cover an unexpected $400 emergency expense or would
have to rely on borrowing or selling something to do so.[8]

This segment of the population is proliferating as income
inequality continues to escalate. Ever-shrinking paychecks
become ever less likely to meet monthly obligations, leaving
people exposed and vulnerable to predation. They are just
one hospital bill away from living with family or friends,
subsidized housing, or on the streets. These are desperate
circumstances in which to care for and raise a family.

In this chapter, we will discuss affordable housing, including what exactly affordable housing is and how it is mea-

sured. We will also look at various economic indicators, such as area median income (AMI), cost (rent) burdened, affordable but not available homes, and how such measurements affect the renting population.

To accomplish this, I will analyze one of the programs established by the Department of Housing and Urban Development (HUD) to assist in the affordability crisis: the Multifamily Tax Exemption (MFTE) program. This will be accomplished through a study of the city of Seattle, Washington. Seattle, like most cities, has been battling a crisis in affordable housing.

In this study, we will consider whether the HUD programs are meeting their objectives and program goals. This chapter shares the results of my affordable-housing study, detailing how Seattle has elected to utilize, among other tools, the MFTE program as part of its mixture of plans designed to meet its increasing needs for affordable housing.

More specifically, the results of my study will determine if those programs meet the city's intended purposes and just how effective the programs are. The city has a responsibility to its taxpayers, per a 2014 city audit of the program, to provide a cost-benefit analysis. I will share the details from the cost-benefit-analysis study to determine if the program costs offer sufficient benefit for the lost tax revenues, a measurement also known as tax shifting.

WHAT IS AFFORDABLE HOUSING?

In this study, "affordable housing" refers to housing units constructed in total or in part with tax subsidies and held for low-income tenants. For reasons of measuring the public and monetary outcomes of affordable housing, the definition is also used to describe housing acquired with vouchers that offer rental assistance to low-income households.

WHAT IS SUBSIDIZED HOUSING?

Subsidized housing, formerly known as public housing, is housing that is made available at below-market rates through government subsidies. Unlike other government programs, such as food stamps or Medicaid, housing subsidies are not an entitlement and are typically limited and challenging to acquire. Most communities have long waiting lists for housing assistance.[9]

For example, in May 2017, reporters for *NPR's All Things Considered* and PBS' *Frontline* traveled to Dallas, Texas, and met Nena Eldridge, who lived in a small bungalow. She paid $550 each month, just about the cheapest she could locate. After an injury left her unable to work, the only income she received was a $780 monthly disability check. Therefore, she had to make tough financial choices, like living without running water.

A building two miles from her house provided subsidized housing with rents of $200 or $300, but it had a waiting list up to four years long. "I'm tired, but I don't have nowhere to go, and I don't have enough money to do it," she said, fighting back the tears. But she added, "I'm not living on the streets. I'm not homeless." Eldridge was among the 11 million people nationwide making these kinds of choices every day.[10]

WHAT IS AREA MEDIAN INCOME (AMI)?

AMI is the midpoint of a region's income distribution—half of the families in a region earn more than the median, and half earn less. For housing policy, income thresholds are set relative to the area median income, such as 50 percent of the AMI, to identify households eligible to live in income-restricted housing units and assess the affordability of housing units to low-income households.

HUD defines cost-burdened families as those "who pay more than 30 percent of their income for housing" and "may have difficulty affording necessities such as food, clothing, transportation, and medical care." A severe rent burden is defined as paying more than 50 percent of one's income on rent.[11]

Therefore, qualifications for these types of units necessitate a household's income be at or below these qualifying levels:

- Low-income level: 80 percent of the area's median income (AMI) or 100 percent of AMI in high-cost areas.

- Moderate-income level: 115 percent of the area AMI, or 150 percent of AMI in high-cost areas.

The Department of Housing and Urban Development calculates each area's AMI and adapts it to the tenant family size.[12] For example, in Figure 1, AMI for a family of four in King County is based on an annual income of $103,400. A family of four earning 80 percent AMI has a yearly salary of $80,250 and can pay monthly housing costs of $2,006 without being cost-burdened. That same family earning 30 percent AMI would calculate a monthly housing cost of $803. However, the average rent in King County at the time was $2,432 per month.[13]

FIGURE 1.

HUD 2017 HOUSEHOLD INCOME LIMITS

	1 Person	2 People	4 People
30% Area Median Income			
Household Income	$22,500	$25,700	$32,100
Corresponding Monthly Rent	$563	$643	$803
50% Area Median Income			
Household Income	$34,450	$42,800	$53,500
Corresponding Monthly Rent	$936	$1,070	$1,338
80% Area Median Income			
Household Income	$56,200	$64,200	$80,250
Corresponding Monthly Rent	$1,405	$1,605	$2,006
Est. Corresponding Purchase Price	$260,400	$297,400	$371,800
125% Area Median Income			
Household Income	$93,625	$107,000	$133,750
Corresponding Monthly Rent	$2,341	$2,675	$3,344
Est. Corresponding Purchase Price	$433,700	$495,700	$619,600

Source: "Final Report and Recommendations for King County, WA," Regional Affordable Housing Task Force, revised March, 2019, https://www.kingcounty. gov/~/media/initiatives/affordablehousing/documents/report/RAH_Report_Final. ashx?la=en.

Understanding how local pay scales impact housing is a critical step in understanding the affordable housing crisis. In most metropolitan areas today, workers earning 80 percent of AMI cannot find and secure housing. However, what about those making under 50 percent or those 66 percent making under twenty dollars an hour? What about them and their families?

COST BURDENING

Cost burdening is one of the critical economic indicators measuring the ability to cover rent costs as a percentage of income. For example, in a study from the King County task force on affordable housing, between 2013 to 2017, the county grew by 32,000 citizens each year; nonetheless, only 10,100 housing units were added each year. From 2006 to 2016, 60 percent of families earned $125,000 or more, while 18 percent earned $50,000 or less annually. Middle-income earners made up only 22 percent of new households.[14]

These inequalities are most glaring when observing low-income workers who are severely cost-burdened, spending more than 50 percent of their wages on housing. These people continuously battle to meet housing costs and are at a high risk of homelessness.

The study I completed revealed that the state of Washington has a massive housing shortage of 225,000 units. The housing shortage has led to severe cost burdening, diminishing homeownership, stifling traffic congestion, negative environmental impacts, gentrification, displacement, growing housing volatility, and homelessness. In every county, at least 25 percent of households experience cost burdening, and in the lion's share of counties, over 30 percent of households are severely cost-burdened. These burdens fall unfairly on those who are most at risk. For families making 51 to 80 percent of AMI in Washington state, 44 percent experience severe cost burdening.[15]

As rent costs have shot up, countless families are left behind. Low-income households (those making 80 percent or less of AMI), must fight individually to locate and hold a home they can afford.[16]

FIGURE 2:

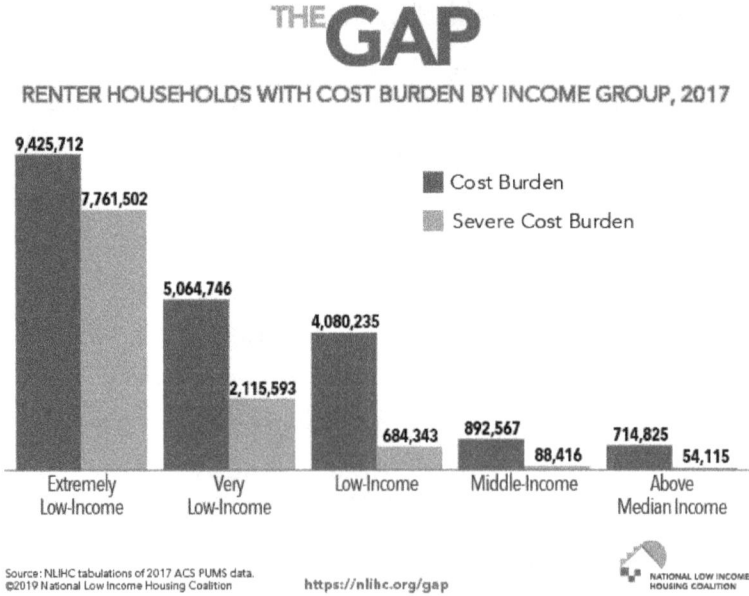

THE**GAP**

RENTER HOUSEHOLDS WITH COST BURDEN BY INCOME GROUP, 2017

Source: NLIHC's *"The Gap: A Shortage of Affordable Homes 2019,"* NLIHC tabulations of 2017 ACS PUMS data. 2019, https://nlihc.org/resource/fact-week-millions-more-lowest-income-renter-households-are-housing-cost-burdened-any.

A severely cost-burdened, low-income family of four with a monthly income of $1,839, for example, has $690 remaining for all other non-housing expenses after renting an average two-bedroom apartment at the fair market rent of $1,149. The US Department of Agriculture's 2018 thrifty food budget for a family of four (two adults and two school-aged children) is $640 per month, leaving only $50 for transportation, childcare, and other necessities.[17]

Furthermore, the GAP study found that only 35 affordable and accessible rental homes exist for every 100 extremely low-income renter households, and 56 exist for every 100 renting households earning 50 percent or below of AMI. There are 93 and 101 affordable and available rental homes for every 100 renting households earning 80 percent or below of AMI or 100 percent or below of AMI, respectively.[18] In Chapter 4, we will look at the housing markets in detail and what is causing this shortage and what is being done to assist these renters.

AFFORDABLE, BUT NOT NECESSARILY AVAILABLE

Another massive problem severely rent-burdened families face is commonly referred to as a housing mismatch analysis; this is the method used to ascertain whether a shortage of affordable housing units meets the needs of extremely low-, very low-, and low-income residents. A mismatch arises when the affordable units that do exist are not available to those who need them, or there is some combination of these factors. A mismatch often occurs when higher-income households occupy units that lower-income families could afford. It can also happen if affordable units are vacant or otherwise held off the market, or if the affordable units are not located where they are needed.

For example, higher-income families can inhabit rental homes in the open market that would be affordable to lower-income families, rendering them unavailable for households with lower wages. Rental units are both reasonably priced and accessible if they are affordable to families with wages below the defined income level and are presently vacant or occupied by a household with wages below the defined income level.

Of the 7.5 million affordable rental units currently held for extremely low-income families, 3.5 million are tied up by higher-income tenants, rendering them inaccessible to extremely low-income renters. Hence, only 4 million affordable and existing rental units are currently available to 11.2 million extremely low-income renter households. This results in a shortage of approximately 7.2 million affordable and accessible rental homes, or only 35 for every 100 extremely low-income renter households.[19]

WHAT IS HAPPENING TO AFFORDABLE HOUSING TODAY?

The extreme scarcity of rental homes affordable and available to the lowest-wage family units precedes the Great Recession but has deteriorated since. In 2017, the Joint Center for Housing Studies revealed that between 2005 and 2015, the total number of homes leasing for $2,000 or more per month increased by 97 percent, or 6.7 million housing units, while the inventory of rental units costing $800 or less dropped by 2 percent, bringing the total drop in 2011–2017 to approximately 4 million units.

The government's approach to the crisis has mainly focused on two avenues: (1) providing vouchers that low-income renters use to help pay rent to private landlords, and (2) providing funding (primarily in the form of tax credits) to increase the production of affordable housing.[20]

An extensive national survey called the American Housing Survey, sponsored by HUD and conducted by the Census Bureau, was completed in 2018 by more than 120,000 households in 25 metropolitan areas, including about 3,000 in Seattle. All told, the rent-subsidized units added up to 12.6 percent of the total rental-housing stock in the Seattle area. Among the 25 metro areas included in the survey, Seattle ranked nineteenth, well into the bottom half.[21]

The data reveal that nearly 75,800 families in the Seattle metro area have their rents reduced through some type of subsidy. Roughly half of the households received a subsidy from the government, such as a housing voucher. About one-third lived in a property owned by the public housing authorities in that area. The rest had reduced rent through some other program or agency that required income verification.[22]

It is critical to recognize that without housing investments for the most impoverished communities with vulnerable populations, increases in homelessness, illness, and mortality will occur. Perhaps for this reason, historically, various federal programs have targeted or provided more significant resources to communities with the most need.

There has been a great deal of controversy growing within the HUD builder/investor tax-exempt programs regarding whether the programs really benefit the rent-burdened, or if the benefit is actually directed to the investors. In Chapter 4, I will discuss what is happening in the markets today and whether HUD is meeting its responsibilities in building sufficient affordable housing.

THE MULTIFAMILY TAX EXEMPTION PROGRAM

Mission: "To expand the inventory of affordable Multifamily Housing projects within the city for low-income households and moderate-income households, and to promote fair housing, provide housing choice, and address displacement."[23]

THE MFTE PROGRAM HAS THREE GOALS:

1. To aid in establishing residential building projects in cost-burdened neighborhoods with insufficient building activity and minimal affordable housing construction.
2. To assist in the construction of affordable-housing projects in urban neighborhoods by stimulating housing construction by lowering operating costs and thereby improving profitability.
3. To help nonprofit housing entities that serve low- and moderate-income earners who do not qualify for the state's other low-income-housing property tax exemptions.

INCOME AND RENT RESTRICTIONS:

MFTE units are income- and rent-restricted, as established by a percentage of the AMI. The AMI percent is controlled by two factors: (1) the type of unit and (2) the period in which the owner or applicant applies to the tax exemption program.[24]

THE BENEFIT TO BUILDERS: TAX-EXEMPT STATUS:

Developers or builders may apply for an eight- or twelve-year property tax incentive for constructing or rehabilitating affordable multifamily housing units. The twelve-year exemption requires owners to offer at least 20 percent of their units as affordable housing. Cities have the authority to approve or reject individual projects. The preference has no maturity date. The program provides a tax exemption on the residential improvements of multifamily projects that meet those guidelines. Over the past four years, an average of $1.1 billion in new construction value is exempted from taxes each year.[25]

MFTE properties must make their best effort to lease designated units to income-eligible households during the compliance period. Typically, this requires that owners lease units to income-qualified tenants at affordable rents before applying for the Final Certificate of Tax Exemption. The process confirms that the designated units comply from the beginning of the compliance period.

IS THE MFTE A MARKET DRIVER OR A BENEFACTOR?

Through a case study of Seattle, I sought to determine whether the MFTE program was responsible for generating the current growth in multifamily housing projects and, therefore, worth the loss of tax revenue. The city of Seattle is scarcely alone in confronting a massive shortage of affordable housing. It's a national challenge, and all of the larger metropolitan areas in the US are struggling to provide sufficient low-income housing to meet the demand.

My case study is limited to the MFTE program. However, it's essential to acknowledge that another program established to increase affordable housing, the Low-Income Housing Tax Credit (LIHTC), has been a critical policy tool for preserving and expanding the supply of affordable rental housing. Between 1987 and 2015, 45,905 projects and 2.97 million housing units have been placed in service.[26]

WHAT ARE THE GOALS FOR MFTE HOUSING UNITS?

The goals are to increase housing supply and other support for the lowest-income households. This will both secure housing stability for these households and also reduce pressure on existing and future housing, improving housing access for those of all income levels across the region.[27]

The city of Seattle, based on its assessments, needed 156,000 more affordable homes in 2018 and another 88,000 affordable homes by 2040 to ensure that no low-income or working households are cost-burdened. In total, then, Seattle needs to build, preserve, or subsidize 244,000 new homes over twenty years if they are to guarantee all low-income family units have a crime-free and safe home that costs less than 30 percent of their income.[28]

Seattle has a plan to continue its growth of affordable housing units. The city has made a commitment to complete its plans. However, the economy will continue to play a key role in the city's desire to meet its obligations to its most vulnerable citizens.[29]

IS THE CITY OF SEATTLE MEETING ITS
TOTAL-UNITS-PRESERVED GOAL?

Seattle's MFTE program is a vital tool to increase the amount of affordable housing, reduce transportation costs, and help fulfill the city's affordable-housing goals. Because the MFTE program limits the number of years the tax-exemption exists, the biggest problem is the likelihood that the owners will exit the program once the tax-exemption status ends, regardless of whether or not the city offers an extension.

Since the MFTE program's inception, 11 projects containing 451 total affordable units were withdrawn from the program at the end of the period. Currently, Seattle faces the effects of having lost another 2,000 units in 2019, which, if and when they are lost, will toss families into a housing nightmare. Simply put, those properties terminating the MFTE program would raise rents from 80 percent AMI to the median market rent, a $325 increase per month. Furthermore, the city's economy would see $7.8 million less in annual available discretionary spending from these households, and families would lose $7.8 million in savings for needed expenses.[30]

IS THE CITY OF SEATTLE MEETING ITS AFFORDABILITY GOALS?

In December 2018, Seattle's mayor, Jenny Durkan, unveiled the biggest low-income housing increase in Seattle history, an investment of over $75 million to build and preserve affordable homes across the city. In total, the mayor proposed targeting approximately 4,000 new affordable homes by 2022, with immediate investment to support the construction of ten new buildings, housing 1,197 apartments, and preserve nine existing buildings, housing 238 apartments. "Too many people are getting pushed out of Seattle and can't afford to live here," said Durkan in a press conference announcing the new investment.[31]

Between 2005 and 2014, 7,000 new units were built in Seattle. A steep drop in housing production followed due to the Great Recession, but production has increased swiftly since the economy recovered. Since 2014 and continuing through 2018, Seattle built more rental units than they had in the past twenty years.[32] The units were accessible at or below 80 percent of AMI, and an additional 1,000 were affordable at 80 to 90 percent of AMI.[33] The city continues its attempts to provide affordable housing; however, the creation of over 12,000 units a year may be hard to achieve.[34] "Affordability is really one of the most moral challenges of our time," said Mayor Durkan.[35]

DID THE MFTE PROGRAM GENERATE THE INCREASE IN HOUSING?

The questions remain: Is the recent spike in construction a result of the free market, or is the MFTE program providing an incentive that attracts the needed builders? To begin with, the city's solid fundamental goals continue to attract investors, with nearly $2.3 billion in multifamily assets trading in the first ten months of 2018. Roughly 8,200 units were delivered in the metropolitan area last year through November, with an additional 24,470 apartment units underway.[36]

According to a recent national report from CBRE, a commercial real estate firm, 80 percent of all apartments completed in 2019 were in the top twenty markets. Below is a list of the top four urban areas that saw the greatest number of apartments built:

- New York Metro – 32,300 units completed

- Dallas / Fort Worth – 20,500 units completed

- Los Angeles / Southern California – 20,000 units completed

- Seattle – 14,400 units[37]

Why are builders constructing so many multifamily units largely in higher-cost urban areas? The year 2017 was the most active year on record for multifamily and commercial real estate finance. Mortgage bankers closed a record high of $530 billion in loans backed by multifamily and commercial properties, and most builders stayed fixated on areas that claim strong job growth, improving demographic trends and therefore more-profitable rents. There is little evidence that the MFTE program brought additional construction into the larger metro areas that wouldn't have been constructed anyway.

THE COST-BENEFIT ANALYSIS

I used a cost-benefit analysis to evaluate rational solutions that meet the goal of providing affordable housing and also explored alternative housing programs based on the results of the study.

I compared the MFTE-model average rents that were collected against the open market–model collected income (rents). I consider the data adequate to evaluate both the MFTE and open market models.

The MFTE program's benefit was that it provided a rental savings of $331,257 for affordable housing programs. The

total average rental income is $3,937,011, and the tax
amount collected is $46,510.

FIGURE 3.

CASH FLOW ANALYSIS - TAX ADVANTAGE - MFTE

	Example 1 Axle Apts	Example 2 Chroma 1232	Example 3 Cityline	Example 4 Crew Apts	MFTE Totals
Income					
Rental Income	$5,765,820	3,760,908	4,516,368	1,704,948	**3,937,011**
Parking Income	667,152	321,768	457,560	206,640	**413,280**
Less: Vacancy	(321,648)	(204,134)	(248,696)	(95,579)	**(196,851)**
Effective Gross Income	6,111,324	3,878,542	4,725,232	1,816,009	*4,153,440*
Expenses					
Taxes	28,212	43,414	68,096	46,316	**46,510**
Management Fees	244,453	155,141	189,009	72,640	**165,311**
Operating Expenses	2,179,909	969,635	1,687,852	481,605	**1,329,750**
Total Operating Expenses	2,452,574	1,168,190	1,944,957	600,561	*1,541,571*
Net Operating Income	3,658,750	2,710,352	2,780,275	1,215,448	2,611,870
Debt Service	2,209,618	1,876,382	1,692,571	1,052,011	1,707,645
DSCR	1.66	1.44	1.64	1.16	1.53
Depreciation	1,748,778	1,395,630	1,150,626	828,981	1,281,004

FIGURE 4.

CASH FLOW ANALYSIS - NO TAX ADVANTAGE

	Example 1 Axle Apts	Example 2 Chroma 1232	Example 3 Cityline	Example 4 Crew Apts	Open Market Totals
Income					
Gross Scheduled Income	6,170,100	4,206,144	4,849,272	1,847,556	**4,268,268**
Parking Income	667,152	321,768	457,560	206,640	
Less: Vacancy	(341,863)	(226,396)	(265,342)	(102,710)	**(213,413)**
Effective Gross Income	6,495,389	4,301,516	5,041,490	1,951,486	*4,054,855*
Expenses					
Taxes	285,642	274,285	163,582	125,640	**212,287**
Management Fees	259,816	172,061	201,659	78,059	**177,899**
Operating Expenses	2,316,905	1,075,379	1,800,820	517,534	**1,427,660**
Total Operating Expenses	2,862,363	1,521,725	2,166,061	721,233	*1,817,846*
Net Operating Income	3,633,026	2,779,791	2,875,429	1,230,253	2,237,009
Debt Service	2,209,618	1,876,382	1,692,571	1,052,011	1,707,645
DSCR	1.64	1.48	1.70	1.17	1.31
Depreciation	1,748,778	1,395,630	1,150,626	828,981	1,281,004

In the open market model, the total average rental income (gross scheduled income) is $4,268,268, and the average tax amount collected is $212,287.

COST AND BENEFIT COMPARISON

This section compares the costs and benefits of the project's examples. The first part of the comparison examines the benefit or value of subsidized rents, and the second part examines the forgone tax benefits. The purpose of this comparison is to identify whether the benefits equal or outweigh the total cost of the MFTE program.

FIGURE 5.

COST-BENEFIT ANALYSIS OF MFTE

Project Owner Rental Savings

MFTE TOTALS	3,937,011
OPEN MARKET TOTALS	4,268,268
Rent Savings	*331,257*

Tax Revenue Loss		Tax Revenue Make Up to Cover Services	Total Tax Revenue Loss to City Programs
MFTE Collected	46,510	0	0
OPEN MARKET TOTALS - Forgone	212,287	165,778	0
Diff Lost Tax Revenue	*165,778*	*165,778*	*331,556*

COST TO TAX PAYERS	-299

I compared the MFTE-model average taxes collected ($46,510) against the open market–model collected taxes ($212,287). The MFTE program forgoes $165,778 in assessed taxes, and per the economic theory, the city must also collect an additional $165,778 in taxes to cover their expenses (known as tax shifting). The cost of MFTE, then, is the total tax cost to the city of Seattle, which is $331,556.

I compared the rental savings of $331,257 against the costs of forgoing taxes in the amount of $331,556 yields; I consider the result of the program to mean that the cost-benefit analysis will break even.

KEY FINDINGS

From these empirical findings, some conclusions can be drawn. First, the benefits can be quantified with the assistance of the cost-benefit analysis, and the results can quantify both the rents in the MFTE program matched against the rents in the open market and the net result as rent savings or benefit.

Secondly, the factors influencing costs related to tax shifting are multifaceted, with no single factor explaining all or most of the value of the tax consequences affecting affordable housing. However, the model does allow me to quantify the amount of the tax consequence, or foregone tax revenues, to provide the cost of the analysis.

The model provided a net result of a break-even program as a result of the cost-benefit analysis. In other words, the cost of the program is basically equal to the benefits of the forgone taxes. Therefore, the success or failure of the MFTE program is dependent on the allotted rooms being occupied by those who meet the eligibility requirement. Otherwise, the loss to the city of Seattle is double the original forgone tax revenues and then even triple to the tenant, who loses a benefit but must pay high rents in the open market.

Industry leaders seem to agree with my findings. The following comes from an interview between *Bisnow* and Bob

Faith, CEO of Greystar, the largest property management company:

> *Bisnow*: "There has been much buzz over the past few months over the tax benefits of this program and what it could do for communities. Is that something you're thinking about?"

> Faith [emphasis added]: "We're interested in it. *It is going to be a marginal benefit to certain sites and locations; I don't know that it's going to be such a huge incentive* that it's going to make deals that shouldn't be built get built, which would be something you might worry about."[38]

THE HIGH-RISK GAMBLE OF THE MFTE PROGRAM

In the MFTE program, for every tax dollar the city forgoes—if, say, the property owner cheats the program a dollar—the cost would actually be three dollars. That's because for each dollar forgone due to the tax exemption, a second dollar must be raised by the city to cover the services the forgone tax would have covered, referred to as tax shifting.

None of those funds replace the lost benefit to the tenant of reduced rents, therefore also costing the tenant a dollar in benefits. In fact, both second and third dollars are carried by the end user, the tenant. The incident of cheating withholds the benefit (one dollar) in the form of lower rents in the MFTE unit, then compounds the financial hit for the tenant, who then must find a way to pay out of pocket the third cheated dollar to their open-market landlord in the form of higher rents. The third dollar will come from renters' already meager, cost-burdened wages.

FIGURE 6.

THE THREE TO ONE RISK FACTOR
CAUSED BY A PROPERTY OWNER CHEAT

PROPERTY OWNER	TENANT	TAXPAYER
MFTE Foregone Tax: -1	Pays higher rent	Raise Taxes*: -1
Original Tax: 1	in open market: -1	Tax-Shift: 0
	Lost MFTE Benefit: -1	
NET CHANGE: 0	**-2**	**-1**

TOTAL LOST DOLLARS: 3   *– City services must be covered as
                                    the apartment complex is open

Note: "The rent would be $1,500" is an estimated rent the tenant would pay in the MFTE program. The tenant actually "pays open-market rent of $2,500," which is significantly over the reduced rent. The cost-burdened tenant is the real loser in this cheating scenario.

Hence, to take advantage of the MFTE program opportunities and lower the cost of securing units utilized for affordable housing in Seattle, additional precautions must be put into place to safeguard the city against losing vast tax revenues and receiving little rent benefit in return. The study reveals that the onerous responsibility of verifying the properties comply with all the rules and regulations, and property managers do not cheat the program, falls directly onto the city.

Therefore, to the extent that providing affordable housing to rent-burdened citizens is one of the goals of the city's affordable-housing policy, a greater emphasis must be placed on ensuring that the properties complete their annual reviews and that the number of assigned units for the MFTE program is the same number actually being utilized within the program.

Furthermore, the MFTE program is only as effective as the time and effort placed into the oversight of the program. For example, the state of Washington performed an audit and found that at least five cities failed to submit a report during the period examined, and a minimum of eleven were unable to report in one or more years.[39] This means cities may not be ensuring that the forgone taxes result in additional affordable rental units, instead leaving the results up to chance.

Unfortunately, another problem was discovered when an investigation uncovered evidence that some property managers were engaged in discriminatory practices against minorities (see Chapter 5 for additional details on discrimination). The building owners agreed to settlements but didn't admit their guilt.[40]

TAX SHIFTING

As we've seen, beneficiary tax savings could result in a property tax shift or forgone revenue. A property tax shift means that other taxpaying citizens are required to pay the sum that would have been received on the exempt property. Forgone revenue means that the tax is never collected from anyone. Complications arise because taxing jurisdictions extend beyond city limits; some of the impacts occur outside the city's authority.

For example, in Seattle, issuing a property tax exemption to the building will affect the allocation of property taxes.

Property taxes are levied at a set rate, then dispersed; for example, if the city needed one hundred dollars to operate, they will collect the one hundred dollars. Therefore, the city must increase the burden on properties that aren't tax exempted. In 2016, Doug Trumm reported his findings in *The Urbanist*. "Assuming a current median residence value of $480,000 and total real property value of $407.4 billion, based on the most recent 2016 figures as determined by the Department of Assessments, the MFTE program will result in tax shifting an additional tax payment for the median Seattle homeowner of $10.84 in 2017, an amount that changes from year to year."[41]

Before a city embarks on the MFTE program, they should ask whether the aggregate rent savings for each of the unit types are comparable to what the owner is collecting in the way of a property tax exemption. Furthermore, the city needs to set firm policies, procedures, and oversight of the program; otherwise, the voucher program is likely the better fit for their housing program.

"I have never seen this question sufficiently answered," Seattle Councilmember Lisa Herbold said. "There are confusing statements about the purpose of the program, which makes measuring what we are getting for the tax-exemption incentive very difficult."[42]

Cities may well find that they could possibly ensure increased affordability with a voucher program, using the forgone property-tax proceeds, rather than the existing programs. Seattle estimated that 12 million tax dollars were shifted or lost in 2015, which would equal a $143-per-month rent voucher for 7,000 family units—lost revenue would be about half that. Therefore, enticing multifamily construction with tax incentives is almost certainly more cost-effective. Although rent vouchers may boost aggregate demand, builders would most likely select the more straightforward calculation and the more significant assured twelve-year benefit, without the property taxes.[43]

TAX SUBSIDY PROGRAMS TEND TO BENEFIT INVESTORS OVER RECIPIENTS

The Low-Income Housing Tax Credit (LIHTC) is a complex but crucial tool for the production and preservation of affordable rental housing. Feasibly, the principal drawback of the LIHTC, as compared to other affordable housing programs, is its high cost. The Government Accountability Office (GAO) found that LIHTC units cost 19 to 44 percent more than units subsidized using housing vouchers.[44] The GAO also found that LIHTC units typically cost more than units funded by other supply-side aid programs. However, the cost isn't the only problem; many cities tend to build these facilities in less-than-safe locations.

In November 2019, Jacqueline Rabe Thomas reported on *ProPublica* the following story:

> Romeo Lugo, a six-year-old autistic child, has witnessed gun violence firsthand. His mother grabbed Romeo and ducked. "Bam, bam, bam," Aida Lugo recalls hearing seconds later. "I couldn't move." After the incident, they explored moving from Frog Hollow, one of the state's most impoverished and dangerous areas. However, the only units in her price range were located no more than a few blocks from the gunshots and the drug dealers in her neighborhood, so she remains marooned there—in the same apartment.[45]

Connecticut officials have elected, time and time again, to direct the vast majority of public funding for affordable housing to their state's most impoverished and dangerous communities. In fact, a recent federal study of twenty-one states revealed that Connecticut has the second-highest concentration of affordable housing in impoverished and crime-ridden neighborhoods, second only to Mississippi.[46]

The primary purpose of the LIHTC is to lower rents to those tenants suffering from cost or rent burdening; however, recent studies indicate the real benefit flows to investors, developers, and financial companies. Unfortunately, the program is very complex, is prone to abuse, and produces expensive low-income housing. An analysis by Gregory Burge found that "the LIHTC program may significantly benefit project developers and owners, with approximately one-third of the program's cost going to low-income households in the form of rent savings."[47]

ACCESS TO AFFORDABLE HOUSING CAN ENHANCE FINANCIAL RESOURCES

Increasing reliable access to affordable housing frees up a family's financial reserves to cover health care and insurance, thus eliminating additional risks to physical and mental health. We know that uninsured tenants devote a much larger share of their wages to housing, food, and education than the insured population. This suggests that poor households shy away from purchasing health insurance because they need to cover other basic necessities.

The 2014 California Affordable Housing Cost Study on social and economic research suggests that access to affordable housing can generate significant benefits for cities like Seattle. This research proposes that access to affordable housing can lead to improved educational awareness, overall health and well-being, economic activity, and significantly lower social services costs for state and local governments, among other benefits.[48]

In Chapter 1, we saw that since the creation of HUD, there have been several periods in which the United States had housing shortages; for example, after WWII. In the 1950s, HUD proposed and implemented a housing plan, and the same occurred in the late 1960s. The question remains: Why does the nation have such a shortage of affordable housing, and why is so little being done by HUD? We will continue this discussion in Chapter 3, and look at what, precisely, is happening at HUD today, which I call the chaos.

Is Howe's proclamation, from Chapter 1, that every child born into this country has an equal opportunity under the law, still relevant today? Are all of the country's children equally protected from the influence of vice, crime, and physical degeneration? Does each child have a safe place to lay their head?

In California, 134,000 people were homeless during HUD's 2016 annual census, a 14 percent jump from 2015. About two-thirds of these people were unsheltered, the highest rate in the nation. The homeless population is skyrocketing, up 47 percent from 2012. At least ten cities on the West Coast have declared states of emergency in recent years.[49] And children are twice as likely to be homeless as adults.

This is a crisis.

CHAPTER 3

CHAOS AND WHAT IS HAPPENING AT HUD TODAY

IN 2008, THE housing industry created trillions of dollars in lost wealth. Who is driving the housing markets, and who is making the decisions? Who is really setting policy? In this chapter, we will look at HUD and, more specifically, the Government Sponsored Enterprises (GSEs) Fannie Mae and Freddie Mac. We will explore the regulatory oversight of these entities as they remain in conservatorship. Who is running the operations, who is making the decisions, and what do they aim to accomplish? Finally, we will look into the protections afforded the taxpayers—the guarantors of GSE lending activities.

In June 2018, the Office of Management and Budget released recommendations to reform the federal government in many areas, including housing finance. The recommendations proposed privatizing the Enterprises.[1]

CONSERVATORSHIP

In September 2008, the Federal Housing Finance Agency (FHFA) placed two government-sponsored GSEs—the

Federal National Mortgage Association (Fannie Mae) and the Federal Home Loan Mortgage Corporation (Freddie Mac), two of the largest financial institutions in the country—into conservatorships.[2] However, putting the Enterprises into conservatorships has proven far easier than ending them; the conservatorships have now entered their eleventh year.

The FHFA was created by the Housing and Economic Recovery Act (HERA) of 2008. HERA serves a unique role as both conservator and regulator of the Enterprises, establishing authorities for providing capital support to the Enterprises. It also authorizes the FHFA director to appoint the agency as a conservator or receiver for the Enterprises. Moreover, the FHFA delegated authority and can revoke its delegated authority at any time. (It retains the authority for certain significant decisions.)[3]

On April 15, 2019, in Washington, DC, Mark A. Calabria was appointed to head the agency by President Donald Trump. Before his work in the White House, Calabria was director of financial regulation studies at the Cato Institute. He had also held a variety of positions, including at Harvard University's Joint Center for Housing Studies, the National Association of Home Builders, and the National Association of Realtors. Calabria was most recently Vice President Mike Pence's chief economist,[4] which means his assignment came from inside the Trump administration.

REGULATORY OVERSIGHT—OFFICE
OF THE INSPECTOR GENERAL

The FHFA's Office of Inspector General (OIG) fosters efficiency and effectiveness. It protects the FHFA and the entities it regulates against fraud, waste, and the abuse of the nation's housing finance system. The office accomplishes this mission by providing independent, relevant, timely, and transparent oversight of the agency through robust enforcement efforts to protect the interests of American taxpayers. Since October 2010, OIG has made more than 425 recommendations.[5]

The OIG's oversight role includes the Enterprises—recipients of $191.5 billion—to ensure that they satisfy their obligations under the authority delegated to them in the conservatorships. Through oversight, OIG seeks to be a voice for and protect the interests of those who have funded the treasury's investment in the Enterprises—the American taxpayers.[6]

In summarizing their findings, the OIG made recommendations intended to protect the Federal Housing Administration (FHA) and Ginnie Mae programs. According to those findings, OIG has concluded that HUD is confronted with the following:

1. A lack of sufficient safeguards in FHA's mortgage insurance program
2. Substantial losses to insurance programs
3. An increase in Ginnie Mae's nonbank issuers
4. Potential emerging risks related to a market shift toward an entirely digital mortgage life cycle[7]

Let's now take a closer look at those weaknesses pointed out by the OIG and perhaps ascertain if a correlation exists between the chaos and this administration's rush to privatize the GSEs.

OIG OUTLINES THE PRIMARY SYSTEMATIC
PROBLEMS PLAGUING THE GSES

The OIG found that the FHFA has delegated a significant portion of day-to-day management to the GSEs. As of 2018, the OIG issued thirty-seven reports that address critical issues regarding the FHFA's conservatorship of the Enterprises.

One such audit found that the FHFA limited its oversight of delegated matters primarily to sending FHFA employees to observe, taking no part in the discussions and taking no actions on any rule-breaking. The findings also show that the FHFA, as conservator, had not assessed the reasonableness of enterprise actions taken according to delegated authority, nor had it assessed the adequacy of the director's oversight of management's actions.

Furthermore, the Enterprises failed to provide GSE directors with accurate, timely, and sufficient information to enable them to exercise their oversight duties. The OIG found a lack of rigor by some enterprise directors in seeking information from managers about matters for which they are responsible. The audit also identified instances in which corporate governance decisions typically reserved to a board of directors had been delegated to enterprise management and third-party participants.

The OIG outlined four primary areas of great concern regarding the Enterprises and their lack of cooperation in adequately addressing those concerns:

1. Consolidation and Relocation of Fannie Mae's Northern Virginia Workforce

As a conservator of Fannie Mae, the FHFA has a statutory duty to "preserve and conserve" Fannie Mae's assets, while operating it in a manner consistent with the public interest.[8] On September 6, 2018, the Office of Inspector General received information from an anonymous source alleging excessive spending in connection with Fannie Mae's consolidation and relocation of its offices to the metro Washington, DC, and Dallas (Plano), Texas, areas.

After completing its investigation, the OIG issued a special report that set forth its assessment of the FHFA's oversight of the costs of the build-out of leased space over the previous year. The report said that the FHFA advised the OIG that Fannie Mae's management was better able to select appropriate features and finishes for the build-out and that it relied on Fannie Mae's management to make those selections and keep the FHFA informed (the observing practice).

Fannie had apparently retained an outside expert to review the reasonableness of certain structural upgrades compared to the amenities and aesthetics in the headquarters of major financial institutions and large public-sector agencies. The OIG found that the FHFA, as conservator, never determined whether the structural upgrades over and above class space (defined as features, finishes, and quality factors, such as amenities and aesthetics) were appropriate expenditures for an entity in conservatorship with an uncertain future.

Four FHFA officials responsible for the oversight of Fannie Mae's consolidation and the relocation of its offices separately reported to the OIG that Fannie Mae's management drove the consolidation. Those same officials acknowledged to the OIG that Fannie Mae could have continued to operate out of its previous offices without a negative impact on its operations.

Fannie Mae directors should all have been aware of prior OIG reports challenging the build-out costs. Yet, the OIG found no evidence that any director ever questioned the managers' decisions.

2.   OIG REVIEW OF CONFLICTS OF INTEREST

The OIG audit of the FHFA included Fannie Mae's responsibility for the resolution of conflicts of interest involving its senior executive officers (SEOs). The OIG sought to determine what practice, if any, had been consistently followed by the National Guideline Clearinghouse (NGC) over the five-year review period between January 2012 and December 2016 concerning SEO conflicts. The OIG identified a total of fifty-seven potential conflicts involving SEOs, which were documented in the company's case management system, NGC meeting materials, and minutes.

Of these fifty-seven potential conflicts involving SEOs, the OIG found that the GSEs' internal ethics group determined, on its own, whether or not a potential conflict of interest involving an SEO existed and took steps to resolve any dispute. This evaluation found failures, both by Fannie Mae's NGC and by the FHFA, which created a weakness in Fannie Mae's risk management structure. Without enhancements to the NGC's oversight, there was a significant risk that the NGC would continue to fall short in exercising its governance responsibilities.[9] In other words, for all practical purposes, there was no real oversight of the many reported conflicts of interest.

One example of a conflict of interest is that, according to their respective single-family selling guides, neither Fannie Mae nor Freddie Mac allows the delivery of loans with a credit score other than classic FICO. Congress, federal regulatory agencies, and policy advocates have long considered whether FICO excludes a large number of creditworthy potential homeowners. Many have suggested that perhaps alternative credit scoring models should be accepted.

Therefore, the FHFA directed the Enterprises to assess the potential impact of updating enterprise credit score requirements from classic FICO to also include traditional FICO, FICO 9, and VantageScore 3.0. Nevertheless, the FHFA publicly acknowledged that its decision on alternative credit scoring models would have significant impacts on the industry. Therefore, a decision of this magnitude must be subject to a well-controlled process.[10] However, little debate took place outside of secluded boardrooms, and on May 24, 2018, President Trump signed the Economic Growth, Regulatory Relief, and Consumer Protection Act into law.

Below are the OIG's findings:

"Based on the Review of Fannie Mae's Corporate Records, It Appears **REDACTED** Did Not Make Complete Disclosures of a Potential, Apparent, or Actual Conflict of Interest Arising from the Potential and Actual Employment of **REDACTED** and FHFA's Decision on the Enterprises' Use of Alternative Credit Scoring Models."[11]

The OIG both discovered and reported numerous such findings to the FHFA; however, the FHFA maintains its policy of observation and taking no action, resulting in taxpayers receiving little to no protection from such abuse.

In addition, the inspector general found that both Fannie and Freddie failed to disclose significant conflicts of interest in maintaining security while using contractors to install AI technology. HUD's entire accounting and software systems remained unsecured and vulnerable to predation. The audit was unable to determine if outside contractors had shared critical passcodes and logins with third-party interests, and the contractors were equally unsure of security protocols.[12]

These deficiencies could allow powerful capabilities to be at the disposal of unauthorized users. They also increase risk, because the privileged accounts could allow unauthorized access to an organization's infrastructure. Another concern is the potential for an agency to be unable to assess contractor performance or the potential risks associated with a user, and this increases the likelihood that erroneous or fraudulent transactions could be processed.

In fact, when employees separate from the FHFA, they are required to go through an offboarding process that includes educating employees about post-employment restrictions and financial disclosure requirements. However, in 2018, the OIG identified at least five separate employees and two departed contractors who still had active enterprise access cards and passcodes. The OIG determined that the FHFA did not maintain a list of separated employees or departed contractors who maintained access to the platform, and the FHFA did not have written procedures for the collection and deactivation of access cards and passcodes.

The OIG further found that Ginnie Mae allowed its contractors to control the process for contracted employees to obtain access to the platform and did not require the contractors to notify Ginnie Mae when a contract employee was granted access, dismissed, or no longer performing duties requiring access to the application platform.[13]

Ginnie Mae still faces contracting and staffing challenges. It continues to rely heavily on contractors because it has the authority to use certain fee revenues to fund contractors but not its own in-house staff.[14] In one instance, Ginnie Mae relied heavily on contractors for accounting expertise and accepted their advice without said contractors being thoroughly evaluated by objective, independent, and well-informed Ginnie Mae executives.[15]

3. FHFA's Approval of Senior Executive Succession Planning

The former FHFA director awarded annual target compensation of $4 million to each enterprise CEO. Their reason was to "promote CEO retention, allow reliable succession planning, and ensure the continuity, efficiency, and stability of enterprise operations."[16] The House and Senate, however, passed the Equity in Government Compensation Act of 2015 to limit this type of abuse, suspending those awards and imposing a cap of $600,000 on the compensation for each enterprise CEO.[17]

In June 2018, however, the board chair submitted the Board Transition Plan to the FHFA for approval. In it, the board recommended a change to Fannie Mae's management structure by filling the positions of president and CEO with separate individuals. Under the board plan, they were provided $3.25 million in compensation. The FHFA's director approved the Board Transition Plan in July 2018.

The OIG found that "First, FHFA's approval of the Board Transition Plan acted to circumvent the congressionally mandated cap of $600,000 on the compensation for enterprise CEOs. Second, the former FHFA director overrode internal controls for conservator review and approval of the Board Transition Plan."[18]

On March 27, 2019, Fannie Mae announced that Hugh R. Frater was appointed CEO. Before his appointment, he had served as Fannie Mae's interim CEO since October 16, 2018, and on Fannie Mae's board since 2016. Frater held several executive and management roles throughout his career, including his current position as a non-executive chairman of the board of VEREIT, Inc. He previously led Berkadia Commercial Mortgage LLC, a national commercial real estate company providing comprehensive capital solutions, and investment sales advisory and research services for multifamily and commercial properties. We will discuss Frater's past connections and how they relate to the story line later in the chapter.

The first responsibility of FHFA should be repaying the taxpayers, not defying congressional intent by granting more than $8 million in compensation to four people doing the same jobs that two people were approved to undertake for $1.2 million. In other words, currently, the two entities (Fannie and Freddie) each have their own CEO, who also holds the title of president, and per regulations should receive $600,000 each annually. However, the board plan called for four executives who could each be paid $2 million each year—or, apparently, as Fannie Mae chose, one person who could be paid a salary for each position, for $3.25 million total.

4. MANAGEMENT AND PERFORMANCE CHALLENGES FOR THE 2019 FISCAL YEAR AND BEYOND

The OIG also identified management challenges that impact HUD's ability to meet the needs of its beneficiaries and protect taxpayer dollars.[19]

The first was ensuring the availability of affordable housing that is decent, safe, sanitary, and in good repair. The crisis in affordable housing was covered in Chapter 2. We will discuss the housing markets in detail in Chapter 4.

The second was protecting the Federal Housing Administration's Mortgage Insurance Funds. Through the FHA, HUD's Mutual Mortgage Insurance (MMI) Fund Program, which is sustained entirely by borrower premiums, insures approximately eight million mortgages with an outstanding principal balance of nearly $1.2 trillion.

From April 2017 through March 2018, the MMI fund paid out almost $14 billion. For those claims for which the lender conveyed the property to HUD and HUD resold the property, HUD recovered only about 54 percent of the funds paid out.[20] The losses, according to the OIG, were due to management failures in policy and failures in monitoring its lending programs.

HUD is challenged in protecting the FHA mortgage insurance program. The insurance protects lenders against losses from homeowners, approximately 25 percent of all mortgages in the United States, from defaulting on their mortgage loans. Without sufficient controls, oversight, and effective rules, FHA's MMI fund is at risk of unnecessary losses. If insurance fees collected from borrowers cannot support the fund, additional funding from the treasury is required, as authorized for federal credit programs.[21]

The third concern was providing adequate monitoring and oversight of FHFA's operations and program participants (FHFA's Supervision of its Regulated Entities). The Division of Enterprise Regulation (DER) is charged with supervision through ongoing monitoring and targeted examinations of the Federal Home Loan Banks (FHLB) and the Office of Finance. According to the FHFA, the activities are complementary: targeted examinations enable examiners to conduct an in-depth or comprehensive assessment of the areas found to be of high importance or risk.

The OIG audit concluded that DER examiners failed to verify that the GSEs' audit committee chairs received the supervisory correspondence from those audits and examinations. Instead of implementing the OIG recommendation, the OIG accused DER of preserving the status quo. Furthermore, DER had been cautioned against preserving the status quo in the evaluation because it "creates a significant risk that management will put its own spin on the deficiencies found by OIG; or, management will filter the information it provides to the Board."[22]

Furthermore, based on the OIG assessments of different elements of DER's supervision program, they identified four recurring themes. The first was that the FHFA lacked adequate assurance that DER's supervisory resources were devoted to examining the highest risks of the Enterprises. Sound prudent policy dictated that board members should

be made aware of serious deficiencies in policies and procedures, and this could only be attained through extensive
examinations into the riskiest activities. For example, management should be made aware of whether or not lenders
followed loan policies when underwriting loans.

Secondly, supervisory standards and guidance issued by
the FHFA and DER lacked the rigor of those issued by
other federal financial regulators. Policies that were established to protect against risky behaviors were not being
reviewed, and their explanations were very similar to the
FHFA's policy to observe and take no action. Third, the flexible and less prescriptive nature of many requirements and
guidance promulgated by FHFA and DER resulted in inconsistent supervisory practices. The inconsistencies could be
traced back to the lack of communication with the board
of directors and their audit committee. For example, when
the examiners prepared for their audits, the purpose and
scope were not outlined and approved by the appropriate
oversight authorities.

And lastly, where precise requirements and guidance for
specific elements of DER's supervisory program existed,
DER examiners-in-charge and subordinate examiners had
not consistently followed them.[23]

THE IMPORTANCE OF INTERNAL AUDITING PROGRAMS

The primary focus of banking supervision and regulation
is the safety and soundness of financial institutions. These
are evaluated in the nature of the bank's operations, the
adequacy of the bank's internal controls and its internal
audit function, and its compliance with regulations. Internal

audits provide an objective, independent review of lending activities, internal controls, and management information systems to help the board and management monitor and evaluate internal control adequacy and effectiveness. Sound internal control objectives and effective internal control provide management and examiners reasonable assurances that operations are efficient and effective. They also ensure that recorded transactions are accurate; financial reporting is reliable; risk management systems are effective; and the GSEs comply with laws and regulations, internal policies, and internal procedures.

The significance, visibility, and role of internal auditing have become critical components of a financial institution's Enterprise Risk Management (ERM) strategy. To ensure the safe and sound operation of a financial institution, the board of directors and senior management must enforce an effective system of internal controls, including internal audits that challenge management to adopt appropriate policies, procedures, and adequate controls.

At the end of the day, it is the responsibility of the board of directors to determine the extent of auditing that will effectively monitor the institution's system of internal controls. When the internal audit function is accurately defined and conducted, it gives directors and senior management critical information about the condition of internal controls. It identifies weaknesses so that management can take prompt, remedial action.

Prudent thought should be given to the placement of the audit in an institution's management structure. The internal audit should be positioned so that the board has confidence that the examination will perform its duties with impartiality, not unduly influenced by managers of day-to-day operations.[24] The failure to enact the program tends to leave directors and those tasked with the responsibility of oversight in the dark as to the current state of the business. Furthermore, the potential for fraud and high-risk bets get lost until losses begin to appear in the balance sheet.

Regulatory guidelines require that all financial institutions maintain an adequate internal audit function commensurate with the size and complexity of its operations. As the conservator of the Enterprises—which together reported assets of approximately $5.4 trillion as of December 31, 2017—the FHFA has the ultimate authority and responsibility for all business, policy, and risk decisions, which influence and affect the entire mortgage finance industry. As a conservator, the FHFA must ensure that both Enterprises are effectively governed and employ sound risk-management practices. Yet the FHFA holds to the failed principle of observing and taking no action.

INSUFFICIENT MONITORING OF ITS OPERATIONS

For years, the OIG has reported on HUD's lack of compliance with the United States Government Accountability Office's (GAO's) internal control standards. GAO's Standards for Internal Control in the Federal Government provide the framework for establishing and maintaining internal control, known as management control.[25] Beginning in 2015 and carrying on through 2017, the OIG reported that HUD was not conducting routine or timely Management Control Reviews (MCRs) and could not ensure that its programs were operating as intended.[26] This is significant because the inconsistent performance of MCRs deprives management of a critical monitoring tool that should provide vital feedback on the effectiveness and efficiency of departmental operations.[27] For example, in the 2018 fiscal year, the OIG's reports identified more than $1.3 billion in questioned costs and nearly $4.7 billion in funds that could have been put to better use.[28] In this example, robust MCRs should have caught this massive waste of resources, so that the money could have financed affordable housing.

COMMISSIONED INTERNAL EXAMINER PROGRAM

The OIG's recent reports on the status of the FHFA's Housing Finance Examiner Commissioning Program (HFE) highlights shortcomings in the FHFA's supervision of its regulated entities. The audit found that during an almost seven-year period, the agency invested approximately $7.7 million in developing, implementing, and staffing the HFE Program. Of the sixty-six examiners who enrolled in 2013, only six completed the HFE Program and passed its final examination. By June 2018, more than half (thirty-six) were no longer employed in the HFE.[29]

FAILURE IN MONITORING THE BANK
SECRECY ACT—KNOW YOUR CUSTOMER

The OIG also found that the FHFA does not make any documented, systematic use of the content of the Enterprises' fraud reports. In response, the FHFA advised the OIG that it recently began to analyze trends of the information in the enterprises' fraud reports.[30]

Furthermore, in a recent report, the OIG explained that the Enterprises face the risk of fraud throughout the mortgage life cycle.[31] Under the Bank Secrecy Act rule, each enterprise must implement an anti-money-laundering program and report suspicious activities—including suspected money laundering and mortgage fraud—to the US Treasury Department's Financial Crimes Enforcement Network in Suspicious Activity Reports (SARs).[32]

In the world of finance, money laundering is a substantial risk to the safety and soundness of the industry, as well as to the country. Through sound operations, financial institutions play an essential role in assisting the investigations and regulatory agencies in identifying money-laundering entities and taking appropriate action. Otherwise, lenders do not know the people with whom they are doing business, and the probability of malfeasance escalates.

The fourth management challenge is the modernizing of technology and the management and oversight of information technology. The mortgage industry is moving toward an entirely digital loan process. The FHA and Ginnie Mae intend to do the same. However, HUD, particularly the FHA and GSEs, have well-known technological challenges, detailed in many reports over the years. Adding the new platforms and security measures required for digital mortgages presents potentially significant risks to the agency, industry, and consumer, which include the security of information, data transfers, platform integration, and system functionality, all of which could lead to fraudulent activities.[33]

The *2014 Strategic Plan for the Conservatorships of Fannie Mae and Freddie Mac* includes the FHFA's strategic goal of developing a new securitization infrastructure (platform) for mortgage loans backed by single-family properties. To achieve this goal, Common Securitization Solutions (CSS), a joint venture owned by the Enterprises, is developing a Common Securitization Platform (CSP) under the FHFA's direction and guidance.[34]

COMMON SECURITIZATION PLATFORM

The Common Securitization Platform is intended to function as one collective, flexible, technological, and operational platform to support single-family securitization. These activities involve storing, processing, and transmitting large volumes of data so that investing in a single platform and carrying out the accompanying operational capabilities to support these functions will benefit companies and, ultimately, taxpayers.[35]

Since the implementation of Release 1, for example, Freddie Mac has used CSP for the monthly issuance and settlement of approximately one thousand new securities, representing about $59 billion in unpaid principal balance. For monthly bond administration functions related to 257,000 securities backed by nearly 10 million loans, Freddie Mac used CSP for approximately $1.7 trillion in outstanding principal balance.[36]

The GSEs claim that CSP operations benefit housing finance. First, the CSP will act as the agent for customers and serve as the standard mechanism for mortgage securitization. Second, the platform through CSS will administer $125 to $175 billion in monthly issuance volume and direct payments on over $4.8 trillion in securities.[37]

However, the technology utilized in the platform is advanced, and the GSEs' lack of oversight and accountability remains a veritable obstacle to ensuring the safety and soundness of the program's architecture. For example, a separate OIG audit revealed that the FHFA did not complete planned supervisory activities related to cybersecurity risks at the GSEs for the 2016 or the 2017 examination cycles.[38] This amounts to another example of failed management decisions in protecting the private data of the borrowers and market participants.

The fifth management challenge relates to the instituting of sound financial management governance, internal controls, and systems. The OIG has determined that the FHFA is challenged with ensuring that its existing controls, including its written policies and procedures, are sufficiently robust and that its personnel is adequately trained on these internal controls and comply fully with them.[39] The OIG found a lack of continuity of management and failure of oversight of the Enterprises' relationships with counterparties and third parties.

HUD, for example, had several senior-level positions in Ginnie Mae that remained vacant for an extended period. In 2018, as in previous years, Ginnie Mae relied heavily on contractors for accounting expertise and accepted the advice of these contractors without objective, independent, and well-informed Ginnie Mae executives thoroughly evaluating the claims.[40] The Enterprises also relied heavily on counterparties. They also relied on third parties for services, including mortgage origination and servicing. The possibility that a counterparty would not meet its contractual obligations or engage in fraudulent conduct was left up to chance.

The OIG determined that the FHFA remains challenged to effectively oversee the Enterprises' management of risks related to their counterparties.[41] Despite this, HUD had been unable to achieve an unmodified audit opinion on its financial statements for six years, instead receiving a disclaimer of opinion for five of those years, including the accounting for its non-pooled loan asset portfolio, which totaled as much as $6 billion at one point.[42] HUD's unstable financial management environment, according to the OIG, weakened public confidence in the government programs HUD administers and prevented HUD's stakeholders from being able to rely upon the department's financial position.[43]

UNRELIABLE ALLOWANCE FOR LOAN AND LEASE LOSSES (ALLL)

Per the US Generally Accepted Accounting Principles (GAAP), Ginnie Mae is required to measure potential loan losses based on the fair value of the loans' underlying collateral (e.g., uninsured loans). On September 30, 2018, Ginnie Mae was unable to obtain the updated fair value of the underlying collateral to fully comply with US GAAP requirements for impaired loans. This remained an open issue at the end of the fiscal year 2018. Therefore, the OIG determined that the balances of the allowance for loan loss account reported in Ginnie Mae's financial statements as of September 30, 2018, remained unreliable.[44]

In banking and finance, the Allowance for Loan and Lease Losses (ALLL)—a reserve for bad debts—is a calculated reserve that financial institutions are required by law to establish. The bad-debt reserve is a ratio that determines the estimated credit risk within the institution's loan portfolio of assets. Also, the ratio sets the required dollar amount of loss reserves that must be held to cover that credit risk. This is the first line of defense in preparations for losses in periods of economic turmoil. For example, taxpayers ponied up $191 billion to HUD after the Great Recession of 2008. In hindsight, if the Enterprises had maintained the ALLL accurately, there would not have been a need for a bailout of the GSEs, ever!

THE ROAD TO PRIVATIZATION AND THE MANY CONFLICTS OF INTEREST

Before FHFA Director Mark Calabria, Acting Director Joseph Otting oversaw the FHFA. Otting previously served as CEO of OneWest Bank, founded by Treasury Secretary Steven Mnuchin, an ally of Jared Kushner's in the West Wing.[45] Calabria, addressing the Mortgage Bankers Association in 2017, laid out plans for the future of Fannie Mae and Freddie Mac that included the end of their conservatorship.

In 2017, Calabria revealed that the Trump administration is "committed" to ending the conservatorship of the Government Sponsored Enterprises. Furthermore, in an interview with *HousingWire*, Calabria stated, "I see my role is to structure that roadmap. Fannie and Freddie, however, are the ones who got to get in the car and drive it," explaining that while some of the objectives needed to remove the GSEs from conservatorship rest on his shoulders, others are dependent on Fannie and Freddie themselves. "As Fannie and

Freddie are given more and more control of their destiny, such as being able to raise capital, they will grow closer to exiting conservatorship," Calabria continued.[46]

What this means is, before the GSEs' privatization, the entities need a great deal more in loss and operating reserves (the ALLL discussed earlier). On September 30, 2019, the US Department of the Treasury and the Federal Housing Finance Agency announced that they had agreed to modifications to Preferred Stock Purchase Agreements (PSPAs). The agreement will permit Fannie Mae and Freddie Mac to retain additional earnings above the $3 billion capital reserves that had been previously allowed. Under the modifications, Fannie Mae and Freddie Mac would be allowed to maintain capital reserves of $25 billion and $20 billion, respectively. "These modifications are an important step toward implementing Treasury's recommended reforms that will define a limited role for the federal government in the housing finance system and protect taxpayers against future bailouts," said Mnuchin.[47]

As we saw earlier, Hugh R. Frater, Fannie Mae's chief executive officer, previously led Berkadia Commercial Mortgage LLC, a national commercial real estate company providing comprehensive capital solutions and investment sales advisory and research services for multifamily and commercial properties. In fact, he served as chairman of Berkadia from 2010 to 2014.[48] Earlier in his career, Frater had been an executive vice president at PNC Financial Services, where he led the real estate division. PNC has been one of the top five loan syndicators for each of the last five years, beginning in 2015. Real estate syndication is an effective way for investors to pool their financial and intellectual resources to invest in properties. PNC, one of the largest publicly traded investment management firms in the country, also provides risk management, investment system outsourcing, and financial advisory services to a growing number of institutional investors.[49]

Frater was also a founding partner and managing director of BlackRock, Inc.[50] BlackRock currently maintains $6.28 trillion in assets under management and is one of the largest investment management companies in the world, with a market capitalization of over $86 billion. In early 2016, BlackRock saw its revenues decrease for the first time since the financial crisis, which is probably the reason the asset manager decided to completely overhaul its actively managed equity business.[51] In Chapter 8, we will discuss Frater and these relationships in greater detail and the ways they have woven their way into the housing industry. I posed this question in Chapter 1: What would happen to the consumers should AI technology be controlled by a large financial group with strong ties inside the government? The answer is conflicts of interest. It has happened before, as outlined in the 1934 Pecora Report.

Fannie and Freddie's long history of conflicts of interest is sure to play a role in the final outcome of the GSEs and the housing markets. We will look more closely at them in the following chapters.

Still more conflicts of interest, which are playing out in real time, are Director Calabria's ties to the Cato Institute, the National Association of Realtors, and Vice President Mike Pence. The Cato Institute was allowed to read its study and memorandum of support to the March 2017 GOP-led hearings on the Consumer Financial Protection

Bureau (CFPB). The GOP-led hearings were an attack on the CFPB's (perceived) illegal structure, and expressed the administration's desire to have the US Supreme Court rule the bureau to be unlawful. The National Association of Realtors filed an amicus brief in support of the administration's case before the Supreme Court to have the CFPB ruled as illegal. Vice President Mike Pence agreed with and signed onto the administration's legal claim to have the CFPB ordered as unlawful.

The Cato Institute was co-founded by Edward Crane and Charles Koch in the 1970s with Koch's money. Rupert Murdoch was on the board. GOP operatives in the Cato Institute include Mark Calabria, the former director of Cato's Financial Regulation Studies.

On April 20, 2012, Mark Ames, a reporter with *The Nation*, said, "The more you get to know the real Cato Institute, the more you see a rank, powerful right-wing corporate front group deeply woven into the Republican Party machinery. The group is viewed as unprincipled and cynical in its relentless service of the 1 percent's interests as it is hostile to the progressive cause."[52]

What do these conflicts have in common? They each want the destruction of the CFPB. The CFPB's current director now stands before the Supreme Court in agreement that the CFPB is illegal in its design—yes, this statement is correct.

Chapter 7 will detail why this is so dangerous, and why the CFPB is critical to the survival of the American taxpayer, and especially the rent-burdened sectors of the economy. The dismantling of the CFPB is tied to Artificial Intelligence–driven technology—it's always about the money.

WHO IS IN CHARGE AT FANNIE MAE?

In response to the OIG, Fannie Mae management provided the following explanation as to why they should now have full autonomy and the independence to make decisions:

> While there are several factual and analytical flaws in the draft Alert, some of which are discussed below, the key to the conclusions in the OIG's Alert are two faulty premises:
>
> 1. That Fannie Mae should operate in a state of suspended animation and avoid affirmative management decisions of the type responsible management officials of ongoing business entities make, while it remains in the conservatorship of uncertain duration; and
>
> 2. That the OIG, rather than FHFA, has the prerogative to determine what management decisions can be responsibly made by Fannie Mae during this protracted period of conservatorship.[53]

This information is vital to understanding how the leadership chain of command actually works within the GSE. Fannie Mae's management has taken the position that because there is no plan in place to either fix or privatize the GSEs, their legal status is in suspended animation. Furthermore, managers at Fannie Mae have made their own interpretations of what suspended animation means and now operate under the assumption that the GSEs are allowed to make their own management decisions without the approval of the FHFA, the legally designated receiver.

This and other chapters will report in detail the consequences and significance of these management decisions.
At issue is that the FHFA refuses to defend the American
taxpayers, who have not taken any action against the GSEs
since 2017, revealing signs of failure in the management of
an entity that has been beleaguered by conflicts of interest.

In another matter, an OIG audit found that the FHFA
continued to lack transparency in other critical financial
reports. For example, the Common Securitization Platform,
powered by Artificial Intelligence–driven technology solely
for use by the Enterprises to issue a single type of security,
cost $2.08 billion.[54] In the OIG's March 2017 update, the
FHFA projected a total of $1.12 billion in platform devel-
opment costs. In making that same update, the FHFA reit-
erated its commitment to transparency.

Furthermore, the OIG addressed the move of Fannie Mae
to close its northern Virginia offices, which include most
of its personnel. The OIG, in further discussing the relocation, noted that the selected new locations were in areas
known to have a vast, highly trained employee base. The
OIG also questioned Fannie Mae's implied intention to
shed the company of career employees they determined to
be deadweight personnel.

Mick Mulvaney, then acting White House chief of staff,
got caught on a phone call, bragging that he had gotten
rid of the crusty old workers at the USDA. On August 9,
2019, Charles P. Pierce reported through *Esquire* magazine
that, "Speaking to the South Carolina Republican Party
at a gala, Mulvaney brought up the USDA move and how
many workers decided to resign because of it, calling it 'a
wonderful way to sort of streamline government.'"[55]

"'Guess what happened?' Mulvaney said. 'More than half the people quit. Now, it's nearly impossible to fire a federal worker. I know that because a lot of them work for me, and I've tried. You can't do it . . . By simply saying to people, 'You know what, we're going to take you outside the bubble, outside the Beltway, outside this liberal haven of Washington, DC, and move you out to the real part of the country' . . . they quit.'"[56] The consequence of Mulvaney's actions was the loss of centuries of knowledge centered on processes and procedures. Once again, employees who have critical awareness and understanding of the operations are now gone.

On August 7, 2019, reporter Dave Jamieson at *HuffPost* reported the following:

> Now the inspector general says USDA leadership didn't follow the law as it carried out the plan. In a report released, the watchdog said that, while the agency has the legal power to move the two offices, it did not obtain budgetary approval from Congress and also failed to meet reporting deadlines. As a matter of record, the inspector general's findings themselves cannot stop the relocation from moving forward.[57]

However, the FHFA could have stopped them, and the question remains: Why have they refused to take any actions since before 2017? The answer, as we have seen, is because their modus operandi has been to observe and take no action. Moving headquarters appears to be the process the Trump administration uses to set its agenda into action. It is, therefore, not a stretch to imagine this is the same reason for the move the administration has taken in the case of the GSEs, as well.

Fannie Mae decided to spend nearly $1 billion on setting up a new location in extravagant facilities, and then to spend over $2 billion to upgrade their IT technology, without acquiring approval from Congress to cover these expenses. This shows another absolute failure to adhere to the policy of maintaining and preserving funds.

In fact, HUD is acquiring the same AI technology that property managers utilize in the multifamily housing markets. We will discuss this technology, as well as the possible interconnectedness between the users of AI technology, in detail in Chapters 5, 6, and 7.

WHAT ABOUT THE TAXPAYERS AND THE $191 BILLION BAILOUT?

Fannie Mae, as of September 30, 2019, still owes $114 billion,[58] and Freddie Mac's debt increased from $75.6 billion to $77.5 billion.[59] The combined debt to the taxpayer remains its original $191 billion. For the billions of dollars in profits touted by the GSEs, American taxpayers have seen no relief from the tax liability they are required to pay.

In the Trump administration's mad rush to push the GSEs into privatization, the entire HUD organization has been driven into absolute chaos. For a federal financial regulator responsible for supervising two enterprises that together own or guarantee more than $5 trillion in mortgage assets and, furthermore, that operate in conservatorship, to fail to complete a substantial number of planned, targeted internal examinations is an unsound supervisory practice and strategy.[60]

The lack of timely policymaking has cost the taxpayers $2.23 billion in losses. In October 2016, the OIG projected that HUD paid claims for nearly 239,000 properties that servicers did not foreclose upon or convey on time. As a result, over five years, HUD paid an estimated $2.23 billion in unreasonable and unnecessary holding costs. The reason? HUD regulations do not establish a maximum period for filing a claim, even though the law places such limitations.

The OIG also estimates that, in one transaction, the FHA, through its approved lenders, insured more than 9,500 ineligible loans worth $1.9 billion. Loans to borrowers designated ineligible for financing had two- and three-month delinquency rates—twice as high as those of the general population.[61]

Further, the OIG found instances of fraudulent appraisals. OIG investigations have revealed situations in which appraisers claim that property values increased by 60 to 100 percent, while other properties in the same area are appreciating only 3 to 4 percent.[62]

Finally, the OIG found that the agency makes limited to no use of reported data on its customers. Consequently, the required fraud reports are of limited utility concerning the risks posed on the Enterprises.[63] A lack of response has led to the Enterprises' inability to accurately report who their customers are because, apparently, they don't care.

According to the OIG, HUD struggles to remain compliant with federal IT regulations. Furthermore, HUD has failed to address its IT challenges.[64] And the OIG is absolutely right: HUD and its many counterparts have been unable to maintain even the simplest and most basic levels of computer soundness and safety. Artificial Intelligence–driven technology is a game changer. Once a person gains even the smallest bit of knowledge about this technology, it becomes difficult to not understand the immense power it has in the development of the new age, the age of big data.

Yet here we are, about to convert the entire HUD system to a program powered by an Artificial Intelligence–driven technology so advanced that the directive includes the authority to hire the most advanced technologists. In stark contrast, the FHFA's management cannot provide a complete list of all those who have access to the new AI-driven system platforms, passcode holders, and, more critically, those who hold the highest levels of clearance to all online activity and databases.

Prudent policy and procedures have been bypassed and overlooked, as pointed out repeatedly by the OIG. The most basic of functions, such as internal audits and exams to ensure the organizations adhere to policies and procedures, haven't been completed in years. In fact, the internal audit program established for the regulator FHFA, at the cost of over $7.7 million to the taxpayer, sits in shambles. The GSEs haven't been able to balance their books in accordance with GAAP for more than five years. Worst of all, the GSEs' Allowance for Loan and Lease Losses was deemed unreliable by the OIG as of September 2018. In the real world, should regulators find a bank operating under such reckless behavior, the bank would immediately be placed under a Cease and Desist Consent Order and likely would be closed indefinitely.

In Chapter 4, we will take an in-depth look at the housing markets, and what lies inside the loans this group is financing under such chaotic circumstances. In Chapter 8, we will take a much more in-depth look into management practices, and all those conflicts of interest the OIG has pointed out.

After reviewing the many facts, it becomes apparent that Fannie and Freddie are setting themselves up to be privatized at a high price tag to the American taxpayer. That privatization comes at the expense of failed management under the FHFA, allowing the entire HUD organization to operate in a state of chaos. All the while, it fails in its mission and original intent—affordable housing. We are over seven million units short. Why?

On December 18, 2018, in a letter addressed to Congress, nearly 2,000 groups supporting affordable housing wrote, "We, the undersigned 1,894 organizations, write to express the support for the national Housing Trust Fund and to urge Congress to expand this critical resource, as part of a broader commitment to access and affordability throughout the housing market."[65] Yet the affordable housing crisis continues unanswered.

This is chaos!

CHAPTER 4

TO LIVE IN A WORLD WITHOUT CONSEQUENCES: THE MULTIFAMILY FINANCIAL MARKETS

IN CHAPTER 3, we saw that the Enterprises (Fannie Mae and Freddie Mac) failed to provide GSE directors with accurate, timely, and sufficient information to enable them to exercise their oversight duties. The OIG warned that the GSEs' regulator DER preserved the status quo (observe, but take no actions), which "creates a significant risk that management will put its own spin on the deficiencies or will filter the information it provides to the Board."[1] Those responsible for the quality and types of loans have been purposefully kept out of the decision-making process, creating a potential blind spot.

What is behind those loans and offsetting bonds? How solid are they? The 2008 Great Recession saw nearly 30 percent of multifamily CMBS loans end in default, and the entire multifamily housing sector suffered catastrophic losses. Nevertheless, today, rental incomes show an ever-increasing profit margin based on rental rate increases. Are those ever-rising rental rates sustainable?

In Chapter 1, we discovered that, once soldiers began returning home after World War II, a severe housing shortage occurred. This also happened in 1968, where Congress found "that the supply of the Nation's housing was not increasing rapidly enough to meet the national housing goal." As our predecessors did in the 1950s, they used the Housing Act of 1949—which grants Congress the power to intervene in the markets—to realize the goal of a decent home and a suitable living environment for every American family.

Why hasn't Congress enacted similar legislation today? What changed in policy and procedure that might hinder such action?

A study by Charles J. Orlebeke in 2000, published by the University of Illinois at Chicago, looked at the evolving federal role in low-income rental housing. Orlebeke divided the evolution of policy into roughly two segments. The first ran from the adoption of the 1949 act to about 1969. The second started with the Nixon administration, which, as we've seen, was marked by a diminished federal leadership role and an intent to engage the "free (for-profit) market" into the production of affordable housing.[2]

The 1970s policy changes shifted the burden of affordable housing to the markets, which created significant disruptions and eventually caused the financial failure of the savings and loans in the 1990s and the Great Recession in 2008.

We know that HUD played a significant role in the 2008 Great Recession. Fannie Mae and Freddie Mac reportedly received $191.5 billion in taxpayer bailouts. Do we see a repeat of HUD's role in another pending economic crash, or has HUD been tamed?

THE 2008 FINANCIAL CRISIS INQUIRY COMMISSION (FCIC): FIVE TOP CAUSES OF THE GREAT RECESSION

The commission was established to examine the causes of the 2008 Great Recession and to explain those causes to the American people. They concluded that the financial crisis of 2007 and 2008 was not a single event but a series of crises that rippled through the financial system and, ultimately, the economy. Distress in one area of the financial markets led to failures in other areas by way of interconnections and vulnerabilities that bankers, government officials, and others had missed or dismissed.[3]

The commission identified five primary causes of the economic crash:

1. CONSOLIDATIONS AND CONCENTRATIONS IN THE INDUSTRY

From 1978 to 2007, the amount of debt held by the financial sector soared from $3 trillion to $36 trillion. The nature of many Wall Street firms changed from relatively straight private partnerships to publicly traded corporations taking greater and more diverse risks. By 2005, the ten largest US commercial banks held 55 percent of the industry's assets, more than double the level held in 1990.[4] As a result, two parallel financial systems of enormous scale emerged—shadow banks and commercial banks. As codependent competitors, their new activities were very profitable and, it turned out, very risky.

The phenomenal growth of the shadow banking system freely operated in capital markets, still beyond the reach of the regulatory agencies that had been put in place in the wake of the crash of 1929 and the Great Depression.

2.   DEREGULATION

Deregulation went beyond dismantling regulations; its supporters were also disinclined to adopt new rules or challenge industry on the risks of innovations. Federal Reserve officials argued that financial institutions, with strong incentives to protect shareholders, would regulate themselves by carefully managing their own risks. In a 2003 speech, Federal Reserve Vice Chairman Roger Ferguson praised "the truly impressive improvement in methods of risk measurement and management and the growing adoption of these technologies by mostly large banks and other financial intermediaries."[5]

3.   CREDIT EXPANSION AND RAPID GROWTH

By the end of the 2000s, the economy had grown for thirty-nine straight quarters. Federal Reserve Chairman Alan Greenspan boasted that the financial system had achieved unprecedented resilience. Large financial companies appeared to be profitable, diversified, and—executives and regulators agreed—protected from catastrophe by sophisticated new techniques of managing risk.

The housing market was also strong. Between 1995 and 2000, prices rose at an annual rate of 5.2 percent. Between 2005 and 2010, the rate hit 11.5 percent. Lower interest rates for mortgage borrowers were partly the reason, as was greater access to mortgage credit for households that had traditionally been left out—called subprime borrowers. The subprime loans would also include other risky loans such as credit cards and auto loans.

John Taylor, a Stanford University economist and former undersecretary of the Treasury, blamed the crisis primarily on this action. If the Fed had followed its usual pattern, he told the FCIC, short-term interest rates would have been much higher, discouraging excessive investment in mortgages. "The boom in housing construction starts would have been much milder, might not even call it a boom, and the bust as well would have been mild," Taylor said.[6]

The commission concluded that the monetary policy of the Federal Reserve, along with capital flows from abroad, created conditions in which a housing bubble could develop.

For example, in 2003 alone, the housing market refinanced over 15 million mortgages, more than one in four— an unprecedented level. Lending standards collapsed, and there was a significant failure of accountability. Loans were often premised on the assumption of ever-increasing home prices and were made regardless of the borrower's ability to pay. Then to further weaken the lending standards in May 2008, Fannie Mae introduced approvals for mortgages with debt-to-income (DTI) ratios between 55 and 65 percent.

4.   THE RISE OF SHADOW BANKING

As Yale economist Gary Gorton put it in his book *Misunderstanding Financial Crises: Why We Don't See Them Coming*, the 2008 financial crisis was triggered by a run on short-term bank debt. Gorton found that illiquidity in the commercial paper market and a sudden lack of confidence in the money market mutual fund industry led to the financial crisis. All three are part of what is called the "shadow banking system," which does not depend on the safety net of either a lender of last resort like the Fed or regulatory agencies that can intervene to deal with the volatility of a run.[7] In other words, the shadow banks are not covered by FDIC insurance, and the government does not have a mechanism to bail the shadow banks out of financial ruin.

During the 1990s, the shadow banking system had steadily gained ground on the traditional banking sector, and briefly surpassed the banking sector after 2000. Investment bankers like Lehman Brothers and Bear Stearns were two of the more infamous non-banking financial companies (NBFCs) at the center of the meltdown. Banks argued that their inability to compete stemmed from the 1933 Glass-Steagall Act, which strictly limited commercial banks' participation in the securities markets.[8]

The shadow banking proliferated for a reason: free from the shackles of regulation, it got money where it was needed. The chief obstacle, however, was controlling the greed.

5. SECURITIZATION AND STRUCTURED FINANCE SECURITIES

Private securitizations, or structured finance securities, had two critical benefits for investors: pooling and tranching. If many loans were pooled into one security, a few defaults would have minimal impact. Structured finance securities could also be sliced up and sold in portions, known as tranches.

Securitization was designed to benefit lenders, investment bankers, and investors. Lenders earned massive fees for originating and selling loans. Investment banks made massive fees for issuing mortgage-backed securities. Securitization was not just a boon for commercial banks; it was also a lucrative new line of business for the Wall Street investment banks with which the commercial banks worked to create the new securities.

The commission concluded that the nonprime mortgage securitization process created a pipeline through which risky mortgages were conveyed and sold throughout the financial system. This pipeline was essential to the origination of the burgeoning numbers of high-risk mortgages.[9]

SUBPRIME LENDING

Of the $600 billion of subprime loans originated in the housing market of 2006, most were securitized. That year, subprime lending accounted for 23.5 percent of all mortgage originations. As private-label securitization took hold, new computer and modeling technologies were reshaping the mortgage market.[10]

Accordingly, multifamily GSEs assumed an expected loss of only 6 percent on subprime CMBS defaults because their models did not accommodate the possibility of a severe recession where mortgage owners could default *en masse*. The end result was that the defaults were much higher than 6 percent—in fact, 29.9 percent of all CMBS loans defaulted. This was a staggering loss.[11]

Vincent Reinhart, a former director of the Federal Reserve's Division of Monetary Affairs, told the commission that he and other regulators failed to appreciate the complexity of the new financial instruments. Securitization "was diversifying the risk," said Lawrence Lindsey, the former Federal Reserve governor. "But it wasn't reducing the risk . . . You, as an individual, can diversify your risk. The system as a whole, though, cannot reduce the risk. And that's where the confusion lies."[12]

NOTABLE TRENDS IN THE CURRENT HOUSING MARKETS

INVESTING IN ARTIFICIAL INTELLIGENCE–DRIVEN TECHNOLOGY

In March 2019, the website Multifamily Insiders surveyed leading property management companies regarding their plans to invest or continue to invest in AI technology. Most respondents expressed why they made significant investments, with answers primarily pointing to the cost dynamics of projects and capabilities, clear ROI objectives, and efficiency or improvement of resident experience. Only 10 percent responded that they would spend less. Respondents further expressed that they were beefing up their platforms to carry out a precise growth strategy, which increased technology spending.[13]

THE HOUSING MARKETS

According to a recent Reis report, the United States now has more multifamily units under construction than at any time since the mid-1970s.[14] The year 2017 was the most active on record for multifamily and commercial real estate finance.[15] In contrast, the single-family residential housing market (SFR) maintains a combined shortage as demand outperforms supply. Total SFR housing completions averaged 1.1 million housing units each year over the past three years. However, total households increased, on average, by 1.4 million annually over those same years.[16]

Both crucial measures of SFR supply are at their smallest levels since the National Association of Realtors began tracking in 1982. In 2017, Zillow put supply at just three months, with inventories in roughly one-third of ninety-three metros under two months.[17] A balanced market is considered to be six months of inventory.

LENDING IN THE GSEs

In 2019, there was more government-backed housing debt than at any other point in US history, according to data from the Urban Institute. Fannie Mae, Freddie Mac, and the Federal Housing Administration guaranteed almost $7 trillion in mortgage-related debt, 33 percent more than before the housing crisis.[18]

WHERE IS NEW CONSTRUCTION
BEING BUILT, AND WHY?

While there may seem to be a lot of multifamily units under construction, at a national level, the potential demand for new units is expected to be in balance with current supply underway. Unfortunately, the match between supply and demand varies greatly among metropolitan areas, which means that several cities could end up with an oversupply of newer, more expensive units. That, in turn, would negatively impact the ongoing lack of affordable multifamily rental housing.[19]

FIGURE 1.

MULTIFAMILY APARTMENT UNITS UNDERWAY – SELECT METROPOLITAN AREAS

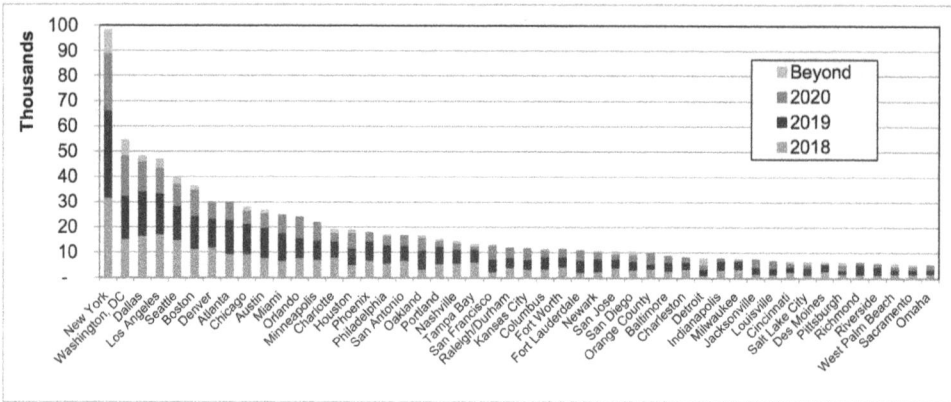

Source: "Multifamily Market Commentary–July 2019 Multifamily Supply and Demand Varies by Metropolitan Areas," Fanniemae.com, accessed December 2019, https://multifamily.fanniemae.com/sites/g/files/koqyhd161/files/2019-07/MF_Market_Commentary_071619_0.pdf.

Why are builders constructing so many multifamily units in higher-cost urban areas? One consideration is rising construction costs. According to data from RS Means, multifamily building costs have increased 5.3 percent on average every year from 2016 through 2018. Yet, the cost of most building materials doesn't change that much by locality. The result is that most builders fixate on urban areas with strong job growth, improving demographic trends, and more profitable rents.

Kim Betancourt, director of economics, and Tim Komosa, economist manager, at the Multifamily Economics and Market Research at Fannie Mae, explain:

But the average asking rent in both St. Louis and Birmingham are estimated at about $950, according to
CoStar. That rent level is not much of an incentive for
multifamily developers to break ground. That's because
there is not much of a project cost differential between
lower-cost metropolitan areas such as Birmingham and
a higher-priced metro area, such as Seattle. But there
is a significant differential in the amount of rent that
can be commanded. With an average asking rent of
$1,730 coupled with annualized rent growth of nearly
4.0 percent, it is easy to understand how Seattle now
has more than 21,000 units underway.[20]

The construction location, in other words, is driven by
developer profits and projection-based pro forma data,
which is centered on ever-increasing rents and an economy
that will never endure a market correction. Neither scenario
is considered realistic.

IS NEW CONSTRUCTION AFFORDABLE?

Between 2006 and 2016, the lowest-cost rental inventory
shrank by more than 10 percent in 153 of the nation's
381 metros and by more than 20 percent in the larger 89
metros. These losses indicate that older rental units have
not filtered down to more affordable levels in many parts
of the country.[21]

The supply of affordable homes at the bottom end is
exceptionally scarce. Virtually all of the 88 metros with
data available had more homes for sale in the top third of
the market by price than in the bottom third. In 46 metros,
more than half of the available supply was at the high end.

Furthermore, there was a conversion of 3.9 million affordable single-family homes to rentals (mostly converted to
vacation rentals) between 2006 and 2016.[22]

A recent study by Freddie Mac cites high housing costs
as the main factor in keeping young adults from purchasing
homes.[23] For example, in October 2018, the median purchase
price for a house in Seattle was $706,000 and $813,000 in
East King County. The high prices put homeownership out
of reach even for families earning 100 percent AMI.[24] To
make matters worse, Freddie Mac is failing its (congressionally enacted) affordable-housing production goals.[25]

Now that we have explored the primary causes of the
2008 Great Recession, discussed the current housing
markets, and examined how these issues might again prove
as pernicious as they did in 2008, we must look more deeply
into those loans. How solid are they? We completed a study
on some of those loans in order to determine whether HUD
is administering its Fannie and Freddie Delegated Underwriting and Servicing (DUS) loans program per its regulations policies and procedures.

LOOSENING OF CREDIT STANDARDS

In January 2019, the Government Accountability Office
(GAO) reported to Congress, as presented in Highlights of
GAO-19-239:

> GSE loan officers indicate a loosening of underwriting
> standards in recent years. Specifically, average com-
> bined loan-to-value ratios (for all loans on the prop-
> erty) and debt-to-income ratios have increased, while
> average borrower credit scores have also declined.[26]

General underwriting guidelines in banking make some requirements for underwriters to resolve questions of collateral (the subject property) weaknesses within the loan, generally referred to as "mitigating risk." Many loans do not meet all lending guidelines, and yet the loans are considered to be safe as the identified weakness is mitigated.

For example, let's say that a potential property owner failed to meet their minimum debt coverage ratio (DCR) of 1.25x, instead coming in at 1.20x. However, their loan-to-value ratio (LTV) was far below the required 75 percent, coming in at 40 percent LTV. The weakness in their DCR would be mitigated by the additional strength of LTV.

Freddie and Fannie are the only GSE entities that have not strengthened their lending standards since the 2008 crash. For example, the Small Business Administration (SBA) requires full guarantees, as well as pledging of additional assets on an as-needed basis, and complete financial disclosure is required of every other type of GSE or conventional financing.

How are the GSEs handling their loan approvals? Let's take a closer look at some of those rules.

BAD BOY CARVE-OUTS

Loans, in general, are non-recourse, which means that a borrower is not personally responsible for the repayment of the loan. The main exception to this is what is known as "bad boy" carve-outs for intentionally causing harm to the property—a mostly useless and unenforceable policy. This type of lending is considered very high risk, because the borrower has little skin in the game.

Conversely, homeowners are held by HUD to be personally liable for their loans, with no exceptions.

High LTV Ratios

Prohibited by policies or regulatory requirements, FDIC-insured lenders are required to use higher overall LTV ratios to limit banks from lending more than 75 percent of the appraised value of the property. Nevertheless, CMBS lenders (shadow banks) are not bound by such policies and regulatory requirements. It is common to see a CMBS loan with an LTV of 80 percent or, in combination with a mezzanine loan, even higher.

FRAUDULENT APPRAISALS AND PRICE-FIXING

In a December 17, 2019, Reuters article, "Big Banks Settle Fannie Mae, Freddie Mac Bond-Rigging Litigation in U.S.," Jonathan Stempel states the following:

> Thirteen dominant banks and financial services companies consented to pay some $337 million to resolve claims by investors that they conspired to fix prices of bonds issued by mortgage companies Fannie Mae (FNMA.PK) and Freddie Mac (FMCC.PK) for a decade. Investors accused the defendants of abusing their market dominance to overcharge for Fannie Mae and Freddie Mac bonds from Jan. 1, 2009, to Jan. 1, 2019, and keep more profit for themselves. According to an amended complaint, the 16 defendants underwrote $3.97 trillion, or 77.2%, of Fannie

Mae and Freddie Mac bonds from Jan. 1, 2009, to
Jan. 1, 2016.[27]

At about the same time, the OIG found previously-de-
scribed instances of fraudulent appraisals being used by
Fannie and Freddie to increase loan amounts to qualify
borrowers for larger loans.[28]

The GSE has set specific policy standards for appraisals:

> The GSEs delegated underwriting and servicing respon-
> sibility to risk sharing lenders, which aligns risk, pro-
> vides certainty of execution, and leverages the lenders'
> capabilities. Appraisals must estimate the as-is leased
> fee market value of the Property ("leased fee" as
> defined in the current edition of *The Appraisal of
> Real Estate*, published by the Appraisal Institute) as
> of the effective date of the Appraisal, subject to stated
> assumptions and limiting conditions. Although other
> valuation scenarios may be appropriate for a particu-
> lar Appraisal, at minimum, all Appraisals must provide
> an as-is estimate of market value.[29]

HISTORY OF PRO FORMA–BASED APPRAISAL THEORY

In 1982, when I first started to work as a federal bank
examiner, the Farm Credit System had already been experiencing economic upheaval due to their ill-conceived decision to lend in the aquatic industry—fishing vessels. In a
rush to grow loan volume and increase their bottom line,
the Farm Credit System began financing an industry they
knew little about. Part of their process included weaken-

ing their credit and underwriting policies, including their policy on appraisals.

By the time I arrived, the inside joke among federal regulators was that appraisals completed by MAI (Member of the Appraisal Institute), once a benchmark of trust, now had the derogatory meaning "Made as Instructed." Farm Credit Banks took on massive credit losses due to their weak underwriting standards and, in part, to federal regulators' lax oversight throughout the system.

At the center of the crisis were the appraisals (theories) themselves, which had weakened as a result of constant pressure from member banks to lessen credit standards. The banks deemed those standards to be the roadblock to loan growth and the source of their inability to compete against big banks like Wells Fargo and Bank of America.

Initially, the aquatic lending program was authorized by Congress, and the rules were established as part of the approval process. Appraisals were required to provide a value based on the theory of "as-is" market value—the value of the property at the time of loan consideration.

However, because the original credit standards were weakened, appraisals were allowed to provide values based on certain assumptions, such as ever-increasing market growth and/or ever-increasing market prices. This assumption was known as pro forma–based theory. This theory includes, among other aspects, the ability to forecast and give present value to future events such as price increases and allow those projected future possibilities to influence the current value. The result of the changes in theory (credit policy) was that Farm Credit achieved and surpassed its loan goals, and the cost of fishing vessels skyrocketed. Those ever-increasing values were supported by pro forma–based appraisals.

There is a correlation between ease of access to seemingly endless amounts of credit and skyrocketing values of financed property—in this instance, fishing vessels.

Unfortunately for the Farm Credit System, the entire agriculture industry would enter into one of its worst economic downturns, which lasted for decades. Most unfortunate was the fact that Farm Credit had severely depleted their loan-loss reserves to cover loan losses from the aquatics division, which left them entirely unprepared financially for the oncoming crisis. The taxpayers would provide bailouts to save the lending system.

Today, appraisers are utilizing pro forma–based values supported by projected rents rather than values based on historical data. The practice of using pro forma–based income statements to support appraised values, which are dependent on sizable rental rate increases going forward, has become the norm for well-funded investment groups. However, no one seems to be paying attention to the ability or sustainability of those projections. Can tenants continue to afford those rental rate increases?

Historical data helps us understand how the GSEs are valuing their collateral and the ability to rely on those pro forma assumptions. The historical approach to evaluating an income-earning property provides a number based on the historical performance of cash flows. In contrast, a pro forma approach relies on ever-increasing rents. Therefore, we must examine the data behind the pro forma financials to determine their reliability.

FINDINGS FROM THE INDEPENDENT STUDY

We completed a study to determine whether the GSEs are administering Fannie and Freddie underwriting programs per their regulations policies and procedures. More specifically, we monitored and reviewed the closing of four multifamily projects (a combination of apartments and mobile home parks, from four different states) to determine whether the lenders (risk sharers) sourcing and closing those loans are meeting their lender requirements and the GSEs' underwriting standards. We will discuss those findings in the examples below.

The Infrastructure Study below concludes that less than 20 percent of infrastructure repair costs are being reported by the lender, leaving massive costs unaccounted for, and the quality of life for the tenants as substandard and, in many cases, dangerous.

Per Table 1, the historical value (HV) is established on the date of the appraisal by a certified and HUD-approved appraiser. The pro forma value (PV) assigns a higher value based on future rent increases. The inflated value (IV) is that portion of the value assigned to future rent increases (Table 4, below). Therefore, the risk to the taxpayer is the inflated portion of the appraisal and the infrastructure costs (IC).

TABLE 1.

RISKY LOANS UNCOVERED

	Example 1	Example 2	Example 3	Example 4
Historic Value	8,385,250	9,376,212	4,341,723	9,256,000
Proforma Value	9,000,000	11,500,000	5,150,000	9,900,000
Inflated Value	614,750	2,123,788	808,277	644,000
Infrastructure Cost	1,332,625	1,020,100	955,750	381,674
Risk to Tax Payers	**1,947,375**	**3,143,888**	**1,764,027**	**1,025,674**
Over Value	7.33%	22.65%	18.62%	6.96%
Combined OverValue	23.22%	33.53%	40.63%	11.08%

The risk (R) equals the IV plus the IC (discussed later), which is the amount of projected collateral shortfall should the property be taken back in default. This loss is then charged to the American taxpayer as the Treasury issues bonds backing those losses; the projected combined loan losses range from a low of 11.08 percent to a high of 40.64 percent.

CONVENTIONAL LOANS PROTECT AGAINST LOSS, BUT GSE LOANS ARE RISKY

In today's world of commercial lending, the community banking system (under $10 billion) maintains more robust credit policy standards, such as requirements for bigger down payments. The amount of required down payment can, as we will see, protect the taxpayer from excessive financial bailouts.

When we carry the risk (R) to the taxpayer from Table 1, and looking at the additional required down payment (EDP) on conventional loans, the additional down payment is the requirement by federal banking policy. The traditional lenders are protecting their investments with stricter lending guidelines, whereas GSEs are offering the best rates and terms to the riskiest of borrowers and lenders.

TABLE 2.

CONVENTIONAL LOANS PROTECT AGAINST LOSS – GSEs LOANS ARE RISKY

	Example 1	Example 2	Example 3	Example 4
CMBS Down Payment	1,700,000	2,300,000	1,030,000	1,460,000
Risk to Taxpayers (R) (From Table 1)	1,947,377	3,143,888	1,764,027	1,524,824
Extra Down Payment Required by Conventional Lenders (EDP) (Table 3)	1,700,000	2,300,000	1,030,000	1,460,000
Estimated Possible Losses after Extra Down Payment (R - EDP)	247,377	843,888	734,027	64,824
Total Risk to Taxpayer Lowered by EDP (as a percent of R)	87%	73%	58%	96%

This can be seen by revealing the dollar risk (R) to the taxpayers and then matching the additional down payment (EDP) required by commercial banks. The final loss results (R - EDP) yield the final estimated loss results. As we see in Table 2, traditional lenders take more exceptional care to protect their investment in the loans. In fact, the study shows that commercial banks' loan losses are projected to be between 58 to 96 percent lower than the GSEs' projected loan losses. This research supports the finding from the OIG in Chapter 3 that the nonbanks are making much riskier (CMBS) loans.

Traditional lenders, therefore, are less likely to sustain significant losses on their portfolio within this example, or with *en masse* defaults, and would be more likely to withstand the financial storm. This theory of lending also equally protects taxpayers from unnecessary risks.

GSE LOAN VERSUS CONVENTIONAL LOAN

Now let's compare GSE loans against conventional loans to determine if GSEs are giving investors a fair and balanced lending program with reasonable risk to the American taxpayer.

The CMBS loans in the table below are characterized by much higher loan-to-value ratios (LTV), lower interest rates, and extended terms yielding lower monthly payments. The conventional loans collect larger down payments and charge more reasonable interest rates, which are priced on risk-based asset quality.

In this example, the top portion details the pricing of four CMBS loans, and the bottom part contains the pricing details of the conventional loans, which require the larger down payments (Table 2). Table 3 explains how the additional cash down payment is accounted for in the example. The additional down payment will be analyzed as an opportunity cost, which is the cost associated with the conventional loan.

TABLE 3.

TOTAL SAVINGS OF CMBS LOANS VERSUS CONVENTIONAL LOANS

CMBS LOAN	Example 1	Example 2	Example 3	Example 4	
Loan Request Amount	6,800,000	9,200,000	4,120,000	5,840,000	
Interest Rate (%)	4.18%	4.18%	4.18%	4.18%	
Total Interest	5,142,582	6,957,610	3,115,800	4,413,570	
Total Principal	6,800,000	9,200,000	4,120,000	5,840,000	
Total Cost	11,942,582	16,157,610	7,235,800	10,253,570	
Conventional Loan					
Loan Request Amount	5,100,000	6,900,000	3,090,000	4,380,000	
Interest Rate (%)	5.65%	5.65%	5.65%	5.65%	
Total Interest	4,433,086	5,997,705	2,685,829	3,807,239	
Total Principal	5,100,000	6,900,000	3,090,000	4,380,000	
Additional Down Payment	1,700,000	2,300,000	1,030,000	1,460,000	
Opportunity Cost	1,664,313	2,057,528	1,056,390	1,362,040	
Total Cost	12,897,399	17,255,233	7,862,219	11,009,279	
					Average Savings
CMBS Savings	954,817	1,097,623	626,419	755,709	*858,642*
Savings Over Conv. Loans	8.00%	6.79%	8.66%	7.37%	*7.70%*

Opportunity cost is the value of what those additional down-payment funds could earn if invested in the market, and the rate assigned is the capitalization rate (CAP rate), the method of establishing value from the appraisal. Put simply, the rate of return is based on what those funds could earn invested in another project.

In this example, the CMBS loan will save its borrowers an average of $860,000, or about 7.7 percent in total financing costs over the life of the loan. The savings is massive when compared to conventional loans, so enormous as to give the borrowers little option in loan financing product choice. The weakening of credit standards is indeed placing massive volumes of loans into the pipelines of production, and all at the risk of the taxpayer. (Pipelines are discussed in more detail in Chapter 5.)

ARE THOSE EVER-INCREASING RENTS SUSTAINABLE?

According to the Joint Center for Housing Studies at Harvard University in 2018, the median renter's income grew only 5 percent between 1960 and 2016, adjusting for inflation. In contrast, for the three years ending in the third quarter of 2018, multifamily property prices increased by 10.7 percent annually. The cumulative cost of rent has risen by 14.1 percent.[30]

Apartment investments continue to provide stable and safe returns for investors compared with other investments.[31] However, are those ever-increasing rental rates sustainable?

Table 4 reflects the changes in rental rates that are happening upon the acquisition of these properties. The question to answer is whether or not the tenant will have funds available to meet future rent increases. To determine the sustainability of the rental rate increases, let's review the four examples. As each of the four cases is from a different state, specific demographic information will be utilized to determine the tenant's ability to meet the projected rental rate increases as proposed by the buyers of the properties. As it happens, the appraisal contains demographic information (Figure 2) needed for this review and is copied in our review materials for analysis purposes. The tenants are considered by the lender to be the source of repayment to the loans financing the property; therefore, assessing their ability to meet the rental rate increases is deemed to be critical to the analysis.

Historic rent (HR) is the amount of rent the tenants have been paying. The pro forma rent (PR) is the amount of rent projected to be paid once the properties are acquired. The following tables summarize the historic rents versus projected rents, the cost to the renter, and how those rent increases affect their ability to make the required rent increase payment.

TABLE 4.

RENTERS HIT WITH SKYROCKETING RENTS

Proposed Rent Increase	Example 1	Example 2	Example 3	Example 4
Historic Rents (HR)	1,528	1,629	1,577	1,493
Proforma Rents (PR)	1,788	1,890	1,719	1,747
Annual Rent Increase in Dollars (RI $)	3,117	3,128	1,703	3,046
Proposed Rent Increase Percentage (RI %)	17%	16%	9%	17%
Average R.I. ($)	*2748.50*			
Average R.I. (%)	*14.76%*			
Estimated Increase in Tenant Income				
Tenant Increase in Annual Income	1,535	(145)	1,300	737
Increase as a percent	8.37%	-0.74%	6.87%	4.10%
Average Increase in Dollars	*856.75*			
Average Percentage Increase	*4.65%*			
Net Effect of Rent Increase– Tenant Ability				
Effect on Budget	(1,582)	(3,273)	(403)	(2,309)
Annual Tenant Budget Shortfall (Dollars)	*(1,891.75)*			
Annual Tenant Budget Shortfall (Percent)	*-10.11%*			

The average annual rent increase upon acquisition is $2,794, or 14.76 percent. This is the average amount of money the renter must pay in additional rents due to the purchase (and for no other reason). The annual estimated increase in tenant income is $857, or 4.65 percent. The findings from this study correlate with and support the results of the Joint Center for Housing Studies discussed above.

The estimated increase in annual tenant income (per the appraisal study in Figure 2) is then compared to the rise in rents occurring within each property. The net effect of yearly income (tenant ability) versus annual rent increases represents the effect on the tenant budget.

To continue our example from the study, we will look at the appraisal information for Figure 2 (from example 3), which reflects information all appraisals are required to contain. The report reveals that tenant gross incomes are going to increase only 4 percent over the next five years. The per capita income number is utilized in this example, and also the number the appraiser used in their analysis. However, the loan was approved based on a 9 percent annual rent increase.

FIGURE 2.

LOCAL AREA DEMOGRAPHICS							
DESCRIPTION	1 MILE	3 MILES	5 MILES	DESCRIPTION	1 MILE	3 MILES	5 MIL
POPULATION				AVERAGE HOUSEHOLD INCOME			
2000 Population	2,669	39,876	105,299	2017	$86,983	$96,705	$91,0
2010 Population	3,109	47,137	128,393	2022	$92,955	$105,256	$98,3
2017 Population	3,727	54,120	146,593	Change 2017-2022	6.87%	8.84%	8.0€
2022 Population	4,173	60,682	162,936	MEDIAN HOUSEHOLD INCOME			
Change 2000-2010	16.49%	18.21%	21.93%	2017	$60,571	$78,014	$73,0
Change 2010-2017	19.88%	14.81%	14.18%	2022	$63,503	$80,536	$75,0
Change 2017-2022	11.97%	12.12%	11.15%	Change 2017-2022	4.84%	3.23%	2.72
POPULATION 65+				PER CAPITA INCOME			
2010 Population	455	4,506	13,139	2017	$32,943	$34,615	$33,0
2017 Population	605	6,537	18,373	2022	$34,264	$36,598	$34,7
2022 Population	768	8,281	23,074	Change 2017-2022	4.01%	5.73%	4.8€

In all four scenarios, the report reveals that the tenants' gross incomes are increasing at rates well below the projected rental rate increases. Per Table 4, tenants will come up short by $1,892, or 10.11 percent annually. Also, with the median annual household income of $60,571 (per Figure 2), the tenant must find a way to fund the $1,892 shortfall. This is what rent burdening, as explained in Chapter 2, looks like. Therefore, the findings show that the lender's source of repayment—the tenant—is doubtful and loan losses are likely.

The loans were approved on the theory that rents would be increased annually. However, per the appraisals along with economic data, the increased rents are not sustainable. The value of the property as proposed cannot be defended or supported. As the future payment is in doubt, the pro forma basis to value is not supportable.

Our research also reveals that without the increased rents, the loans will fall into default on their loan covenants. Pending infrastructure costs typically associated with older apartment complexes and older mobile home parks also loom unaccounted for within the appraisal.

THE CRISIS IN INFRASTRUCTURE STUDY

"Infrastructure" is a term used to describe vital systems, services, and organizational structures for everyday use by citizens. The systems are known as "public works," and we expect them to work for us, although we do not like to pay for them.

Infrastructure costs add significant risk to loans, because should the property be taken back through the default process, the government (as the beneficiary and now owner of the property) will be required to resolve any problems before or during the liquidation process.

Our study, therefore, sought to determine if infrastructure costs address the actual cost of the needed improvements versus the reporting to GSEs. Second, we sought to determine the cost needed for infrastructure improvements and how the cost is impacting appraised values.

There are two types of reports utilized in the acquisition process: buyer-ordered reports and lender-ordered reports, as follows:

1. BUYER-ORDERED INFRASTRUCTURE REPORTS

Licensed general contractors complete this task. The reports are invasive to the property—for example, the sewer report includes sending a telescoping camera through the entire sewer system, and the report is considered to be the most comprehensive and accurate of all reports and investigations. Each report (electrical, water lines, gas lines, and sewer/septic system) costs between $5,000 and $10,000. The reports also typically lead to real costs needed to bring the property up to code. Our findings were that lenders do not generally ask for this information except when the reports are clean.

2. LENDER-ORDERED INFRASTRUCTURE REPORTS

Most lenders use the Property Condition Report. Its purpose is to provide an assessment of the condition of the property and to make recommendations for the expected capital repair and replacement cost that the property may need. However, the assessments and recommendations are based upon a walk-through survey of the site and buildings. Furthermore, the reports are limited, and observations of the building systems are completed without removing components or looking beneath the system. The real cost is left unknown, and this is by design—similar to "observe and take no action."

Our study sample consisted of six older properties that sold. Table 5 is the final average of the six examples, representing the current status of the infrastructure. The Infrastructure Cost Reported comes from the lender-ordered reports; Infrastructure Cost Not Reported comes from the buyer-ordered reports.

TABLE 5.

ACTUAL VERSUS SUBMITTED INFRASTRUCTURE COSTS

	Cost (In $)	Percentage
Infrastructure Cost Reported	223,886	19.64%
Infrastructure Cost Not Reported	1,139,768	80.36%

The study concludes that less than 20 percent of infrastructure costs are being reported to the lender, leaving massive amounts of infrastructure costs unaccounted.

Furthermore, the buyer-ordered infrastructure reports substantiate the fact that quite a bit of our infrastructure has reached its end. Utility and power systems within the properties were between ten and twenty years beyond their expected useful life.

Before the 2008 crash, the housing market was strong. Between 1995 and 2000, home prices rose at an annual rate of 5.2 percent annually, and the consensus opinion was that the single-family residences (SFR) market values would continue to increase forever. However, like the increase in home values of 1995–2008, these rental rate increases today are not sustainable. Nevertheless, the American taxpayer will be required to honor the loan guarantee the GSEs have entered into on our behalf.

"Greystar Credit Partners maintains a credit strategy that involves acquiring subordinated and securitized debt issued by US government–sponsored entities. It is a logical progression for us," Greystar founder and CEO Bob Faith said in a statement. "Our vertically-integrated rental housing platform, together with our intimate knowledge of the origination and underwriting guidelines utilized by the GSEs, positions us well to invest in the most subordinate part of the capital structure."[32] In Chapter 5, we will discuss how some of these entities operate and how their entities are interconnected.

At the beginning of this chapter, we discussed that the OIG pointed out that those responsible for the quality and types of housing loans have been purposefully kept out of the decision-making process. The loan examples we used in our study point to a massive blind spot: pro forma appraisals, lax underwriting policies, and a lack of rigor in assessing infrastructure costs all lead to problematic outcomes once the economy heads south.

THE INVESTORS' MASSIVE BETS: WHEN WE WIN, YOU LOSE—WE ALWAYS WIN!

There is an attitude that buyers can pay any price for a property because higher prices will be supported by higher rents. The purchase price is no longer the most critical part of the purchase price equation. Interest rates, for example, are just as important over the life of the loan, and the buyer will pay nearly the same on interest as on the principal. In the end, it is all about the rents and the ability to increase them indiscriminately.

Currently, GSEs have the most liberal lending standards within the industry, with minimal oversight and within a state of chaos. The borrowers of loan products do so with double the risk of conventional loans—minimal skin in the game and high leverage. These new buyers are electing to use the GSEs' below-market rates and better-than-market terms; in fact, buyers can purchase two properties with the same down payment (capital) as one loan under conventional standards. Risk is growing exponentially within the multifamily financial bubble.

Regardless of how this plays out, the investors win, and the homeowner and taxpayer are the big losers. Taxpayers are required to fund and guarantee risky investments, even though the US Securities and Exchange Commission (SEC) regulations prohibit over 95 percent of Americans from participating in this type of loan program. We are paying for a party we will never get to attend.

Tenants work hard and have taxes withheld from their meager paychecks to fund the guarantees and investments of wealthy billionaire investors. Currently, GSEs are allowing those investors to raise rents without consequence and at the expense of and great detriment to the tenant. The result requires the tenant to guarantee the rights of the investor to raise rents, possibly being forced into financial ruin. In essence, the tenant has no voice in this process, in direct violation of HUD's mission statement.

Today, millions of Americans are in peril of being forced out of their homes because of escalating rents, and millions of Americans have to make critical decisions every day as to where they are going to sleep that night. To make matters worse, the GSEs' lax standards have the potential to cost the American taxpayer hundreds of billions of dollars in losses should the investors' gamble not pay off. The tenants are left with little recourse while their lives are in turmoil.

This is a crisis.

CHAPTER 5

PROPERTY MANAGERS AND ARTIFICIAL INTELLIGENCE– DRIVEN TECHNOLOGY

As we saw in the last chapter, according to the 2008 Financial Crisis Inquiry Commission (FCIC), the number one cause of the Great Recession of 2008 was "consolidations and concentrations in the industry." A tightly interconnected web of companies created not just a single disruption but a series of crises that rippled through the financial system and, ultimately, the economy. Distress in one area of the financial markets led to failures in others via interconnections and vulnerabilities that bankers, government officials, and others either missed or dismissed.[1]

In this chapter, we are going to look more deeply into those consolidations and at the interconnectedness that has developed in the multifamily real estate industry and seeped into our financial system. We will see who the actors are, and we will evaluate and discuss the dangers and vulnerabilities this market structure has once again created.

PROPERTY OWNERS

Beginning in 2015, property ownership changed significantly. Previously, most multifamily units were sold to a single person or a firm, which either contracted a property management company to run day-to-day activities or took care of things on their own. Today, it's private buyers, backed with unlimited funds from unknown and largely unregulated investors, who are taking on significant debt from the GSEs.

The tax-credit syndicators capable of generating the institutional investor-owned properties are forming complex, fragmented ownership-style structures. These structures have become so complex, and the structures the owners create to hold their assets have equally become so complex, that in response, in November 2018, Julie Segal reported in the *Institutional Investor* that J. P. Morgan had issued a new study for the firm's wealthiest clients, warning that those assets may be hard to sell once the economy goes south.[2]

The new owners are buying an increasing portion of the multifamily housing market, making the institutional investor–owned property the new normal. In fact, the top four multifamily property owners in the United States, measured by number of units, are now institutional investor–owned.

Alden Torch Financial took the top spot for 2016, after acquiring Hunt Companies' tax-credit syndication platform. Hunt was the largest syndicator in 2015, but their real value to Alden Torch was their platform and their senior leadership, who possessed deep experience in the Low-Income Housing Tax Credit (LIHTC) industry and were all about consolidation.[3]

In 2017, sales of apartment properties jumped 32 percent to $150 billion, which significantly impacted the National Multifamily Housing Council (NMHC) Top 50 Owners list. When questioned about the impact of this explosive growth in apartment construction, Greystar CEO Bob Faith (now recognized as the largest property manager) said, "Well, I think a lot of it has to do with the tailwinds of the institutionalization of the multifamily sector. Everybody is moving to the city, and multifamily is a massive component of that."[4]

When we consider the growth in apartment units and the change in ownership structures, we must ask: Who are the actors taking possession of that growth, and how have they impacted the overall multifamily industry?

PROPERTY MANAGERS

Historically, property managers are a company engaged by property owners and/or investors to watch over the day-to-day operations of a property. Property managers make sure the real estate they care for operates smoothly, maintains its structural quality, and increases value. The owner's return on investment (ROI) typically determines the property manager's compensation.

With property ownership falling to larger firms and investors, property management companies are also changing. As we will discuss in more detail later, the number of property management companies is decreasing as firms merge and buy each other out in order to keep pace with the larger owners and investors they are working to accommodate.

BUILDERS

The builder is the firm contracted by a property owner to construct a new dwelling. Like the property owner and property management industry, the building industry has seen increased concentration and consolidation, with the market share of the top twenty builders jumping from 21 percent in 2008 to 29 percent in 2018.[5]

The concentrations have led to massive builder abuse. For example, a USA TODAY Network investigation found that Ryan Homes, the country's fourth-largest home builder, disregarded warranty claims made by customers. The builder forced customers into restrictive arbitration agreements, forbidding them from publicly discussing their cases or repairs.

According to a recent study by economists Luis Quintero and Jacob Cosman at Johns Hopkins University, between 2013 and 2017 home prices escalated more than twice as fast as they would have if the market hadn't consolidated.[6]

GROWING CONCENTRATIONS

What is driving these extreme market-share concentrations in the multifamily real estate market? Over the last two decades, AI-driven technology in IT networks seems to be a main factor. The same pattern of automation and disruption we have seen in other industries has also made its way into multifamily housing.

The pattern looks like this: Firms within a specific industry look to technology to drive their efficiency and growth. Usually, one particular technology company's platform becomes widely used, creating greater industry integration. Global traffic in that industry then flows through increasingly concentrated areas. Once firms operate on the same platform, a merger become easier. The allure of economies of scale prompts firms to unite or buy smaller firms. Thus, market shares eventually concentrate.

The multifamily real estate market is a $12 trillion industry,[7] and firms quickly picked up on the capability to make better-quality, AI technology–driven decisions that save time and earn vast sums of wealth. One particular platform, RealPage, has become the most widely used in the industry, creating greater integration and global traffic.

We are at the beginning of an era in which intricate networks of businesses across industries collaborate to deliver seamless experiences for their clientele. Traditional firms, especially those under the impending threat of competition, are digitally transforming to try to remain relevant and succeed in a data-flush economy. The financial opportunities are substantial and unprecedented—as are the risks.[8]

However, when the economies of scale and network effects of proprietary systems are robust and reliable, they may give rise to "winner-take-all" or "winner-take-most" markets. Rising concentration makes failures in the financial system more likely to occur. The economy, leading up to the 2008 financial crisis, was beleaguered by concentrations at every level. The phrase "too big to fail" entered public discourse to describe these organizations.

AI WITHIN THE MULTIFAMILY MARKET: A SOURCE OF GROWTH, BIAS, AND MASSIVE DATA

What is this technology, and what are developers of the technology promising in exchange for the billions of dollars the property managers are investing?

Machine Learning and Deep Learning

AI-driven technology, like humans, can be taught various policies, principles, and procedures, including discrimination. In theory, over time, AI will no longer accept commands from its human operators and instead will learn from itself. One of the unfortunate side effects of that is that the discrimination will, over time, become the norm within the model itself.

Historically, software programs were hard-coded by people who had been instructed on specific tasks or assignments. In contrast, it is possible to set up algorithms—a process or set of rules followed in calculations or other problem-solving operations, especially by a computer that "learns" from data without the need for human programming.[9] These programs, in short, are trained instead of being human-programmed.

Machine-learning theories postulate that by giving the algorithm a vast quantity of "experiences" (data) and a broad base for learning, AI should be able to recognize outlines, connections, and awareness.

Deep learning, the cutting edge of machine learning, utilizes neural networks with many sublevels of data to push the boundaries of machine learning, hence the label "deep." Data scientists continue to innovate, training deep learning to recognize objects and faces and to comprehend more complex data.

As they continue to automate programs and processes, the likelihood of consumer and labor abuse from corporate America remains relatively high. After all, corporate America has tended to seek outcomes that best benefit themselves.[10]

REALPAGE

In the housing markets, property managers utilize AI-driven technology to both drive profits to the bottom line and to drive the renter experience. As mentioned above, RealPage is considered to be the primary provider of software and data analytics within the real estate industry. The RealPage Market Analytics platform serves as a system for all of the groups in the rental real estate ecosystem, from tenant to property owner, and supports all stages of the renting cycle. They currently serve nearly 12,200 clients.[11]

The RealPage platform has been functioning on an AI-based screening app since 2006, using the newest technology to communicate with prospective and existing residents. The company employs specialists in social media, search engine optimization, website administration, and paid search.[12]

We can see the technology within the multifamily real estate market by following the RealPage platform, breaking it down to three of the primary categories of solutions the platform offers: property management, leasing and marketing, and resident services. We will explore how the RealPage platform, particularly its Experian RentBureau database, allows property managers and property owners to drive efficiency and execution with massive amounts of data. Later, in Chapter 6, we will further discuss RealPage's revenue management and how rental rates are set through the platform.

The RealPage *Property Management Solutions* manage core business processes including leasing, accounting, budgeting, and purchasing. This includes a central database of prospects, applicants, renters, and property data that is accessible in real time by their users. It interfaces with the most popular general ledger accounting systems through the RealPage Exchange platform.

Just as a platform like Microsoft Office offers a seamless experience with its products such as Word, Excel, and PowerPoint, the RealPage Exchange platform works similarly, allowing users to access and move data, spreadsheets, and models across software and between users. All information is available to the manager through a comprehensive reporting system.

The flexibility of the RealPage system allows tracking of revenues based on client preference, which we will discuss later in more detail. The platform can also propose to increase rent and charge premiums for high-valued items, such as views, proximity to amenities, what floor the apartment is on, and other desirable features. [13]

The solutions offered to support *Leasing And Marketing Processes* include websites and syndication, paid lead generation, organic lead generation, real-time unit availability, automatic online apartment leasing, and applicant screening. State-of-the-art technology and marketing packages provide industry-leading solutions to generate traffic, ensure managers never miss a sales opportunity, and deliver prompt customer service at every point of interaction.[14]

Resident Services via RealPage provide a platform intended to improve the leasing and social experience of tenants, thus enhancing the property's value. This platform assists core renter processes including utility billing, service requests, contract renewal, and renters insurance.

SHARING DATA IS EASY

The process is quick and appears seamless. For example, Experian RentBureau does not charge the platform or its members for reporting rental payment data, which we will look at in more detail below. After the initial setup, data is securely transmitted directly from the property management software without any modification to existing software or any impact on operations.[15]

In the past during the prescreening process, property managers relied on credit bureau reports, which did not contain the rental history data. It took six to eight months to view adverse rental history through traditional collection efforts. Today, the massive amount of data RealPage produces can be used to compare eviction rates at other properties or perhaps to appraise a website to ascertain if applicants are quitting in the rental process or looking for a new place.[16]

Additionally, RealPage offers a connection to Experian RentBureau, which provides two ways for property owners/managers to benefit from its collective national repository of rental payment history data:

- *Access*—Real-time rental payment history data as part of the screening process. This data predicts a tenant's likelihood to pay rent.

- *Share*—RealPage participants supply rental payment data. This rental history is immediately available to all managers in all communities and can be incorporated in the applicant screening process.[17] The shared platform integrates with a central repository of lease transaction information, including prospect, renter, and property information. The open archi-

tecture allows third-party applications to access the
solutions using the RealPage Exchange platform.

The companies using RealPage have access to 30 million
actual lease outcomes (full lease performance history and
historical information) to evaluate tenant performance,
along with third-party consumer financial data and extensive rental credit and criminal background checks.[18]

Experian RentBureau reveals balances, charge-offs, and
collections information to the entire multifamily industry. When this data is combined in the resident screening process, the technology enables property managers to
prevent applicants who are trying to leave another community with money owed from getting a new lease until they
satisfy their outstanding debt obligation. Managers connected to the platform can support each other by not allowing tenants to move without the "group's" consent. This
broad visibility and transparency to bad-debt balances benefits everyone using the process, providing improved bad-
debt recovery for communities and enabling more accurate,
comprehensive applicant screening.[19]

Once reported, a firm's uploaded rental history data is
immediately available to other owners/managers through
the resident screening partners. When this information is
incorporated in another community's screening, all collab-
orating firms benefit.[20]

Operators can easily incorporate automated rental
payment history from a provider, like Alliance Residential, the fourth-largest property manager and platform user,
does with Experian RentBureau.

After Alliance incorporated the changes offered by Experian RentBureau and began accessing and sharing the data in their tenant prescreening process, a study evaluated the positive and negative impacts of using data from submarkets using manual screening compared to ones that used Experian RentBureau. The study revealed that bad debt was 15 percent higher at properties that used manual screening history checks compared to those utilizing the automated system.[21]

THE ACCESSING PROCESS

Every twenty-four hours, Experian RentBureau updates rental payment history data and makes that information available to the entire multifamily industry. This quick turnaround impacts every point of management decision-making, giving unprecedented insight into an applicant's likelihood to pay rent, and enabling on-site teams to make better leasing decisions and reduce manual verifications.[22] Access to this data expands the management firm's internal collections department and lessens the need for listing outstanding bad debt with third-party collection agencies.[23]

In 2012, the former Riverstone Residential Group supplied its residents' payment history to Experian RentBureau. Brannan Johnston, vice president and managing director for Experian RentBureau, explained, "By furnishing resident rental payment history data to Experian RentBureau, Riverstone Residential will immediately enhance the effectiveness of its rental collections while decreasing bad-debt levels and encouraging proactive rental payment practices among its residents (hefty fees for pushing timely payments), leading directly to increases in net operating income (NOI) to the bottom line."[24]

Since beginning the collaboration with Experian Rent-Bureau, Riverstone Residential has already received more than four hundred "hits" of rental applicants attempting to move into a community while still owing a rental payment debt elsewhere.[25]

This process of access and sharing is what gives the Real-Page platform its value and sets it apart from all other IT tools.

PRESCREENING AND DEBT COLLECTION

Historically, tenant screening was based on credit score and wages. Under the new AI program, applicants are screened for both credit and criminal background, and property managers determine the screening criteria for each property based on location and demographics. Usually, they require a minimum of two-and-a-half times the monthly rent as an income qualifier and deny any applicants currently in bankruptcy.

Beyond prescreening new renters, property management firms have begun leveraging the same information they collected during the application process to aid in their debt collection efforts. RealPage's Debt Collecting program is an incentive-based plan designed to encourage staff to take all possible steps to collect the debt before turning it over to a collection agency based on the information contained within the file.[26] Of course, who is in charge of determining what information is left in the file? This becomes important to the tenant once property managers have found their collection attempts unsuccessful and then turn the delinquent accounts over to the third-party debt collection companies.

Before RealPage, when a tenant failed to pay rent on time—or skipped out on a lease owing rent—property management firms were forced into a lengthy and costly collections process to alleviate the bad debt. Now, property management firms simply allow the debt collection companies with whom they contract to access Experian RentBureau's massive database. Debt collection companies use the intensely personal rental application data—such as home addresses, contact information for employers, cell phone numbers, even locations of tenants' cell phones—to recuperate debts owed. Unsurprisingly, property management firms immediately saw a decrease in skips and evictions under RealPage and annually recovered $400 million in bad debt, an average of $31 per unit per year.[27]

In one case, rental collections information from the Experian RentBureau database resulted in nearly $1.5 million of recovered debt for one national collection agency over seven months. Before the screening, the recovered debt had been outstanding for almost eight hundred days. Once the rental-specific collections information was used in the screening process, however, those amounts were paid off entirely within twenty-five days.[28]

According to Chris Jenkins, vice president of financial planning at Equity Residential, "On the collections side, we have a lot of examples where we don't have to contact former residents. They contact us to clear up an outstanding balance when their rental payment history appears in connection with trying to rent another apartment. So, it absolutely does work."[29]

BIG DATA

The RealPage platforms and the services they offer all mean one thing: massive amounts of timely data allow property owners and managers to drive ROI. The software developers push the theory to the platform users—know who's who and how to calculate risk—without added liability or consequences of violating federal housing laws.

The level of information available is staggering. RealPage offers access to the industry's largest rental payment history database, in-depth criminal background information, and extensive rental credit checks. The database also provides a comprehensive understanding of a consumer's total monthly obligations, such as debt-to-income ratios. The predictive analysis can use the consumer's location, the demographic data they provide, or even the device they use to make contact. If an applicant is found to be highly risky—including by income or race standards—they can be pushed for additional proof of identity.[30]

The developers of the AI technology challenge RealPage users to dive deep into the data and uncover hidden potential through filtering, sorting, highlighting, and drill-down functionalities. AI technology allows tracking of revenues based on the client's preference, meaning that each property owner gets to decide how the AI interacts with the tenants and whether the property adheres to compliance with the law.[31]

Now that we have explored the technology platform that has driven greater market concentrations within the multi-family real estate market, let's turn our attention to concentrations and interconnectedness that ballooned under the new relationships between managers and owners created under the rise of the institutional investor–owned property and examine how these issues might again prove as pernicious as they did in 2008.

CONCENTRATIONS MIXED WITH INTERCONNECTIONS

We've seen how property management firms became more capable of technological improvements and larger under increased mergers and buyouts. Figure 1 reveals the top ten largest property management firms, which are also among the top ten largest property owners. Moreover, those same property management firms are in the top ten largest builder firms, revealing a disturbing level of interconnection.

There are six related entities associated with the ten largest property managers, controlling 51 percent of the market within this subset. They also interrelate with owners and builders within the industry. The combination of the overall financial strength of this group is unmatched within the history of the industry.

For example, Lincoln Property Company, the second-largest property manager, is also involved in property development and construction. Not only is Alliance Residential one of the top ten property managers, but it's also one of the country's largest developers. Meanwhile, many managers like BH Management, LLC (and subsidiaries) provide management, investment, construction, architecture, and design.

It doesn't stop there. BH Management also owns BH Equities, which helps investors underwrite and acquire properties via its developed capital markets experience and its strong relationship with lenders, brokers, and sellers. The list goes on and on.[32]

FIGURE 1.

SIX INTERRELATED ENTITIES AMONG THE TOP TEN PROPERTY MANAGERS

		PROPERTY MANAGERS				OWNERS		DEVELOPERS	
Entities	Rank	# Units	% Units	Interconnected	Rank	# Units	Rank	# Units
Greystar Real Estate Partners	1	418,475	27.92%	27.92%	7	62,045	6	3,454
Lincoln Property Company	2	190,542	12.71%		9	58,375		
Pinnacle	3	162,000	10.81%			0	3	6,223
Alliance Residential	4	110,712	7.39%	7.39%		0		
FPI Management, Inc.	5	107,996	7.21%			0		
WinnCompanies	6	100,020	6.67%			0		
MAA	7	99,792	6.66%	6.66%	1	100,864		
Apartment Management Consultants, LLC	8	91,958	6.14%			0		
BH Management, LLC	9	79,990	5.34%		8	58,411		
Equity Residential	10	78,302	5.22%	5.22%	2	79,260		
Starwood Capital Group	19	59,076	3.94%	3.94%	4	76,932		
Trammell Crow Residential							7	2,787
Top Ten Totals		1,498,863	100%			435,887		12,464
Interrelated Entities Totals		766,357	51.13%					

Decisions within the multifamily housing industry are made by fewer and fewer individuals, as firms' market shares have more than doubled. As property managers fight for fewer available opportunities, they have to promise more and more profits to secure business. These increases generally come at the expense of the tenant, who has to pay more rent and fees needed by the property managers to satisfy the ROI requirements of the property owners and investors.

We know the complex interconnections between actors in the banking and financial system were a dominant cause of the 2008 financial crisis. Connections can be beneficial to some extent, providing diversification, additional liquidity, and products that take advantage of more investment opportunities. However, as these connections deepen and become more complex, they lead to profound vulnerabilities in the market.

In 2013, Goldman Sachs acquired a 20 percent stake in Greystar,[33] creating a significant connection and giving Goldman Sachs access to the growth Greystar was producing. While 20 percent ownership did not give Goldman Sachs majority voting rights, it did give them a measurable amount of influence over Greystar's movements.

This relationship proves favorable to both parties during a solid economic climate. However, if there were suddenly a liquidity crisis in the economy and Goldman Sachs went bankrupt, their creditors could liquidate the 20 percent of Greystar owned by Goldman Sachs, essentially making Greystar fodder for creditors.

Another prime example of deep interconnection is Ryan Homes and NVR. Ryan Homes is part of a publicly traded conglomerate that builds more than 18,000 homes a year and pockets nearly $1 billion a year in profits.[34]

Ryan Homes is also an entity owned by NVR, Inc., which operates two business segments: homebuilding and mortgage banking. NVR also provides a complete range of settlement and title services through the finance portion of the business.[35] To operate, NVR utilizes a $200 million line of credit from Bank of America[36]—one of those warehouse lines of credit discussed in Chapters 4 and 9.

NVR's business model does not purchase land; instead, they obtain finished lots using joint venture arrangements. NVR sells all of the loans it originates into the secondary market (to GSEs such as Fannie Mae and Freddie Mac), and generates income through origination fees, gains on sales of loans, and title fees.[37]

Currently, NVR boasts a return on equity of 46.7 percent, highest among all public builders.[38] However, just how

strong is a company that boasts of such strong balance
sheets? In April 1992, when the markets went south during
the 1990s recession, NVR filed for bankruptcy after their
stock fell from $7.75 to $1.00 a share. The company
defaulted on its bank loan for $12.5 million, and the CEO's
ex-wife claims he still owes her $1.3 million.[39]

If NVR were to go bankrupt again, Ryan Homes would
qualify as an asset that could be liquidated to satisfy creditors.

Beyond owning stake in each other's firms, actors can also
create joint ventures together, pooling their liquidity and
assets to purchase new investments and tying together their
assets and debt obligations. For example, in 2013, Greystar Real Estate Partners and Goldman Sachs & Co. entered
into a joint venture agreement to purchase a $1.5 billion
portfolio of multifamily assets from Equity Residential.[40]

Greystar also created a special fund for pension managers and other large institutional investors seeking exposure
to US student housing.[41] "The evolution and formation of
Greystar Credit Partners was a logical progression for us,"
Bob Faith said in a statement. "Our vertically integrated
rental housing platform, together with our intimate knowledge of the origination and underwriting guidelines utilized
by the GSEs, has made our platform possible as they acquire
subordinated and securitized debt issued by the Government
Sponsored Enterprises, Fannie Mae and Freddie Mac."[42]

COMPLEX AND OPAQUE INTERCONNECTIONS

Interconnections prove especially dangerous the more
complex they become, and Greystar is a prime example.

Headquartered in Charleston, South Carolina, Greystar is the largest property manager in the US, and it has used interconnections extensively as the firm has grown. It is also a leading, fully integrated real estate company with operations in investment, management, and development. Since 2011, Greystar has raised more than $4.5 billion for its value-added fund series.[43]

In fact, this new breed of property manager described throughout the chapter began with Bob Faith. He saw the need for a rental housing industry leader, a bluechip company that could deliver world-class services to property owners and investors.[44] The Riverstone purchase in 2013 gave Greystar ownership and control of the RealPage platform, allowing them to be competitive nationally.

"Having the ability to take care of pretty much every major market in the country certainly gives us a leg up to continue to be a major player in that consolidation that's underway," Faith was quoted as saying. "An organization such as ours, with boots on the ground in all these markets, that can do takeovers very quickly, allows us to do large transactions."[45]

EXTREME INTERCONNECTION

Perhaps the most extreme example of interconnection is vertical trusts. A vertical trust exists when an organization combines all phases of production of a good or service into its operating model. This expansion typically occurs over time, and a firm may backward-integrate by expanding operations closer to the development and construction of apartment projects or forward-integrate by increasing their control over the selling of the structured security bonds or loans for investor portfolios.

According to a study by Dr. Adnan Özyilmaz of Mustafa Kemal University, today's vertical trusts provide a high probability of delivering outperformance benefits to organizations. Trusts enable cooperative behavior, reduce transaction costs, promote adaptive organizational processes and documentation (used throughout the various levels of approval, from breaking ground to issuing bonds), and reduce dysfunctional conflict between employees through the various stages of advancement to the end goal. It improves working relationships between employees of the organization's multiple divisions, improves information sharing between the divisions, and drives productivity.[46]

However, not all types of vertical trusts are legal. In fact, many are incredibly illegal. One of the most common ways to violate the various forms of competition law is in-house vertical integration, when a company seeks to acquire dominance at every level of production. Antitrust legislation is aimed at preventing price-fixing or bid-rigging, infractions that are common with in-house vertical integration.[47]

The new property managers have largely replaced the traditional format with a vertical trust organization that provides better servicing arrangements for the new kind of property owner they serve while maximizing investor returns.

We've seen that property manager roles have greatly expanded, in part because AI-driven technology makes renting easier than ever. The sheer size and scope of the program allows them to offer services not available to renters, partners, employees, or clients from previous property managers.

Through their trust structure, property managers provide unparalleled competitive advantages—for example, the ability to offer a full-scale employee acquisition platform, a property transitions team, and a performance analytics group focused on compiling, analyzing, and interpreting vast amounts of data from more than 180 markets nationally.

SHARING EMPLOYEES

Tangential to this discussion of the interconnection of assets, debts, and future investments lies the discussion of sharing employees, interconnected firm leadership, and connections between financial and political leaders. When companies become overly close in their associations and interconnectedness, sometimes even employees will be "shared."

Typically, sharing occurs when a need arises to accomplish an important task relating to the sharing companies. For example, Kim Hallett is the chief accounting officer for Trammell Crow. Hallett first joined Trammell Crow Residential (TCR) in 2002, and then left for fourteen years, during which she was the executive vice president at Greystar when they acquired the AI technology. Hallett also held various roles at Goldman Sachs.[48]

Before joining Greystar in 1999, Bill Maddux held numerous positions with Trammell Crow.[49] Liza Kunkel is managing director of global public affairs and corporate marketing for Enterprise Services at Greystar, responsible for overseeing the company's public relations, internal and external communications, and corporate marketing. Her role includes advising on crisis communications and government affairs. She joined Greystar in 2017 from Blackstone, where she was a director of global public relations.[50]

In Chapter 4, we saw that the GSEs don't analyze these relationships the way the commercial banks would be required to do. While the act of sharing is not in and of itself pernicious, interrelated leadership and employees reveal how interconnected the companies are and how it can spur further connections through future business ventures.[51]

DANGERS OF CONCENTRATIONS
AND INTERCONNECTEDNESS

To fully illustrate the dangers of concentrations and interconnections in the market, let's look at an example using four interconnected firms. In our example, the four companies have formed joint ventures to carry out their various investment activities throughout the entire life cycles of the apartment building asset.

FIGURE 2.

THE EXAMPLE OF FOUR COMPANIES

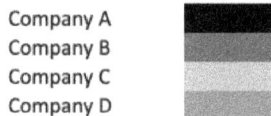

Company A
Company B
Company C
Company D

The six phases include the acquisition/construction phase through the asset disposition phase. We will assess the six stages in Figure 3 through three economic cycles, including a normal market cycle, a market with moderate risk and its

impact, and a market meltdown like the economy leading
up to the 2008 financial crisis, which was beleaguered with
concentrations and interconnectedness at every level.

FIGURE 3.

ANALYSIS OF INTERCONNECTEDNESS THROUGH SIX PHASES OF THE MULTIFAMILY ASSET

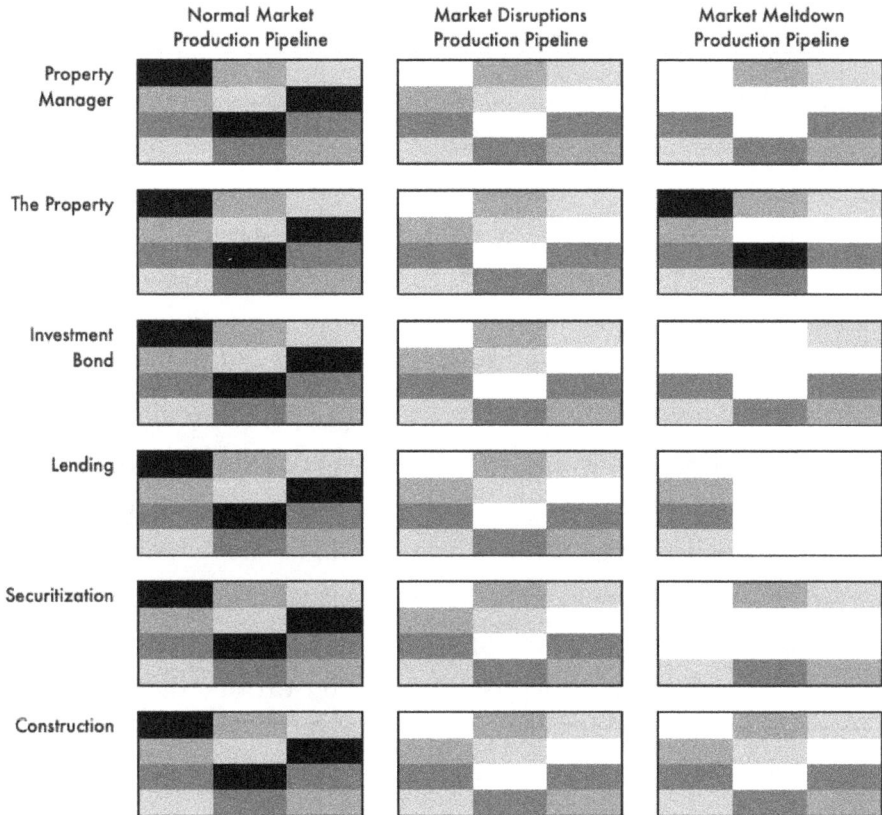

During the normal market cycle, entities are flush with
cash, and in fact, they are boasting returns on investment
above 800 percent. Currently, there is little concern within
the markets, except the multiple warnings issued by OIG
discussed in Chapter 3. As illustrated in Chapter 4, the

ever-increasing rents on which firms are basing their debt acquisition and investment creation are not sustainable. Once the markets head south, the loans and securitized bonds created using inaccurate rents may begin failing.

The four related companies begin to feel the market disruptions once the economic correction begins. Then the weakest link entity begins to fail financially, meaning they begin to miss their required payments into the joint venture's financial arrangements. This phase is marked by company A (black/blank in the cycle column) exiting the financial world.

In this scenario, the remaining three connected entities are now required to make the payments of the now-defunct Company A, which rapidly depletes their once-ample cash reserves. This process furthers the market meltdown cycle, which is now also marked by other companies exiting their weaker areas of the market and the additional blank sectors. During the meltdown phase, many companies elect to hold on to the investments they can save and let the remainder of assets fall to foreclosure, creating further failures and disruptions throughout the financial market. This is reflected in the meltdown cycle, as indicated by various blank sections within each sector.

There have been many studies completed regarding interconnections, all resulting in the recommendation to analyze all interconnected entities on global cash flow and risk basis. In 2008, we saw that once one of the entities in an interconnected relationship blew up financially, all related firms experienced some amount of financial blowback or hardship, if not a complete financial implosion of their own.

In another example of weakness, the blank sections of Figure 3 reveal failures up and down the sectors of the financial system. As we've seen, the 2008 Financial Crisis Inquiry Commission found that these consolidations resulted in an event where the cause was not a single event but a series of crises that rippled through the entire financial system. Figure 3 reveals how the process unfolds and looks.

Today, the vertical trusts, with their ever-increasing interconnectedness and concentrations, make failures in the financial system more likely to occur. In fact, our current markets are beginning to look a lot like 2007, except we now know that our investments are much larger, more complex, and riskier than in 2008.

ANCILLARY FEE INCOME ANALYSIS

We will close this chapter by examining another factor that drives firms toward greater interconnection and growth: fee income. If the AI technology platform is the mechanism for growth in this industry, then fee income is the fuel that powers the growth.

Fee income is the revenue taken in by financial institutions from account-related charges to customers. Lenders earn fees for originating and selling loans, investment banks earn fees for issuing mortgage-backed securities, and the large financial institutions have merger and acquisition fees, wealth management charges, and trading desk fees.

Unsurprisingly, all these fees have been consistently increasing. Securitization of mortgages was not just a boon for commercial banks; it was also a lucrative new line of business for Wall Street investment banks.

This draw of large fees spurred the growth of shadow banks. As we saw in Chapter 4, shadow banks do not take deposits; they only deal in loans. Unlike traditional banks, which use deposits from customers to fund the loans they offer, shadow banks open lines of credit with traditional banks to cover the loans they provide. This means two things: first, because shadow banks do not hold deposits, they are not federally insured or regulated; and second, shadow banks do not have liquidity from which to draw should many of their loans default.

The main type of fee income is the fee with which most Americans are familiar: closing costs. Closing costs cover expenses associated with closing real estate transactions, such as legal and processing fees paid to the originator, and are typically 1 to 5 percent of the mortgage balance.

Shadow-banking fees are typically higher than those of traditional banks. For example, a common complaint on consumer review websites regarding Quicken Loans, the largest shadow bank lender in our data, is its high origination fees relative to other lenders. Using the public closing cost estimators that Quicken Loans and other shadow banks provide for purchases and refinances, we can see their typical closing-cost fees. For the purchase of a $200,000 home with a 20 percent down payment in Illinois, the calculator estimates an origination fee of $8,648, which is 5.4 percent of the principal balance at origination.[52]

In comparison, property owners of multifamily housing also face closing costs. Drawing from Example 1 in Chapter 2, we can see in Figure 4 the closing costs paid on a typical multifamily-unit loan. We see the borrower will pay some 3.32 percent or $1.67 million in upfront fees on a $50 million loan. These fees are enormous, especially when you consider the loan is federally insured under the GSEs, and the investors received more than $4 million in tax savings that more than cover the fees or cost of issuance.

FIGURE 4.

COSTS OF ISSUANCE—ORIGINATION FEES

Due Diligence	25,157	0.05%
Construction Lender Fees	503,145	1.00%
Construction Lender Counsel	35,220	0.07%
Lender Origination Fee	503,145	1.00%
Lender Counsel	45,283	0.09%
Mortgage Banker Counsel	35,220	0.07%
Underwriter	226,415	0.45%
Underwriter Counsel	50,315	0.10%
Rating Agency	18,113	0.04%
Printing	10,063	0.02%
Trustee	12,075	0.02%
Issuer	100,629	0.20%
Bond Counsel	75,472	0.15%
Financial Advisor Issuer	30,189	0.06%
Total	**1,670,441**	**3.32%**

Mortgage balances—the most significant component of household debt—rose by $12 billion in the second quarter of 2019 to $9.4 trillion, surpassing the high of $9.3 trillion in the third quarter of 2008.[53] Figure 5 shows the estimated fees paid on this current mortgage debt. Using 4 percent for the fee rate, there has been an estimated $376 billion paid out in fees.

FIGURE 5. CALCULATION OF THE ESTIMATE OF FEES
PAID ON THE CURRENT MORTGAGE DEBT

Fees Paid on Debt Calculation	Dollar Amount
Total Mortage Debt	$ 9,400,000,000,000
Avg. Fees	4%
Fees Paid on Debt	$ 376,000,000,000

With so much money to be made funding mortgages, it is unsurprising that some unsavory business practices have popped up to take advantage of the large returns. Banks use bonus structures to incentivize their employees to keep issuing more and more loans (of increasingly poor quality) to keep collecting the associated lucrative fees. These loans are then compiled into the mortgage-backed securities we discussed earlier.

On February 9, 2012, federal and state attorneys ruled the five largest mortgage servicers owed $25 billion due to their criminal actions in loan servicing and foreclosure abuses tied to the 2008 financial crash.[54] However, in Figure 5, we know that a $25 billion fine is not going to deter banks from illegal behavior when banks are currently collecting around $376 billion in fees. These paltry fines and penalties provide no real hindrance to unfettered access to profits.

There was a time when we would liken this process to a shark feeding frenzy, as greed takes over in the race for unending massive fee income and profits; investors and traders alike are afraid to miss out on the unrealistic perpetual profits. Unfortunately, in the end, the American taxpayer and homeowner shoulder those massive losses.

LOAN GROWTH AND PIPELINES

The commission tasked with evaluating the causes for the Great Recession of 2008 concluded that the nonprime mortgage securitization process created a pipeline through which risky mortgages were conveyed and sold throughout the financial system. This pipeline was essential to the origination of the burgeoning number of high-risk mortgages.[55]

A loan pipeline needs an inventory, and history has taught us that inventory is easy to acquire. However, as the inventory increases, the quality of mortgage loans it captures decreases. Inventory centered in substandard credit policy causes severe disruptions in the marketplace when that loan inventory begins to severely underperform.

HOW TO GROW LOAN PRODUCTION
THROUGH A PIPELINE

There are basically two ways to grow a pipeline through organic new business growth: manipulations of loan quality and offering more aggressive rates and terms of service. However, loan quality and its rates and terms of service are not just important measures of profitability, they are also the standard of quality on which a loan portfolio is graded. Thus, we see an inverse relationship between the number of loans sent through the pipeline and the quality or profitability of those loans.

To see how loan growth works in practice, say that the market dictates and regulators agree that the loan-to-value ratio (LTV) for a loan should be 65 percent. Therefore, to entice growth, management elects to loosen credit standards and allow their underwriters to increase LTV to, say, 80 percent. Alternatively, say that the market rate for ten-year fixed rates is 4.25 percent. Management can elect to offer rates at 4 percent. Both of these moves will generate substantial loan growth. However, should management elect to hyper-grow their loan portfolio like this, they would lower both credit quality and rates and terms at the same time. This aggressive approach to growth generally arises when short-term corporate profitability becomes key to management. Unfortunately, we have seen that once the credit policy gets changed for a few more aggressive firms, the marketplace follows suit. A loan that once was considered substandard (a tier II or III loan product) is now reassessed as a "prime loan," and the loan product is now deemed a safe investment.

Once growth through rate and loan quality is exhausted, refinancing assets becomes necessary to fill the void in the pipeline. Management will refinance assets that were once deemed safe and sound under new rates and terms, lessening standards and increasing risk.

The pipeline becomes a critical vehicle for management to achieve their goals and should not be underestimated. Without the pipeline, multi-billion-dollar bonds could not be issued, and tranches could not be bundled.

However, pipelines can also create a great deal of nonperforming assets in a short period. For example, the 2008 crash saw nonperforming mortgage loans peak nationally at about 4 percent, which would lead to trillions of dollars in lost wealth in a ripple effect. The end result was a few key players making billions of dollars in fees from overflowing pipelines that delivered a defective and mislabeled investment to investors. Ultimately, the American taxpayer

was left to carry the burden of banks "too big to fail" col-
lapsing in on themselves and destroying all in their wake.

WHAT CAN WE DO? A HISTORICAL PERSPECTIVE

Back in 1929, the United States was suffering not only from
the effects of the Great Depression but also from a great
crisis of confidence in the American financial system. Americans demanded an investigation into the system's failure,
along with transparency of the findings and congressional
action to address and nullify the deviant practices that had
led to the American economy's collapse. President Herbert
Hoover supported a groundbreaking 1932 congressional
investigation into market manipulations he believed had
contributed to the crash.

The Franklin D. Roosevelt administration continued
the investigation, which came to be known as the Pecora
Report, named for Ferdinand Pecora, the chief counsel of
the investigation. The enormous sampling of Wall Street
banks included in the 402-page document showed that the
corruption in Wall Street was not limited to a few bad
actors, but permeated the entire institution and nearly every
bank and person connected to it. The committee's conclusion was that these actors determined who did and did not
earn money and who made entire fortunes off the meager
investments of the working class and the working poor.[56]

As Pecora himself described in a 1933 *New York Times*
article, ". . . [M]en of might—not because of principle
but because of economic power and wealth—have, by the
waving of a hand and adoption of a resolution, taken mil-

lions and millions of the hard-earned pennies of the people [working poor] and turned them into gold for themselves."[57]

Possibly the most significant outcome of the Pecora Report was that bankers had not broken any rules. The financial markets lacked any kind of system to hold bankers accountable. The outrage ignited by these findings led the nation to demand significant reform of Wall Street. Congress established the Securities and Exchange Commission (SEC) and tasked it with regulating the stock market and protecting investors.[58] Congress went on to create the Federal Deposit Insurance Corporation (FDIC), which provided not only regulation of deposit accounts but insurance for them as well.[59]

The country has once again reached a junction, this time one in which property managers control the flow of information on a level the country or world has never witnessed. Technology has far surpassed the current laws' ability to control the damage or minimize ongoing violations. The government has yet to take any measurable role in containing possible damage.

The master puppeteers of AI have sent America's laws into unfamiliar territory, similar to the findings of the Pecora Report. The overall conclusion is that those who control AI-driven technology can determine who will and will not earn money, and who will make entire fortunes off the meager investments of the working class and working poor.

CHAPTER 6

THE CONSEQUENCES OF ARTIFICIAL INTELLIGENCE– DRIVEN TECHNOLOGY

As we discussed in Chapter 5, property managers today are often large property management firms, interconnected from builder to owner to investor, and employing a comprehensive AI-driven platform capable of meeting all needs throughout the renting experience. So what does that mean for tenants? What does the experience look like for renters?

Property managers hold a unique role between their clients, the property owners, and the tenants they serve, and they carry a level of responsibility and obligation to both. A property manager must hold a real estate broker's license because they are deemed a fiduciary for their clients. Fiduciary duties are the highest legal obligations, and are similar to what any professional, such as a doctor or lawyer, owes to their patient or client. For property managers, those obligations include the responsibility to safeguard a property owner's confidence and secrets. However, a property owner may not withhold from a tenant any known material facts concerning the property or misrepresent the condition of the property or its contracts. To do so would impose liability on both the broker and the property owner.[1]

How well have property managers' responsibilities to their tenants been met, given the new data-driven, vertical trust–dominated industry? In this chapter, we will explore the tenant experience under this new system.

THE TENANT EXPERIENCE

Greystar Property Managers maintains an "F" rating from the Better Business Bureau due to failure to respond to 122 complaints filed against the business, and they are not alone. Pinnacle Campus Living received an "F" rating for failure to respond to multiple complaints. WinnCompanies, a multifamily property management corporation that oversees several low-income housing facilities in Boston, over a five-year period, defended itself in 146 civil cases filed by the tenants and defended by the firm.[2]

FIGURE 1.

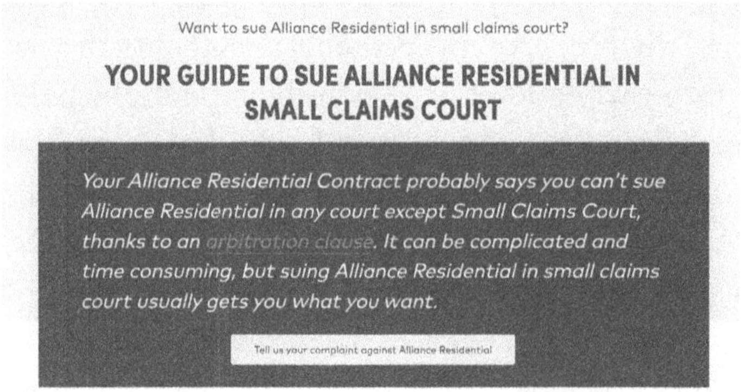

Want to sue Alliance Residential in small claims court?

YOUR GUIDE TO SUE ALLIANCE RESIDENTIAL IN SMALL CLAIMS COURT

Your Alliance Residential Contract probably says you can't sue Alliance Residential in any court except Small Claims Court, thanks to an arbitration clause. It can be complicated and time consuming, but suing Alliance Residential in small claims court usually gets you what you want.

Tell us your complaint against Alliance Residential

Source: "Want to Sue Alliance Residential in Small Claims Court," accessed December 2019, https://myradvocate.com/Your%20Guide%20to%20Sue%20 Alliance%20Residential%20in%20Small%20Claims%20Court.

The relationship between Alliance Residential and their tenants has become so toxic that a website has been established to assist other tenants in claims.

PART I. MAJOR VIOLATIONS OF FAIR HOUSING LAWS THROUGH DISCRIMINATION

Our study uncovered four significant findings regarding the tenant experience. First, the fees charged to tenants are often unreasonable and against current laws and regulations. Second, violations of the Fair Debt Collection Practices Act in the collection of consumer credit are rampant. Third, many property managers and their clients violate fair housing laws by employing the technology platforms they use to discriminate against protected minorities. Finally, predatory leasing and collection practices lead to the loss of due process for the tenants.

UNREASONABLE AND MASSIVE FEES

Multiple courts across the country are ruling against the practice of excessive fees. For example, in 2018, the US District Court for the Western District of Texas, Austin Division, ruled that the fees charged by property managers were unreasonable and against current laws and regulations.[3] A second example is a ruling that charging a late fee as liquidated damage was in violation of California's Unfair Competition Law as well as the Rosenthal Fair Debt Collection Practices Act.[4] A third example is a settlement that has been reached in a class-action lawsuit alleging that Greystar Management Services and Riverstone Residential Group violated the Texas Water Code and Texas Administrative Code by billing residents at certain apartment complexes improper sewer and water fees. Under the terms of the settlement, the defendants will pay $2.7 million.[5]

On May 17, 2018, Dan Kane and Ely Portillo of the *News & Observer* (TNS) of Raleigh explained the following:

> No one tracks the total amount of disputed fees paid by tenants, but North Carolina communities and much of the southeastern United States are home to some of the nation's highest eviction rates. A recent study by a Princeton professor shows [actual court records] that North Carolina had nearly 164,000 eviction proceedings in the 2016–2017 fiscal year.[6]

Though most eviction cases end with tenants settling with the landlord and remaining in their apartments, tenants were still being charged eviction-related fees. To illustrate, look at the case of Jordon Hargrove, twenty-six, in Raleigh, North Carolina. Hargrove struggled with medical bills after a bout with bronchitis. He tried to arrange to pay two-thirds of his $875 monthly rent up front and pay the rest, plus a late fee, when he received his next paycheck. The apartment management was unwilling to cut him a break. His mother stepped in to cover the rent he couldn't pay, the late fee, the court fees, and next month's rent, which the landlord demanded in advance.[7]

This experience is typical for tenants. That's why the dispute arises in North Carolina: Is it legal for a landlord to charge the kinds of eviction-related fees that Hargrove paid?

In Hargrove's case, he paid the fees to stay in his Raleigh apartment, only to discover months later that his record reflected an eviction, which became a barrier as he sought to move elsewhere. "Sadly, this is what it comes to," said Hargrove, who works in sales for a computer manufacturer. "Sadly, this has become a money-making scheme on top of the profit that they are already making from rent."[8]

Debt Collectors and Specialty Credit Reports

Specialty rental reports contain intimate personal information, including past property rental addresses, rental payment performance history, and lease risk scores, just to name a few.[9] For property owners, as we saw in the previous chapter, there is an advantage to utilizing the rental reports about potential tenants. For tenants, however, the stories may become a substantial threat to housing access and stability.

"The number one deterrent of acquiring an apartment is if you've had a prior problem with a landlord," says Andrew Heiberger, the CEO of TOWN Residential. An adverse rental history, Heiberger added, "is the single worst blemish you can have."[10]

On March 28, 2017, the Consumer Financial Protection Bureau (CFPB) issued an official notice to consumers to beware of specialty consumer reports, which collect and report information about a person's history, including housing, employment, medical, and banking records. The federal posting from the CFPB breaks it down into more detail. Reports of the following types may be compiled:

- Opening or using bank accounts (including writing or bouncing checks or overdrafts)

- These companies collect and report information about a person's checking accounts. If someone has had their account closed due to an unpaid negative balance, the bank or credit union would typically report this "involuntary closure" to a checking account reporting company. A person may also be reported if they were suspected of fraudulent activity by the bank or credit union.

- Apartment rental payments
  - Experian uses rental payment and collection information in its credit reports.

- Insurance claims
  - Reports collect information about filed insurance claims via property and casualty policies, such as homeowners' and auto policies. They may also share driving records.

- Renters insurance claims

- Payday lending

- Utility payments

- Phone bill payments

- Employment
  - Employment reports often include credit checks, criminal background checks, public records such as bankruptcy filings and other court documents, and information related to employment history.

- Medical records or payments
  - These agencies may supply reports on prescription drug purchases, medical conditions, data from insurance applications, and data from other sources.[11]

You might not know these reports exist unless you run into a problem, such as not getting a job, housing lease, or insurance, or when a utility company asks you to put down a deposit before starting service with you.[12]

FIGURE 2. REPORTS FOUND TO BE ILLEGAL

STOKES v. REALPAGE, INC., No. 2:2015cv01520 - Document 43 (E.D. Pa. 2016)

Court Description: MEMORANDUM AND OPINION. SIGNED BY HONORABLE JOHN R. PADOVA ON 10/19/16. 10/19/16 ENTERED & E-MAILED.(fdc)

⤓ Download PDF

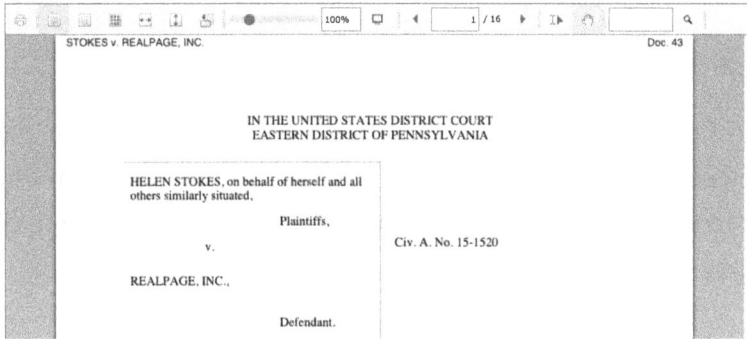

[2] The statute provides that "Whenever a consumer reporting agency prepares a consumer report it shall follow reasonable procedures to assure maximum possible accuracy of the information concerning the individual about whom the report relates." 15 U.S.C. § 1681(b).

[3] The statute provides that "Every consumer reporting agency shall, upon request, and subject to section 1681h(a)(1) of this title, clearly and accurately disclose to the consumer: (1) All information in the consumer's file at the time of the request . . . . (2) The sources of the information . . . ." 15 U.S.C. § 1681g(a)(1)-(2).

Source: Stokes v. RealPage, Inc., No. 2:2015cv01520 - Document 43 (ED Pa. 2016) Justia Law, https://law.justia.com/cases/federal/district-courts/pennsylvania/paedce/2:2015cv01520/502592/43/.

VIOLATION OF PRIVACY LAWS

Specialty consumer reporting agencies fail to adequately disclose how they collect data, how they use data, and how they disseminate or share data. Managers also fail to disclose how they use data against tenants throughout the process of the tenancy and forever after that. Yes, once the tenant signs the application or lease document, their right to curtail future use of data is waived. The data can be used in all future transactions, without the ability to opt out. Other investigations have led to the conclusion that property managers and owners are bending the technology to gain the result they desire, regardless of the law.[13]

The Tenant Experience: Debt Collectors

On October 30, 2018, a tenant filed a complaint with the Better Business Bureau against Apartment Management Consultants (AMC). The tenant reported receipt of an email from AMC, as follows:

> You have a past due account of $1,507.28. This balance is more than 380 days old. Please contact me at the office no later than November 2, 2018, to make a payment on your account. If we do not hear from you by the date above, your account will be turned over to our collection agency, and at that time, the amount will be increased by 50% to cover the collection costs, a judgment will be put on your credit report, and your wages garnished. Once this is on your credit, it will remain there for seven years and will make it difficult to rent an apartment and/or purchase a home.[14]

According to the tenant, until they got the notice, they were unaware of a balance on their old account, and they had not heard from this apartment manager for over a year after moving out.

These are just a few of the thousands of cases of American citizens reaching out in frustration as property managers run roughshod, ignoring housing laws and taking whatever action they can to increase the ROI and keep property-owner clients satisfied. The majority of these tenant complaints are for illegal collection actions by the property managers and third-party collection agencies, and the managers know they are violating the law.

Violations of Fair Housing Laws

In 2017, the largest corporate landlord in the United States was hit with a federal civil rights lawsuit that alleged a blanket refusal to rent to tenants with a criminal record. In a complaint filed in US District Court for the District of Columbia, the nonprofit Equal Rights Center argued that Memphis-based Mid-America Apartments' policy of categorically forbidding anyone from renting an apartment who has a "felony conviction or pending felony charge as well as certain misdemeanors or pending misdemeanor charges" violates the Fair Housing Act of 1968 because it has a "disproportionate adverse impact on African Americans and Latinos."[15]

From 2018 through 2019, my studies discovered so many intertwining connections, from bond price-fixing by the shadow banking markets—part of the vertical integration by the property managers—to massive profits being acquired by this AI technology and the many cases of abuse discovered through the various court cases and the tenant experience.

Through my research, a court case in Texas was discovered, which began to connect the many dots from all the research I had completed. The AI technology had been taught to discriminate against certain classes of people based on race, skin color, or other demographics. As outlined in documents contained in the US District Court for the Northern District of Texas, Dallas Division, one property management company and a member of the RealPage platform were caught deceptively assigning criminal records to the reports of potential tenants they did not want to live in the apartment community. The AI knew the criminal records did not belong to the applicant; however, according to court records, the technology had been educated by RealPage to accomplish this task. RealPage paid a $3 million fine to halt the investigation into their practices.[16]

The Federal Trade Commission (FTC) vote authorizing staff to file the complaint and stipulated final order was 5–0—a rare consensus, especially for Texas. The Commission files a complaint when it has "reason to believe" that the law has been or is being violated, and it appeared to the Commission that a proceeding was in the public interest. Stipulated final orders have the force of law when approved and signed by the district court judge.[17]

We know that AI technology allows tracking of revenues based on client preference, which means that each property owner gets to decide how their AI technology interacts with the tenants and whether the property will adhere to compliance with the law. Discrimination is an ROI choice in the world of property managers.

The continued use of Artificial Intelligence for tenant screening could lead to further violations of the law, especially since application denials will be obscured by algorithms and alternative data. Deep-learning standards or desired outcomes are obscure, at best, and can erect barriers to understanding in specific applications. Currently, it is difficult to understand how profoundly such networks influence or manipulate the learning insights and assumptions within the algorithms, causing grave concern for the use of the data in cases where transparency of decision-making may be essential for regulatory purposes.

There are moral questions encompassing machine intelligence. One set of moral trepidations relates to the possibility wherein prejudices can be embedded into training data. Who is in control of the algorithm's conclusions? And who regulates the abuses?

In Chapter 10, we will discuss that during 2019, HUD proposed making changes to the nation's disparate impact rule, a move that fair housing advocates claim is part of a Trump administration effort to "gut" federal protections against housing discrimination.[18] They want to be allowed to hide the discrimination within the algorithms, the horcrux hidden within Pandora's box—a move that will surely rip our country's soul apart in the process.

Will there ever be a price too high for greed and power?

PART II: RENTAL RATE PRICE-FIXING AND PRICE-SURGING

Free and open markets are the foundation of a vibrant and stable economy. Aggressive competition among sellers in an open marketplace gives consumers—both individuals and businesses—the benefits of lower prices, higher-quality products and services, more choices, and greater opportunities for innovation. Unfortunately, the multifamily real estate market has seen a degradation of its free-market policies.

The conclusions of my four housing-market studies provide strong evidence that suggests that property managers have implemented the practice of rental rate price-fixing and rental rate price-surging by employing RealPage to manipulate rental rates. This has led to increased homelessness and excessive rent burdening. The RealPage platform works as an intermediary, allowing competitors to relay information and agree with each other on the most competitive fees to charge.

Are independent property managers sharing data through RealPage that competitors would normally not share? This might include personal and private rent roll information, along with other financial information from the tenant.

If so, what are they doing with the rental information they are sharing, and what is the purpose of sharing? What are they trying to accomplish? And does the sharing of said information make them, by definition, a cartel? If so, then they are either bid-rigging or price-fixing, as that is the sole purpose of a cartel—to control the supply and prices of a good or service.

Opportunity to Collude

The RealPage platform provides the opportunity to collude, as we've seen, and there is ample evidence that property managers are doing just that because they have had to promise property owners and investors unsustainable increases in the rate of return on investments.

The Federal Trade Commission (FTC) defines a cartel as "an association built from a formal or informal agreement between a group of producers of a good or service to control supply or to influence prices." In this case, a cartel is a collection of otherwise independent property managers that act together as if they were a single property manager and thus can fix prices for the goods they produce and the services they render without competition.[19]

According to the FTC website, price-fixing is defined as follows:

> An agreement (written, verbal, or inferred from conduct) among competitors that raises, lowers, or stabilizes prices or competitive terms. Generally, antitrust laws require that each company establish prices and other terms on its own, without agreeing with a competitor. When consumers make choices about what products and services to buy, they expect that the price has been determined freely based on supply and demand, not by an agreement among competitors. When competitors agree to restrict competition, the result is often higher prices. Accordingly, price-fixing is a major concern of government antitrust enforcement.
>
> A plain agreement among competitors to fix prices is almost always illegal, whether prices are fixed at a minimum, maximum, or within some range. Illicit price fixing occurs whenever two or more competitors agree to take actions that have the effect of raising, lower-

ing, or stabilizing the price of any product or service
without any legitimate justification.[20]

Explicit Agreement

In order to collude with each other and set prices, competitors need to have an explicit agreement. RealPage contains the explicit agreement that property managers have set for colluding with each other. RealPage is the hub or intermediary that speaks to each of the competitors and then relays each competitor's "agreement" to increase prices.

The shared RealPage platform began in 2006 and now has 12,200 clients in four hundred markets. The platform is powered with AI-driven technology. RealPage and its clients have repeatedly affirmed that the prime directive of the platform is to give property managers the ability to drive performance by 2 to 7 percent over open-market rents in order to drive higher profits for property owners.[21] Furthermore, RealPage improves bad-debt collections by 15 percent.[22]

The RealPage platform shares massive amounts of data between members that would not otherwise be available to property managers were it not for their association with the platform, including the Experian RentBureau processes discussed in Chapter 5. We'll now take a more in-depth look into the various AI-enhanced technology programs and how the RealPage Exchange platform utilizes those programs. Our goal is to establish how rental rates are fixed through accessing and sharing, which sets the platform apart from other IT tools, and indeed, creates its value.

How Rental Rate Pricing Works

Market rental surveys compare the rental rates and occupancy of available and comparable properties. They can show owners and property managers what comparable rents are in their area and where the competition is within a market.

Through the Asset & Investment Management (AIM) software program, the software program LARA can propose increases to rent and charge premiums for high-valued items, such as views, proximity to amenities, what floor the apartment is on, and other desirable features. The shared platform integrates this information with a central repository of lease transaction information, including prospect, renter, and property information. The open architecture allows third-party applications to access the solutions using the RealPage Exchange platform.[23]

The Axiometrics application, for example, offers tools to analyze the data by multiple variables such as asset class, age, and competitive floor plans and location. Axiometrics provides its customers with timely market intelligence on apartment markets that is accumulated from the software program (Yardi) survey and research data.

In other words, RealPage designates each available apartment unit to a specific class based on factors such as the number of bed- and bathrooms, floor plan, square footage, property location, and property condition. This allows for each apartment unit within the 13 million units represented to be priced just like each similar property.

Per their website, RealPage promises visibility into real submarket performance that no one else can produce. Real-

Page Market Analytics is the industry's only lease transaction–driven platform that delivers broad transparency into real-time rent roll and revenue, revealing the most current and accurate data critical to making investment decisions.[24]

RealPage boasts, "Asking rents and survey data can't determine when you need to shift gears to accelerate return [rental rate surging]. Only RealPage Market Analytics can. We've reimagined market research, building on the *Axiometrics®* foundation, to drive higher ROI for investors."[25]

The Yardi Matrix website claims that gathering effective rental survey data is difficult to do consistently. Critical potential sampling errors in traditional rental rate surveys and reporting–including issues such as reluctance to disclose the gap between asking (published) and effective (actual quoted) rent to surveyors—result in distortion of actual rental market conditions. Yardi Matrix surveys, on the other hand, are actual rents, not published street rents, and include concessions being offered to attract new renters. Yardi Matrix surveys establish the industry standard for accuracy in rental rate reporting, getting its information through the 13 million units in the digital platform.[26]

The shared platform integrates with a central repository of lease transaction information, including prospect, renter, and property information. The open architecture allows third-party applications to access the solutions using the RealPage Exchange platform. However, it is primarily Lease Rent Options' repository of lease transaction data and data science talent with the existing platform of pricing, demand, and credit optimization tools that perfect the process.[27]

PREDICTIVE ANALYTICS

Utilizing and implementing advanced statistical methods follow the same process. First, the machine must be trained and fed a dataset so that it "learns"—assimilates the dataset's intricacy and attempts to evaluate the influence of each dynamic (house characteristics, for example) on the output value (rent).

Second, the testing phase occurs where the previously educated information is verified against a set of data where the output is known. The algorithm predicts the output value, which was found to be extremely accurate. The machine is calibrated and is ready to predict.

Third, the prediction phase utilizes an algorithm to predict the output value of a dataset with an unknown output value. With analytic and simulation technologies mixed with the prospect of integrating datasets, the decision-making horizon for property managers is increasingly profitable and expanding.[28]

THE TECHNOLOGY PROVIDES THE "FIXED" RATE

The property manager engages their AI-driven platform to price their leases based on yesterday's rental rates from comparable properties ("exact type and floor plan"); then the system adds the percentage increase in rents that the property owner desires—say, 5 percent.

The new rental rates are then made available to all users on the RealPage platform, with all 12,200 users pricing their units in unison and while sharing the platform.

In other words, when the property manager enters the property units to be priced, human interaction stops and the system algorithms take over. The AI technology provides the rental rate to be used, and it, rather than the market, dictates what new renters must pay.

We see the evidence of this collusion and price-fixing in improved rental income and debt collection for property managers and owners. Greystar chief legal officer Michael Hoffman, for instance, said that the technology provided annual sales growth for his company of nearly 50 percent, from a loss of $2.4 million to a profit of $16.4 million.[29]

A correlation exists between these findings and the findings of the study we looked at earlier, by economists Luis Quintero and Jacob Cosman at Johns Hopkins University, which showed home prices escalated more than twice as fast as they would have if the market hadn't consolidated. The building industry increased the market share of the top twenty builders from 21 percent in 2008 to 29 percent in 2018.[30]

Motive

The purpose of the RealPage platform is to control supply and to influence prices as if all property managers participating were a single producer, allowing them to fix rents without fear of competition.

The top property management and property owner companies, as we've seen, have become massive in size. Like their financial institutional bank counterparts, they have become too big to fail, and they are behaving in the same manner as those too-big-to-fail banks. Property managers who maintain significant influence over the markets also

maintain significant influence over the AI technology platforms utilized by the industry.

Their concentration also pushes the remaining property
managers to become more aggressive in their tactics and to
make bigger promises regarding bigger profits to the bottom
line. Apartment Management Consultants (AMC), which
we saw earlier, states, "Our mission is to generate value
through maximizing the earnings of our client's investments.
We are focused on delivering value to the bottom line. Every
opportunity is carefully evaluated for its ability to reduce
cost or enhance revenue on each asset we manage. AMC
built its revenue management program to help drive rents
and increase revenue."[31] In addition, companies like Greystar promise to grow rents 5 percent *every year* (and guarantee 2 to 4 percent above markets) as follows:

> As the largest revenue management user in the indus-
> try, Greystar's program facilitates daily pricing and
> asset strategy reviews for more than 115,000 units
> while partnering with more than 100 ownership groups
> in more than sixty unique metropolitan service areas.
> Our in-house experts increase revenue growth by stra-
> tegically calibrating pricing based on ownership goals,
> supply and demand, exposure, and competitor activity.
> With the Greystar Revenue Management program's 99
> percent client retention rate and a 69 percent annual
> growth in the company-wide use of our program, our
> clients enjoy the operational and efficiency benefits
> while consistently maintaining an average of 5 percent
> or higher rent growth. Multi-year users continue to

see 2 percent to 4 percent revenue growth above-average market gains. [32]

To accomplish aggressive goals, aggressive tactics must be implemented. For example, we saw previously that AMC has an aggressive bad-debt collection program that encourages staff to take all steps necessary to collect the debt before turning it over to a collection agency. AMC also has implemented common area maintenance (CAM) and real estate tax chargebacks as a proactive way to drive income. Their goal is to collect 95 to 98 percent of operating costs plus administrative fees on behalf of the property.[33]

Other companies also overcharge for operating expenses and bills to the tenant, as described earlier in the chapter regarding the class-action lawsuit in Texas against Greystar for overcharging fees.[34] Property managers have also implemented an aggressive measure to lower the property owner's liabilities while shifting the expense to the tenant in violation of established laws.

Thus, property management companies have turned to the AI technology platform RealPage to provide the rental rates, not the market.

THE "PLUS FACTORS"

In legal and economic circles, plus factors are the supporting arguments for an anti-trust conclusion. When we consider what we've learned so far, there are quite a few:

1. The prime directive of the AI-driven technology is to drive profits to the bottom line by skirting

and bending the rules around restrictions or regulations—whatever it takes to get to the ROI.

2. Technology had been educated to discriminate against certain classes of people based on race, skin color, or other demographics, also violating the Fair Credit Reporting Act (FCRA).

3. Property managers have access and means to bend AI technology to their will, and their motive lies in the massive profits they can generate.

4. In Chapter 4, we discovered that the Financial Crisis Inquiry Commission (FCIC) often pointed to the moral hazard that guided the markets before the 2008 crash and compared those actions with the bond price-fixing of housing markets in 2019. As the concentrations of power continue to be held by fewer and fewer players, the propensity for maleficence increases. The bond markets have become part of the vertical integration the property managers have interwoven into their business models.

CONCLUSION

The multifamily property managers have formed a cartel that operates through RealPage, a shared platform that provides an intermediary through which various agreements of rental pricing can be made across property management firms. RealPage shares data that would not otherwise be available to those managers and owners. The purpose of the RealPage platform, then, is to control supply and to influence prices, allowing property managers to operate as a single producer to fix rental rates without competition.

We found that a correlation exists between the use of AI technology and the skyrocketing rental rates in metropolitan markets, as well as the ballooning homelessness in these same markets. According to the United Way ALICE Project, nearly 51 million households cannot afford housing in their monthly budgets. This accounts for 43 percent of households in the United States.[35]

Just how much are the inflated rents over the market? To answer, we will utilize the formula that the property managers utilize from RentBureau. If the average rents were $1,500 per month and rents are inflated by 5 percent per year for five years, the rent has been artificially inflated 25 percent, or $375, equaling some $4.8 billion annually. The fines rarely deter the practice due to the vast wealth being acquired by the property managers and property owners at the expense of the tenants.

CHAPTER 7

ONE TIN SOLDIER, THE REGULATOR—THE CONSUMER FINANCIAL PROTECTION BUREAU

WHAT IS A tin soldier? Once a popular toy, tin soldiers represented the symbol of bravery. No price was too high for the tin soldier, as they were willing to offer the ultimate sacrifice in defense of their compatriots.

Let's turn our attention now to the Consumer Financial Protection Bureau (CFPB), the regulator of Artificial Intelligence–driven technology. Who are they, what is their purpose, and why are they essential to the American taxpayer and consumer?

The agency was launched in 2011 in the aftermath of the financial crisis, as part of the Dodd-Frank Wall Street Reform and Consumer Protection Act. Combining authority once held by several agencies, the bureau's goal is to protect consumers from deceptive or misleading practices in the financial industry[1] by enforcing "laws that outlaw discrim-

ination and other unfair treatment in consumer finance"
and "restrict unfair, deceptive or abusive acts or practices."[2]

The CFPB provides a new, single point of accountability for enforcing federal consumer financial laws and protecting consumers in the financial marketplace. No single
agency had the needed tools to set the rules or monitor the
entire market, which led to the economic crash of 2008.
Today, it's the CFPB's primary focus.[3] The CFPB has gone
to great lengths to inform various industries of rules and
regulations, in part because we've learned that corporate
America does not self-regulate in favor of consumers.

WHO REGULATES THE CONSUMER
FINANCIAL PROTECTION BUREAU?

The CFPB is regulated through a series of checks and balances by the Administrative Procedure Act[4] and the Financial Stability Oversight Council. [5] Since it receives funding
from the Treasury, the bureau cannot alone increase its
operating budgets, as the FDIC or the Office of the Comptroller of the Currency can.

The Trump administration and the Republican Congress
have been open about their desire to gut the CFPB. Who is
behind the funding the destruction of the CFPB, and why?
Once again, as we will see, Occam's razor points toward
the money trail.

WHOM DOES THE CFPB REGULATE?

When the CFPB was established, for the first time consumer
reporting agencies and debt collectors became subject to

a federal supervision program. One of the bureau's key responsibilities is assessing compliance with federal consumer financial laws as well as detecting and evaluating additional risks to consumers.

In 2012, CFPB's cases centered on the credit card and debt-relief sectors. In 2013, the bureau added home mortgages, auto loans, and a few land-development deals to its enforcement agenda. In 2014, the bureau expanded to the growing student loan industry and debt-collection companies.

When the bureau began, nine of its first cases involved other federal co-plaintiffs, including the Federal Deposit Insurance Corporation, the US Department of Justice (DOJ), and state attorneys general (AGs). This included the case in Dallas, Texas, described in Chapter 6, where the Federal Trade Commission (FTC) found AI-driven technology to be discriminatory. The CFPB brought the FTC into that case. On February 26, 2019, the FTC's Bureau of Competition began a task force dedicated to supervising the AI technology.

Today, the CFPB supervises banks, credit unions, and their affiliates with total assets of more than $10 billion. The bureau also has the authority to supervise nonbanks, regardless of size, in certain specific markets, including mortgage companies, payday lenders, and private education lenders,[6] and to supervise the activities of debt collectors, credit reporting agencies, and private student loan companies.[7]

The three largest consumer reporting agencies each maintain files on more than 200 million Americans. The reporting industry is a $4 billion market. In addition, the CFPB also oversees a variety of specialty consumer reporting agencies, which report information on alternative financial products and services, including apartment rentals or payday loans. Every year, 3 billion consumer reports are issued, and 36 billion updates are made to consumer files.[8] However, how accurate and helpful is the information?

FIGURE 1.

TYPES OF CREDIT REPORTING COMPLAINTS REPORTED BY CONSUMERS AND SENT TO OTHERS

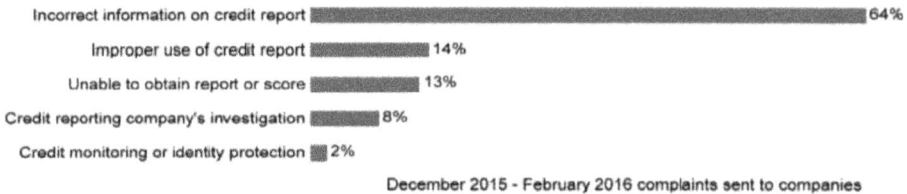

Incorrect information on credit report	64%
Improper use of credit report	14%
Unable to obtain report or score	13%
Credit reporting company's investigation	8%
Credit monitoring or identity protection	2%

December 2015 - February 2016 complaints sent to companies

Source: "Monthly Complaint Report Vol. 11," Consumer Financial Protection Bureau, May 2016, https://files.consumerfinance.gov/f/documents/201605_cfpb_monthly-complaint-report-vol-11.pdf.

In 2017, the consumer credit reporting agency Equifax took six weeks to notify its 143 million customers that their private information was at risk after discovering it had been hacked. During that period, top executives sold off almost $2 million of the company's stocks after discovering the breach. Vox reported that Equifax had spent $1.1 million in 2016 lobbying against regulatory laws, including ones related to data security and breach notification.[9]

In the Texas court case discussed in Chapter 6, RealPage was found guilty of discrimination due to using technology to apply fake records to final documents. One of those companies issuing the fake reports was Sterling Infosystems, Inc. The CFPB instigated legal proceedings to resolve allegations that Sterling violated the Fair Credit Reporting Act, alleging that Sterling's procedures created a heightened risk that its reports would include criminal records belonging to another individual with a similar name as the applicant.[10]

Looking at another branch of CFPB programs, debt collection is now a $10.9 billion industry that employs nearly 120,000 people across approximately 8,000 collection agencies in the United States.[11] More than one-half of the industry's revenue, about $5.9 billion, is generated by firms contracting with creditors to collect their debts on a contingency-fee basis. Another one-third of debt collection revenue, or $3.5 billion, comes from debt buyers who purchase accounts from the original creditor or other debt buyers and then generally seek to collect on that debt, either by themselves or through third-party debt collectors.[12]

The term "contingency-fee basis" means the collection is split between the debt collector and the company claiming to be owed the obligation. Typically the debt collector employee gets to pocket all of the gains over and above the original debt. Their incentive to break the law, then, is enormous in a risk-versus-rewards scenario, and the process that debt collectors use is brutal. The CFPB found the collection process to be aggressive and abusive, and that debt collectors routinely violated collection laws. On the other hand, when salaried personnel collect the debt, abusive tactics are typically not applied because there is no financial incentive to break the rules.

WHO IS FUNDING THE CFPB'S PATH OF DESTRUCTION?

The financial industry contributed more or less evenly to the two major parties until 2010. After this, more and more of their contributions and lobbying efforts heavily favored Republicans. For example, in 2010, over 62 percent of the funds went to Republicans, and since 2012, 70 percent now flows to the GOP.[13]

In the 2017–18 election cycle, Wall Street banks and financial special-interest groups reported spending almost $2 billion to influence lawmakers—more than $2.5 million per day.[14] This vast level of spending exposes the constant battle to restructure the financial system and the industry's dogged efforts to either repeal or acquire privileged exemptions from all or parts of the Dodd-Frank financial-reform law.

Matt Taibbi, reporting for *Rolling Stone*, states that the financial industry followed a strategy established to defeat any regulation:

> The political and economic system has grown too complicated for democratic control. Creating legislation is a grueling process. But undermining legislation through lawsuits and comment letters and committees make the process of destroying the law fairly easy. Companies can't purchase votes in a democracy; nevertheless, the democracy is operated through a bureaucracy. Taxpayers can cast a vote, or attend rallies during protests and elections, but real people—even committed professionals—have limited time and energy.[15]

For example, federal regulators wanted to ensure borrowers of payday loans were able to make their payments—a sound lending policy. However, payday lenders wanted the rules to change, and even worse, they got regulators to

change the rules on basic underwriting standards for borrowers.[16]

Four consumer data facilitators spent $55 million on lob-
bying in 2017, doubling their combined spending of $27.4
million in 2016, and some are spending at a higher rate so
far this year, according to the Center for Responsive Politics. There are 238 people registered to lobby for the four
companies—about 75 percent have formerly served in the
government.[17] The campaigns to influence lawmakers have
become immense.

The Consumer Financial Protection Bureau is the only
bureau ever devised to withstand regulatory interference
by big business. However, that was then.

THE GROUNDWORK TO DESTROY THE CFPB

The Trump administration filed a brief with a federal appeals
court in Washington, arguing that the CFPB is unconstitutional as currently structured. The case has now been
appealed to the US Supreme Court (in *NLRB v. Canning*,
on actions taken by the CFPB).[18] On June 13, 2019, Patricia
A. McCoy of the Boston College Law School wrote about
the topic: "In 2017, after legislation to weaken the Bureau's
structure failed in Congress, and constitutional challenges
to the CFPB's structure became bogged down in the courts,
the GOP leadership turned to the White House to dismantle the CFPB from within."[19]

The Trump administration called on all government
departments and the entire GOP to join in on the war
against the CFPB.[20] On March 21, 2017, the GOP led hearings before the US House of Representatives, stating the

CFPB was unconstitutional. According to the record, Ann Wagner, the chair of the Financial Services subcommittee, said the following:

> For the past eight years, the American people, under the Obama administration, have grown complacent with the unchecked power emanating from Washington and its complete disregard for the Constitution. It is time to bring accountability back to Washington for us, the people. Additionally, the CFPB is unaccountable to the president, as well as by being headed by a single director, who can only be removed for a cause rather than at will. The Constitution vests the executive power in an elected president of the United States of America, and not in various unelected agency and bureau heads.[21]

Saikrishna Prakash, of the Miller Center, said, "First, I'll argue that 'for cause' removal restrictions are unconstitutional under the Constitution. Second, I'll contend that the restriction on the removal of the CFPB's director is deeply problematic under the Supreme Court precedent. Third, I'll address how Congress might resolve the constitutionality difficulties."[22]

Is the US Supreme Court case about presidential power, or is it really about AI-driven technology, which is currently being implemented at HUD? This administration continues to push to privatize parts or all of HUD once the AI-driven technology has been successfully implemented, and they could be thwarted by the CFPB, the regulator of this technology.

In January 2018, the Court of Appeals for the District of Columbia Circuit ruled that the CFPB's structure was constitutional, reversing a 2016 verdict.[23] Then–US Circuit Judge Brett Kavanaugh delivered the dissenting opinion and furthered the Trump administration's position. However, the court would remind Judge Kavanaugh that the Federal Reserve contained the same structure as the CFPB:

> (4) Judge Kavanaugh makes much of the fact that the CFPB Director's five-year term could result in a one-term President being unable to remake the agency by naming a CFPB Director during his or her tenure. Kavanaugh Dissenting O.P. 190-91. However, the same can be said of the Federal Reserve, where, absent the circumstance of a Board Member's early retirement, a President can never appoint a majority of the Board. See 12 U.S.C. 241,242.[24]

In Chapter 11, we will dig deeper into the real reason behind this administration's motives and what they aim to achieve.

CFPB NAMES NEW SENIOR STAFFERS

On May 13, 2019, Ben Lane reported in the *Wall Street Journal* that Mick Mulvaney, the acting White House budget director, had added several new senior staffers at the CFPB. One was Brian Johnson, previously senior counsel at the House Financial Services Committee and an aide to House Financial Services Committee Chairman Jeb Hensarling, known to be Congress's leading critic of the CFPB.[25] Johnson was expected to push the CFPB through the desired transition and was given authority to act on behalf of Mulvaney.[26]

This intent was not a surprise. Chris Arnold had reported via NPR in July 2018 that "Mulvaney says he is changing the bureau's mission to make it a much less aggressive regulator and begin requesting the industry to self-regulate."[27] Furthermore, Mulvaney himself wrote, "The bureau is far too powerful and with precious little oversight of its activities," as reported by Thomas Ahearn in *ESR News Blog*.[28]

On April 25, 2018, Jim Puzzanghera of the *Los Angeles Times* reported in a speech to the American Bankers Association that Mulvaney said that he was "siding with bankers and collectors on legislative steps to limit the bureau's authority . . . [I]n my office, in Congress, if you were a lobbyist who never gave us money, I didn't talk to you." Mulvaney, a former South Carolina representative, said at the banking group's government relations summit, according to a transcript provided by the bureau.[29] Mulvaney, in other words, was asking the financial industry to fund this battle.

In fact, Karl Frisch, the director of watchdog organization Allied Progress, said, "When you tell a room full of big bankers and their lobbyists that you gave more access to lobbyists who gave you more money and that they should continue putting pressure on Congress, it doesn't take a rocket scientist to deduce what you are telling them to do."[30]

KRANINGER TO SERVE AS THE NEXT CFPB DIRECTOR

In furthering the administration's goals of destroying the bureau, the Trump administration then selected an ally to run the bureau and attempt to destroy the bureau from within. On December 6, 2018, the US Senate confirmed the nomination of Kathleen Kraninger to serve as the next director of the Consumer Financial Protection Bureau. Gregg Gelzinis, research associate for economic policy at the Center for American Progress, released the following statement:

> The CFPB was created to fight for consumers, but Acting Director Mick Mulvaney has abandoned that vital mission. From day one, he has served the needs of financial institutions at the expense of consumers.[31]

Tom Jawetz, Center for American Progress vice president of immigration policy, also supported Gelzinis's research when he said, "It is beyond shameful that the US Senate would confirm an individual who played a central role in the separation of thousands of children from their parents at the US southern border—the cruelty of the policy itself that was overseen by Kraninger. Her confirmation represents a dereliction of duty by the US Senate."[32]

Powerful Democrats said Kraninger was not qualified to be the director of the bureau.[33] Her history was tied not just to the detention of immigrants and refugees at the southern border, but to some of the worst fiascos of the Trump administration, including the failed response to Hurricane Maria in Puerto Rico.[34] Democrats and Republicans have recognized—and the Trump administration has effectively conceded—that Kraninger has no experience in consumer finance or protection.

"We have grave concerns about Kraninger's people holding the authority to waive anti-discrimination laws," Jim Saksa wrote in *Roll Call*, August 2019, adding that Kraninger was implementing a regulatory sandbox program in which firms could apply for a two-year safe harbor from CFPB enforcement actions under antidiscrimination and consumer disclosure laws.[35]

The nonprofit coalition Americans for Financial Reform said, "The top official charged with protecting consumers in the financial services marketplace needs to be someone with a track record of doing just that. But there is no sign that Kraninger even understands the various sides of this issue, let alone that she values the mission that Congress gave the CFPB."[36]

Kraninger herself was quoted as saying the following: "I have challenged the staff to take a fresh new look at the entire process—the prioritization and frequency of exams, to ensure a culture of compliance means working confidentially in a back-and-forth process with a financial institution, which needs to self-examine, self-report, and provides restitution where appropriate. It is incumbent upon us to ensure that I do not impose unmanageable burdens while performing the duties."[37]

She went on to say, "I take the responsibility seriously under the law to reduce unwarranted regulatory burden and to consider the impact of the rulemaking on regulated entities and consumers. The CFPB must acknowledge that the costs imposed on regulated entities absolutely affect access to and the availability of credit to consumers."[38]

Kraninger's remarks show that her approach to fulfilling her responsibilities to the taxpayers is based on the theory of cost-benefit analysis. If the financial industry provides credit to consumers, then any rule-breaking by the industry will be overlooked, so long as the financial industry does give credit to the consumer, even if that credit is based on subprime or payday-type loans.

HALTING THE CFPB PROGRAM OF ENFORCEMENT

The Consumer Federation of America's 2019 study "Dormant: The CFPB's Law Enforcement Program in Decline," written by Christopher L. Peterson, found that under the leadership of Mick Mulvaney and Kathy Kraninger, enforcement activity at the CFPB has declined to levels that are either nonexistent or significantly below those of the prior administration. "Troublingly, the bureau has failed to announce or resolve a single anti-discrimination matter."[39]

The CFPB has, for all practical purposes, ceased enforcing laws that protect the consumer. During the terms of Mulvaney and Kraninger, Americans submitted 139,134 complaints regarding credit reporting practices. Yet, the GOP-driven CFPB has not returned any consumer relief to the public under the Fair Credit Reporting Act.[40]

Peterson's report revealed that the total number of enforcement actions in 2018 declined by 80 percent from the peak in 2015, and average per-case monetary relief for victims was down by 96 percent.[41]

When Kraninger stated that she took her responsibility seriously under the law to reduce unwarranted regulatory requirements on the financial industry, we believe her. However, looking at her statement regarding supporting the consumer, not so much. Kraninger would declare the

CFPB to be unconstitutional, revealing that she absolutely does not support consumers or taxpayers.

CFPB'S CONSTITUTIONALITY TESTED

As we'll discuss in more detail in Chapter 11, the CFPB's constitutionality went before the DC Circuit, which was asked to consider the impact of the US Supreme Court's decision in *NLRB v. Canning* on actions taken by the CFPB while Richard Cordray was serving as a recess appointee.[42]

Furthermore, on September 9, 2019, a federal court dismissed the 2017 court action brought by the CFPB against Ocwen Financial Corporation. The CFPB accused the company of "failing borrowers at every stage of the mortgage servicing process."[43]

Less than two weeks after the judge's ruling on Ocwen's dismissal bid, however, CFPB Director Kraninger announced that the bureau would refrain from defending the case. The pivot came as the CFPB joined efforts with the Trump administration and the Department of Justice to lobby the US Supreme Court to appeal the agency's Dodd-Frank Act regarding presidential powers.[44]

DO WE NEED A CONSUMER FINANCIAL PROTECTION BUREAU?

Initially, in 1994, Congress delegated the responsibility of protecting consumers to the Federal Reserve as a means to bar unfair and deceptive mortgage lending. Nevertheless, the central bank viewed consumer protection as a hindrance to ancillary fee income discussed in Chapter 5 and didn't use that power until 2008 after the housing crisis.[45]

This is one of the many examples of failures in so-called self-regulation.

On December 5, 2017, Gillian B. White, a reporter for the *Atlantic*, wrote, "About 178 million American taxpayers have credit cards. Forty percent of adults under the age of 30 have student debt. A record of 107 million (43 percent) of adults has auto debt. And about 80 percent of adults have a credit score. The safety and soundness of the financial products that these hundreds of millions of Americans use are now regulated by the Consumer Financial Protection Bureau."[46] In other words, nearly all taxpayers and consumers interact with the financial industry, and many have been affected by the industry's malfeasance.

The CFPB reported that 27 percent of consumers in lower-income neighborhoods first establish a credit record not through their own efforts to seek credit, but instead through debt collection accounts or in public records. This rate is 240 percent higher for low-income Americans than it is for consumers who live in higher-income neighborhoods, an example of predatory lending and related activities.[47]

The CFPB was the first regulatory entity to protect consumers against the onslaught of predatory lending tactics. To understand why the financial industry has developed such a powerful front against regulation, we only need to review their dark criminal past. Figure 2 reflects the record of illegal offenses, broken down by dollar amounts of penalties, and the number of violations, through mid-2019. It becomes evident why the bankers want to rid themselves of their regulator.

In the beginning, the CFPB made significant improvements in consumers' lives. They recovered more than $13 billion in corporate America's ill-gotten gains and created

stronger safeguards for 35 million consumers against reckless mortgage practices that caused the financial crisis. Furthermore, the CFPB gave consumers a voice by promptly
responding to over 1.9 million complaints, fixing problems
for vast numbers of individuals.

The following information is provided by Violation
Tracker, a national policy resource center for grassroots
groups and public officials.

FIGURE 2.

VIOLATION TRACKER AGENCY SUMMARY PAGE

Top 8 Parent Companies	Total Penalty	# of Records
Bank of America	$82,630,515,262	182
JPMorgan Chase	$34,503,944,885	135
Citigroup	$24,980,998,562	97
Deutsche Bank	$17,970,400,778	51
Wells Fargo	$17,296,835,949	136
UBS	$16,756,803,331	65
Royal Bank of Scotland	$13,349,520,000	25
Goldman Sachs	$13,139,380,987	37

*Source: "Violation Tracker Industry Summary Page," Good Jobs First, accessed
January 2020, https://violationtracker.goodjobsfirst.org/prog.php?major_industry_
sum=financial+services&page=26.*

For example, during 2014, the CFPB publicized that it
had ordered Bank of America, N.A., and FIA Card Services,
N.A., to reimburse $727 million to consumers for illegal
programs related to credit card add-on products and to
pay a $20 million civil penalty. Over 1.4 million consum-
ers were affected by this deceptive marketing.[48]

The penalties below represent some of the worst nonbank
offenders of these laws:

- Ocwen Financial Services (servicer)
  Penalty total: $2,317,651,804; number of settlements: 17

- Equifax Credit Rating Services (credit reporting)
  Penalty total: $721,441,883; number of settlements: 12[49]

AMERICAN TAXPAYERS WANT MORE
REGULATION OF WALL STREET

Taxpayers believe that the practices of Wall Street deserve additional government regulation beyond the measures taken after the 2008 financial crisis. In 2019, an AFR/CRL poll concluded that about three in four voters (73 percent) say that further accountability of business is needed, while only 11 percent say that companies' practices have changed enough that they don't need additional regulation.[50]

FIGURE 3.

**VOTERS CARE ABOUT FINANCIAL REGULATION
AND THE INFLUENCE OF THE INDUSTRY**

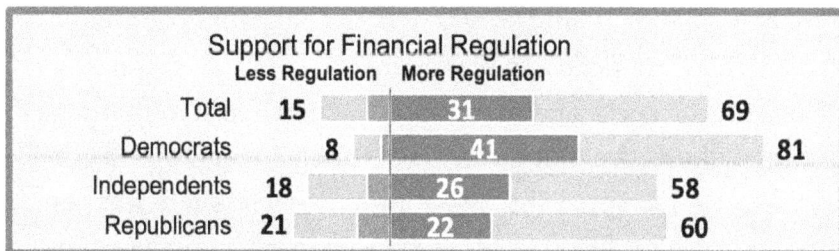

	Support for Financial Regulation		
	Less Regulation	More Regulation	
Total	15	31	69
Democrats	8	41	81
Independents	18	26	58
Republicans	21	22	60

Source: "AFR/CRL Poll: Early State Voters Support Continued Reform of Wall Street," Americans for Financial Reform, October 2019, http://ourfinancialsecurity. org/2019/10/afrcrl-poll-early-state-voters-support-continued-reform-wall-street/.

Now that we have explored the primary causes of the CFPB's demise, we will now take a closer look at how the property managers operate without regulation or supervision (self-regulation). The managers appear to have created a ten-step process to enrich themselves; however, the unintended consequence of this process is the leading cause of our skyrocketing homelessness.

In January 1934, at the first meeting on public housing (referenced in Chapter 1), the presiding head and treasurer of that public housing conference, Herbert B. Swope, shared a warning from the past:

> If I point with pride to the ending of child labor and the elimination of sweatshops, then I must, to be consistent—in fact, to be ordinarily decent—stop the sweating of tenement house dwellers, for that is what the slums are. They would not be continued if they were not profitable, and they are profitable only through operation on a dehumanizing method—through bleeding the tenants until all social justice is debased.[51]

In Chapters 5 and 6, we saw that a correlation exists between how property managers are using AI technology and the skyrocketing rental rates in metropolitan markets; furthermore, we found the property managers to be a contributing factor to the ballooning homelessness in these same markets. We concluded that property managers have become vertically integrated, with ties into the lending industry, and appear to have acquired the lending industry's more controversial programs known as predatory lending. This rather torrid yet lucrative practice works, as Herbert

Swope said, "through bleeding the tenants until all social justice is debased."

In the banking world, predatory lending is a method instituted to get to the billions of dollars the government places through the welfare programs. Similarly, property managers appear to be using what we'll call "predatory leasing."

It appears that property managers instigated this program to improve their return on investments (ROI), their prime directive for the property owners. No price is too high for profits when indifference breeds wealth.

PREDATORY LEASING AND TEN STEPS TO HOMELESSNESS

FIGURE 4.

PAY TO PLAY – OR END IN THE STREETS

A. THE TENANT
Old debts must be paid before
application will be accepted...
No Exceptions!

B. THE PROPERTY MANAGERS
Control access to both
Multifamily Markets and
Subsidized HUD Housing Markets

C. MULTIFAMILY HOUSING MARKETS
- Apartments   • Mobile Homes
- Condos   • Rental Houses

D. SUBSIDIZED HOUSING MARKETS
- HUD Housing
- Subsidized Housing

STEP ONE—THE RENT-BURDENED TENANT

The typical story is usually about severely rent-burdened tenants who can't pay an unexpected $400 hospital bill and no longer have assets to sell or provide as collateral. The tenant falls behind on the rent.

For example, Katrina Wallace had saved up two months' rent to tide her over as she went through brain surgery to correct a dangerous condition. However, when her recovery took longer than expected, she no longer had enough to pay rent for her apartment. She put together enough to cover one-third of the next month's rent and received a commitment from the county's social services department to cover the rest while she waited for her disability payments to start. Her landlord rejected that arrangement and launched eviction proceedings while she was still in the hospital. That triggered an additional $201 in court fees.[52] Of all Americans, 43 percent currently find themselves in this category, a desperate situation in which to raise their children.[53]

STEP TWO—FEE STACKING

After a tenant gets behind with the rent, property managers stack on fees and late charges, often doubling the tenant's debt. The practice of "stacking late fees" by charging additional penalties on late fees even when rent is current is illegal, but still happens.[54]

Multiple courts across the country are ruling against the unlawful practices of excessive fees collections. For example, as we saw in Chapter 6, the US District Court for the Western District of Texas, Austin Division, ruled in 2018 that fees are unreasonable and against current laws and regulations.[55] Late fees are also considered liquidated damage in violation of California's Unfair Competition Law, as well as the Rosenthal Fair Debt Collection Practices Act.[56] And a court found in a recent class-action lawsuit that property managers violated the Texas Water Code and Texas Administrative Code when they billed residents improper sewer and water fees.[57]

In April 2010, Mc Nelly Torres reported on Consumer-Affairs.com the following example:

> [Virginia] Ringstaff felt nothing but relief when the repo-man repossessed her Dodge Caravan. She had endured months of humiliation at the hands of debt collectors who made calls and disclosed her debt to relatives and employers. "They got so hateful on the phone that I wouldn't answer it. A mother of two children, ages 13 and 11. It's embarrassing. I was on the verge of losing my job because they [debt collectors] called my boss at home and called him a liar."[58]

We also saw that on October 30, 2018, another tenant filed a complaint with the Better Business Bureau after receipt of an email: "You have a past due account of $1,507.28. This balance is more than 380 days old . . . If we do not hear from you by the date above, your account will be turned over to our collection agency, and at that time, the amount will be increased by 50%."[59] This was illegal and unenforceable.

STEP THREE—THE EVICTIONS

At this point, tenants may attempt to move to another location. The process is complicated by the technology put into place by a property manager running interference on behalf of the property owner by identifying prospects who are attempting to skip or who have left another community with money owed.[60]

As an example, Experian RentBureau worked with Riverstone Residential, which received more than four hundred acknowledgments that one of their tenants applied to another apartment community. Riverstone Residential, under agreements, informed RentBureau of rental applicants attempting to move into a community while still owing a rental-payment debt elsewhere, enabling the property managers to prevent those tenants from getting a new lease until they satisfied their outstanding debt obligation.[61] As outlined in Chapter 5, the tenants cannot move unless the property manager group consents.

As we've seen, one of the property owners' primary tools in collecting illegal fees is their use of the "specialty" renters reports, which then also become a substantial threat to tenants' housing access and stability. Andrew Heiberger, CEO of TOWN Residential calls an adverse rental history "the single worst blemish you can have."[62]

On May 17, 2018, Dan Kane and Ely Portillo of the Raleigh *News & Observer* reported that North Carolina had reported nearly 164,000 eviction proceedings in the 2016–17 fiscal year. One such eviction case, discussed in Chapter 6, concerned Jordon Hargrove, twenty-six, who, with the help of his family, had paid the eviction fees to stay in his apartment, after the property manager refused a two-week partial payment extension. However, the conclusion to the story is that months later, he discovered his record reflected a false eviction, which became a barrier as he sought to move elsewhere.[63]

Each one has a story behind it, thousands of which are posted with the Better Business Bureau and similar sites.

Once the tenant realizes they neither have the money to pay the excessive fees at their current location nor are able to move into another apartment complex, the tenant may choose to stay with friends or family while trying to sort this whole situation out. The result moves the tenant to either steps four or five below.

STEP FOUR—PROPERTY MANAGERS BEGIN THE DEBT COLLECTION PROCESS

Excessive fees have kept many vulnerable families out of affordable housing. For example, in December 2017, a federal district court judge in Oakland, California, gave the go-ahead for tenants of Equity Residential to pursue a class-action lawsuit alleging unlawful and excessive fees.[64] This was just one of the hundreds of such court cases.

We know that in Washington State, along with many others, tenants can be evicted for missing one monthly payment by only four days—in Seattle, 45 percent of eviction filings were for missing rent for one month or less.[65]

For example, in January 2020, a Seattle youth homeless shelter faced its final days, and its young residents confronted an uncertain future. In King County, 1,200 young people, ages eighteen to twenty-four, were homeless in 2019, and half of them had no shelter at all.[66]

Imagine, if you will, a single young man from an impoverished background who has worked his way through college but acquired significant student loan debt along the way. After graduating with honors, he works long hours at Amazon, making less than twenty dollars per hour.

Now with student debt bills mounting, he cannot keep up on rent payments. "Please, landlord," he pleads. "I just need two additional weeks to make the rent payment. Please don't throw me into the streets, I have nowhere to go."

Step Five—Tenant in Chaos

If friends or family are not able to provide temporary housing, the tenant's plight will take a dangerous turn, and they may attempt to enter shelters. For Jennifer Newman, program director of St. Martin de Porres shelter in Seattle, it can feel overwhelming. The homeless population is aging, a phenomenon that is happening nationally. A 2013 study found that one in three men sleeping in shelters in Boston, New York, and Los Angeles County in 2010 were over the age of forty-six, compared with one in eight in 1990. An ongoing study of homeless individuals in the San Francisco Bay Area found that, in 1990, 11 percent of people struggling with homelessness were over the age of fifty. That number has now skyrocketed to over 50 percent.[67]

Step Six—Third-Party Debt Collectors Are Unleashed

Predatory leasing entails massive illegal collection activities, and at this point in the process, they will send delinquent accounts to collection agencies, and a new round of harassment begins. AI technology is deployed by certain collectors against homeless people, usually pushing the former tenant into bankruptcy as their only means to get into housing.[68]

Just how abusive are the tactics used by the debt collectors? On July 25, 2019, Letitia James, the New York attorney general, alleged that debt-collection key player Douglas

MacKinnon violated the Fair Debt Collection Practices Act. The complaint alleged that MacKinnon purchased millions of dollars' worth of consumer debt, inflated those consumer debts, and relied on illegal tactics to extract as much money as possible from consumers.

MacKinnon also set up a network of at least sixty additional debt collection firms. Companies lied to consumers, telling them that they owed sums they did not owe or were not obligated to pay, and that the companies did not have a legal right to collect. They falsely threatened consumers with legal actions the collectors had no intention of taking, and impersonated law enforcement officials, government agencies, and court officers.

Under the proposed settlement, MacKinnon will be banned from the industry.[69]

However, no relief would be given to those vulnerable tenants who were trapped in the webs. As one of these massive debt collectors is taken down by the law, another one takes its place.

In Chapter 5, we found that property management firms allow their contracted debt collection companies to access information in Experian RentBureau, meaning debt collection companies use the intensely personal application data to recuperate debts. Furthermore, they collect bank account numbers and sources of income, including government welfare payments or child support, as well as how to access those accounts (with or without authority) once the funds hit the bank account. In Chapter 5 we discussed that property management firms have decreased skips and evictions under RealPage and uncovered $400 million for the owners in the process.[70]

How does this behavior affect the tenants? Annette Jaramillo of Apple Valley, California, suffered when a Miami debt collector called her home repeatedly and told her teenage daughter and son in separate calls that their parents were going to jail. Jaramillo said, "You don't do that to a child. My daughter was so scared, and she was fearful that something would happen to us."[71]

Thousands of consumers, including Virginia Ringstaff, have posted complaints on the ConsumerAffairs website alleging that unscrupulous collectors have threatened to arrest and jail them, made harassing phone calls, contacted third parties and disclosed their debts, called their employers, and also tried to collect debts not owed by the consumer—all violations of the Fair Debt Collection Practices Act. More disturbingly, consumers have complained that debt collectors have gained access to their bank accounts and made withdrawals without their consent;[72] the tenant is bled until all social justice is debased. The consequence is that debt collectors are increasingly using courts to arrest and even jail debtors, exposing the most vulnerable consumers to what critics call "a de facto debtors prison."[73]

However, when judgments are in place, and the AI knows the location of all banking accounts, property managers attach all assets (cash and property) that the tenant may have. The fines for these illegal acts rarely deter the practice due to the immense fee income.

STEP SEVEN—PROPERTY MANAGERS
ESTABLISH ROADBLOCKS

The struggle to get back into housing becomes difficult due to the barriers set up by property managers. In tenant applications, all applicants are screened for both bad credit and criminal background. Property managers have a policy to "not rent to people entering bankruptcy, currently in bankruptcy, or leaving bankruptcy [a violation of the law]."[74]

For example, Apartment Management Consultants (AMC) determines the screening criteria for each property based on location and demographics; generally speaking, AMC requires a minimum of 2.5 times the monthly rent as an income qualifier and denies any applicants currently in bankruptcy.[75] They may also exclude those who have criminal background records, including those records that are inaccurate.

Property managers reject applications until the tenant pays the massive fees in step two above. With the courts on their sides, they abuse the laws and collect their illegal fees.

As discussed in Chapter 5, the property managers, through the RealPage platform, worked together to block tenants from getting housing if the manager considered a debt to be owed. For example, Chris Jenkins, VP of financial planning for Equity Residential, said, "We don't have to contact former residents. They contact us to clear up an outstanding balance when their rental payment history appears in connection with trying to rent another apartment. So, it absolutely does work."[76]

The consequence of that process is that tenants receive no protections from bankruptcy if property managers do not accept an application until the tenant has paid the landlord all monies due and payable, including fees. If the tenant cannot make an arrangement to pay the debt, they are left with fewer and fewer housing options.

At issue is that once the fees have been collected or ripped from the tenant, the tenant no longer qualifies as a tenant per qualifications outlined above.

Step Eight—Financial Ruin

In Chapter 4, we discussed how the property owners are financing the facilities through very risky loans that are guaranteed by the taxpayers, while tenants work hard and have taxes withheld from their meager paychecks to fund the investments of billionaire investors. The tenant, in other words, guarantee the rights of the investor to raise rents, indiscriminately, possibly being forced into financial ruin. The tenant receives no protections from bankruptcy.

If the tenant cannot make an arrangement to pay their debt, then they move to step nine.

Step Nine—Tenant Held Hostage by the Property Manager —Aggressive Leasing Tactics

At this point, tenants with outstanding debt are not candidates for subsidized housing either, because they are typically out of funds, and the property managers who handle market value properties also manage subsidized housing. Unfortunately, property managers typically will not accept an application until the tenant has paid all fees and monies owed to their previous landlord.[77]

Figure 4 displays the various actors involved in the predatory leasing process, including the property managers referenced in Section B (private housing) and the property managers in Section D (public housing). These actors are the gatekeepers to the housing markets.

One such example, WinnCompanies, is the sixth-largest property manager per Section B. The National Affordable Housing Management Association also ranked WinnCompanies as the number one provider of federally subsidized homes (Section D) in the country in 2012.[78] Housing clerk magistrate Robert L. Lewis says Winn is one of many realty management companies that have appeared in court.

In fact, this is a nationwide movement in Massachusetts; for example, according to the *Trial Court's Overview of Trends Report*, 10,784 total cases were filed in housing court in 2013, an 11.7 percent increase since the previous year. The report also indicated a 35 percent increase in code enforcement entries, or complaints against the landlords, since 2013.[79]

The multifamily housing cartel has effectively blocked access to the tenant's search for housing. The prime directive of the property managers is to drive profits to the bottom line, return on investment—damn the consequences.

STEP TEN— HOMELESSNESS

In the end, the tenant has no choice but to move onto the streets. Opioid addictions and drug use have become commonplace for once-productive tenants who fell on hard times—some of the many who are only one hospital bill away from the streets. In Seattle, for example, the *Puget Sound Business Journal* reported that ninety-one homeless people died in 2017 in King County, and the region's opioid crisis—the cause of many such deaths—has only gotten worse.[80]

Evictions, including forced relocation due to significant rent increases, are one of the primary causes of homelessness in Seattle, like many metro areas. From 2012 to 2017, one-bedroom apartment rents soared 53 percent, according to Dupre + Scott Apartment Advisors. Zillow concluded that for every 5 percent rate increase, 258 people in Seattle experienced homelessness, and children are twice as likely as adults to be homeless.[81]

Between 2017 and 2018, the number of people experiencing homelessness in Seattle counted on a single night in January jumped 15 percent. In California, 134,000 people were homeless during the annual census for the Department of Housing and Urban Development, a 14 percent jump from 2016. About two-thirds of them were utterly unsheltered, the highest rate in the nation. The nationwide population of those experiencing homelessness is up 47 percent from 2012. Those who would become homeless for the first time jumped 16 percent from 2017. At least ten cities on the West Coast have declared states of emergency in recent years.[82]

A crime committed by a third-party collection agency is forcing people onto the streets. At the same time, property managers and investors sit in their ivory towers, counting their wealth. Why is this acceptable behavior?

It isn't. In 2013, the Consumer Financial Protection Bureau found Global Expert Solutions, the country's biggest debt collector, guilty and ordered it to pay a $3.2 million civil penalty, the largest ever collected from a third-party debt collector.[83] Today, however, the CFPB no longer functions to protect the vulnerable among us. This approach is supported by the Trump administration. Wealth comes with a price—the price of indifference.

HUMAN RIGHTS BEFORE PROPERTY RIGHTS

In 1932, during the great and terrible Depression, Democrats coined the phrase "Human rights before property rights."[84] This statement rings loud today.

Homelessness isn't an unexplained phenomenon; homelessness is a process developed by property managers in an attempt to satisfy management contracts (ancillary incomes) and increase the bottom line.

Homelessness isn't just happening, it's being done to people—property managers are waging war, as described in the 1934 Pecora Report: "Men of might—not because of principle, but because of economic power and wealth—have . . . taken millions and millions of the hard-earned pennies of the people [working poor] and turned them into gold for themselves."[85]

What will society become without a system of laws? The "one tin soldier" built for this onslaught is being sacrificed by those who should be protecting him. This saga will continue in Chapter 11 as the Trump administration takes the case to destroy the CFPB to the US Supreme Court.

CHAPTER 8

THE CHAIN OF COMMAND OVER ARTIFICIAL INTELLIGENCE–DRIVEN TECHNOLOGY

As we saw in Chapter 3, the Trump administration is pushing for the privatization of the Government Sponsored Enterprises (GSEs), and according to the Office of Inspector General (OIG), the GSEs Fannie Mae and Freddie Mac have been plagued with conflicts of interest,[1] including the lack of ability to remain compliant with federal IT regulations and to effectively oversee the Enterprises' management of risks related to their counterparties.[2]

As we discussed in Chapter 3, more troubling is that, to this day, the FHFA's management cannot account for those who have access to the new AI-driven system platform—passcode holders, and, more critically, those who hold the highest levels of clearance to all online activity and databases.[3]

In this chapter, we are going to look more deeply into those conflicts of interest associated with the implementa-

tion of AI technology. Who is implementing the AI algorithm? HUD personnel, or is a shadow leadership chain of
command in charge? And if so, who are they, and why were
they selected by the Trump administration?

Furthermore, is there a correlation between this administration's role in the demise of the CFPB (Chapter 7)—the
only regulator between AI technology and the consumer—
and this administration's drive to privatize the Enterprises?

We will see who the actors are and what they aim to
accomplish. Is HUD's AI-driven algorithm trained to be fair
and equitable, or are their outcomes based on discrimination, as the courts found in Texas?

The process began on February 11, 2019, with the Executive Order on Maintaining American Leadership in Artificial Intelligence. The order emphasized that the United
States must drive technological breakthroughs in AI.[4]

The American AI Initiative fast-tracked the Trump administration's desire to maintain control of the implementation process.[5] According to a GeekWire article by Darwin
McDaniel, the process also granted authority to the National
Coordination Office, which sets initiatives and includes the
funding to increase AI-driven technology research. The
process is to be completed over five years, with the government delivering $1.2 billion in funding for AI technology
research and development. The bill created the National
Quantum Coordination Office and an advisory committee,
supervised by the Office of American Innovation.[6]

THE OFFICE OF AMERICAN INNOVATION

President Trump's son-in-law, Jared Kushner, has a staff
that, among other duties, enlists the most prominent tech-

nology CEOs—Amazon's Jeff Bezos, Apple's Tim Cook, Microsoft's Satya Nadella, IBM's Ginni Rometty, and more. During their first official gathering, it was disclosed during a White House press briefing that the Veterans Administration had decided to acquire a new, multi-billion-dollar, AI-driven IT system. Those in the room realized that $1.2 billion in big tech projects were now on the table.[7]

The tech CEO gathering got the most headlines, but possibly the more enlightening event occurred at the White House during a July 2017 briefing, when Secretary of Veterans Affairs David Shulkin first acknowledged and thanked what he called the "American Office of Innovation." Until this announcement, the American taxpayer had been kept in the dark about its existence.[8]

The Office of American Innovation team currently consists of Kushner; Chris Liddell, a former chief financial officer of both Microsoft and General Motors; Reed Cordish, a former Baltimore real estate developer; and Matt Lira, a veteran Capitol Hill staffer.[9] Each team member has a history of interconnectedness in the multifamily housing industry. The stories are all pretty much alike, and so we can focus on Kushner as a fair representation of the group.

KUSHNER'S TIES WITH THE GSES

By late 2012, Jared Kushner had grown his company's rental-housing portfolio by more than 11,000 units through a complicated transaction refinancing past-due debt with $371 million in new Freddie Mac financing. "We've secured great financing on everything we've bought so far," Kushner said.[10]

On June 21, 2017, Zachary Cohen reported through CNN that Kushner, a thirty-six-year-old commercial real

estate magnate whose marriage to Trump's daughter Ivanka
had thrust him into the center of US foreign relations,
arrived in Israel for meetings with Israeli prime minister
Benjamin Netanyahu's administration.[11]

Later in 2017, however, the Kushner Companies worked
with Israel-based Psagot Investment House, which provided
the financing on the $1.2 billion purchase of Quail Ridge, a
1,032-unit complex in Plainsboro, New Jersey.[12] Were possible conflicts discussed by Kushner and approved by some
White House authority? Was the Israeli visit political, or did
Kushner have an alternative purpose for the meetings? Did
he use his position and influence with his ties to the White
House to acquire financing for the property?

On July 23, 2018, Alec MacGillis reported through Pro-
Publica and the *New York Times Magazine* that a lawsuit
described highly aggressive illegal tactics used by Kushner
Companies to pursue tenants and former tenants at fifteen
apartment complexes in the Baltimore area. The suit claimed
that Kushner's company had been improperly inflating payments owed by tenants by charging them late fees that were
often baseless and in excess of what was allowed by law,
similar to the behavior discussed in Chapter 7. This level
of behavior is based on the concept of "client preference"
imposed by a very real cartel with aggressive processes and
tactics. The lawsuit also alleged that the late fees and court
fees set in motion a vicious churning cycle as tenants were
pressured to pay the snowballing fees while under an imme-
diate threat of eviction.[13]

On May 23, 2019, *Bloomberg* reported that Kushner
Companies received another $800 million in a federally
backed apartment loan—the company's biggest purchase in

a decade. The loan was underwritten by Berkadia Commercial Mortgage, a national commercial real estate company that also provides underwriting for GSEs. Kushner Companies had more than $500 million in loans from Fannie Mae and Freddie Mac at that time, and now has more than $1.2 billion,[14] all guaranteed by the American taxpayer, not Kushner Companies.

In Chapter 3, we discussed the chaos and conflicts of interest at the Enterprises as they rushed to privatization. We further examined the potential for conflicts of interest by Fannie Mae CEO Hugh R. Frater, who previously led Berkadia Commercial Mortgage. He was also an executive vice president at PNC Financial, the largest securitizer for the GSEs, with ties to BlackRock, one of the largest investors in the GSEs and their institutional securitized bond market.[15]

In Chapter 5, we discussed how vertically integrated entities (vertical trusts) will forward or backward integrate to fill their organizational structure with segments from the industries in which they interact. The lending industry is one such example the vertical trusts desire to add to their organization, and the GSEs are their lenders of choice. Companies like Kushner Companies or Greystar and their connections have been consumed with the varied aspects of the GSEs. Greystar founder and CEO Bob Faith said in a statement, "Our vertically-integrated rental housing platform, together with our intimate knowledge of the origination and underwriting guidelines utilized by the GSEs, positions us well to invest in the most subordinate part of the capital structure."[16]

Once you place the financial connections (GSEs) into the property managers' organizational structure, the GSE connection appears to serve two purposes. First, it connects to the pipeline, providing the means to move the billions of dollars of loans and bonds. Second, the connection ensures optimal financing, as Kushner pointed out, through the weak underwriting and the failure of prudent lending policies discussed in Chapter 4. Should a lender elect to hypergrow a pipeline, both the rate of interest charged and credit quality would be decreased.

The risks of such a move would be immense, as we have not witnessed these types of financing arrangements since before the financial crash of 1929. That's because the Glass-Steagall Act of 1933 separated the connections between banks and investment houses, the activities of which contributed to the 1929 crash. But that was then.

WHO ARE THE MULTIFAMILY HOUSING AND AI TECHNOLOGY COMPANIES FUNDING?

The various participants within the housing markets have become very political, and donating vast sums of money furthers this work. In late 2019, Donald Trump kicked off his reelection campaign donation tour with a $3 million luncheon in Northern California, followed with a $5 million Beverly Hills dinner at the home of real estate developer Geoffrey Palmer of G. H. Palmer Associates—who personally donated an additional $7 million.[17] G. H. Palmer Associates began in 1978 and currently holds a portfolio of multifamily real estate valued at more than $4.5 billion. It actively seeks to expand through the acquisition and development of multifamily properties, in alliance with institutional lenders and underwriters for taxable and tax-exempt mortgage revenue bonds.[18]

These connections lead us back to the Office of American Innovation. The property manager vertical-trust operations are concerned with the privatization of the GSEs, as this is a critical segment of their organization. Why? How intertwined and interconnected are they in the implementation process? Not only that, how do they intend to implement the technology, similar to the property managers? And what do they aim to accomplish? The devil's in the details.

The Office of American Innovation legal counsel Brooke Rollins is Jared Kushner's assistant. Kushner, as we've seen, represents the Trump administration in the Office of American Innovation.[19] Before this, Rollins served as Texas governor Rick Perry's deputy general counsel, and later as his policy director.[20] She was also the past president and CEO of the Texas Public Policy Foundation, a think tank in Austin, Texas, that has provided "ultra-conservative" research for almost twenty years. One of their projects, Right on Crime (ROC), is a partnership with the American Conservative Union and includes the "conservative ideas on criminal justice." She was instrumental in assisting Kushner with his push to change the justice system through a legal position that has been considered discriminatory against people of color and minorities.[21]

Another Trump supporter is entrepreneur Peter Thiel, who played a critical role in ensuring a Trump victory in 2016. Thiel donated more than $1 million to Trump's first presidential campaign and then assisted with the transition team. After the election, Thiel's chief of staff, Michael Kratsios, was named deputy chief technology officer (CTO) of the administration, becoming Trump's acting head. At the same time, the top job was left vacant (another example of operating in the shadows). Kratsios previously worked in politics during the George W. Bush era, when he interned for Senator Lindsey Graham of South Carolina while studying political science at Princeton.[22]

Peter Thiel, Kratsios's former boss, is a venture capitalist, the co-founder of PayPal, and an early investor in Facebook. Thiel has sold most of his ownership in Facebook but remains on the social media company's board, and advises Facebook head Mark Zuckerberg on critical issues, such as honesty in political advertising.

Thiel also cofounded the CIA-backed big-data startup Palantir, lately valued at around $20 billion.[23] *Bloomberg Businessweek* has reported that Palantir has some dubious overseas ties. The business worked with Cambridge Analytica, the UK-based data analytics firm that illicitly accessed the personal data of Facebook followers and used it to assist in Trump's 2016 presidential campaign.[24] In this, Thiel's actions can be seen to mirror J. Edgar Hoover's, with an aggressive style in enforcing his views through unconventional tactics.

Now that we have discussed who these actors are, we will now look more closely at what they are trying to accomplish.

RURAL HOUSING DEVELOPMENTS IN HUD

In January 2020, the Trump administration recommended, "Having both USDA and HUD housing programs administered by HUD would allow both agencies to focus on their core missions and, over time, further align the Federal Government's role in housing policy."

Gustavo Sapiurka, of RealPage SVP Enterprise Solutions, did not hesitate to praise HUD—representing one of Real-Page's most extensive customer bases.[25]

Secretary Ben Carson spoke on September 9, 2019, concerning new IT platforms:

> FHA also continues to operate on antiquated technology platforms that inhibit the agency's ability "to appropriately manage risk and fulfill its fiduciary duty to taxpayers." FHA has already developed a detailed technology roadmap that will guide the development of a single platform and baseline architecture to cover all aspects of the mortgage process, from loan origination, through endorsement, servicing, claims, and, as required, disposition. Overall, the investment in the new single platform structure will allow FHA to better adapt to changing the industry, regulatory, and statutory requirements; the modernized systems will be data-driven, and ultimately allow FHA to fully digitize the mortgage process, opening doors to significantly more refined risk analysis and management. To this end, HUD has recommended that FHA explore agreements to share technology with GNMA and other government-supported mortgage programs, including the GSEs, when feasible. Additionally, HUD recommends that Congress appropriate sufficient funds for FHA to complete its multiyear, single-family IT modernization effort.[26]

On August 14, 2018, Secretary Carson announced that the position of HUD's chief information officer (CIO) would report directly to him. He also directed that the IT functions dispersed across the agency be consolidated into the Office of the Chief Information Officer (OCIO), rather than being held separately by each program office. After this reorganization, the CIO would establish knowledge and skills standards for all agency IT personnel and identify positions in which critical hiring needed to exist. If there was a shortage of highly qualified candidates, the CIO could use special hiring authorities to address these staffing risks.[27]

This type of move is unprecedented and critical to understanding the massive and unequally negative impact the AI-driven technology will have on the housing markets. Our history has proven that unregulated industries become toxic in a relatively short period of time.

FIGURE 1. OFFICE OF THE CHIEF INFORMATION OFFICER

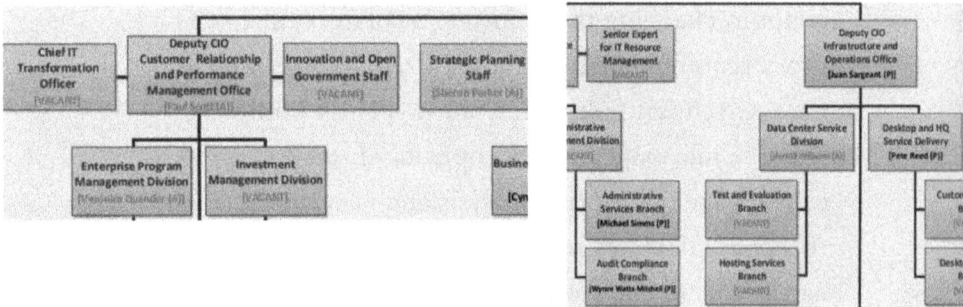

Source: "Organization Chart," Office of the Chief Information Officer, December 2019, https://www.hud.gov/sites/dfiles/OCIO/documents/cio_Orgchart.pdf.

As we see on the organization chart in Figure 1, nearly every position is either vacant or "acting," leaving us to question the authenticity of this group and their ability to function, and to wonder whether the department is actually being governed by a shadow group, and if so, who are they?

THE LEADERSHIP CHAIN OF COMMAND
OVER AI TECHNOLOGY

On May 5, 2016, Trump's presidential campaign announced that it had hired investment banker Steven Mnuchin as national finance chairman. Mnuchin had deep ties to Wall Street and Hollywood, and was appointed to lead the campaign's fundraising efforts.[28]

After the election, Trump nominated Steven Mnuchin for secretary of the Treasury and Wilber Ross as secretary of Commerce. For both men, their primary qualification was personal loyalty to Trump, with little experience in politics or policy.[29] Mnuchin was involved deeply at the time in developing the president-elect's tax proposals—$6 trillion in tax reductions for the wealthiest corporations.[30]

"Steve Mnuchin is a world-class financier, banker, and businessman," Trump said in a statement on November 30, 2016. "His expertise and pro-growth ideas make him the ideal candidate to serve as Secretary of the Treasury. He purchased IndyMac Bank for $1.6 billion and ran it very professionally, selling it for $3.4 billion plus a return of capital. That's the kind of people I want in my administration representing our country."[31]

Mnuchin went on to select his AI implementation "management team" from the failed IndyMac group of investors that acquired and managed the bank as OneWest Bank, then sold the bank to investors at CIT.

President Trump, as we've learned, does what he thinks will most benefit his causes. Why would he choose this group? Of all the investors who have acquired large banking entities and sold them for profits, why this group? What made them unique, what skills were visible during the auditions for the roles?

We find some of the answers in the July 2018 Executive Order Establishing the President's National Council for the American Worker, which says in part:

> In addition to the Co-Chairs, the Council shall include the following officials or their designees:
>
> (i) the Secretary of the Treasury; Steven Mnuchin, Chief Information Officer. [32]

Throughout the Executive Order, Trump laid out his plans to interface AI technology into federal housing markets. Steve Mnuchin was chosen to lead this process.

Mnuchin's experience began when he joined investment bank Goldman Sachs in 1985 and later became the firm's chief information officer (CIO), responsible for the management, implementation, testing, and use of information and computer technologies.[33]

Today, two separate factions or connected groups appear to control the implementation of AI technology. First, and most dominant, are the former executives hailing from the acquisition and sale of Mnuchin's failed IndyMac. The second group appears to center around IT provider DXC Technology.

The former IndyMac leaders took over the operations of implementing and controlling AI-driven technology. Team members included Secretary of Commerce Wilber Ross, Secretary of Treasury Steve Mnuchin, and Comptroller of the Currency Joseph Otting. As a reminder, Otting was also the acting director of FHFA, the organization that supervises and maintains control of Fannie Mae and Freddie Mac.[34] Otting also previously served as CEO of OneWest Bank.[35] In addition, Brian P. Brooks, former chief legal officer at OneWest, became the chief legal officer for Fannie Mae over the program,[36] and Frank Nazzaro, the former chief technology officer of CIT, became Freddie Mac's chief legal officer.

In Figure 2, the color shaded highlights point out how the group knows each other and what their past connections are.

FIGURE 2.

THE FAILED INDYMAC ACQUISITION

	NAME AND POSITIONS	COMPANY	POSITIONS	INDUSTRY
Feb 2017	**Steven Mnuchin** Secretary of the Treasury	Goldman Sachs	Chief Information Officer	Financial Investments Firms
		OneWest Bank N.A.	Chairman of the Board	Banking and Finance
Dec 2018 Nov 2017	**Joseph M. Otting** Acting Director FHFA Comptroller of the Currency	OneWest Bank N.A.	President & CEO	Banking and Finance
	FANNIE MAE			
Mar 2019	**Brian P. Brooks** Strategic Initiatives & Technology Committee	Coinbase Global, Inc.	Chief Legal Officer	Cryptocurrency
		OneWest Bank N.A.	Chief Legal Officer	Banking and Finance
		Spring Labs Inc.		AI Tech Fincen compensating financial institutions for data sharing
Sep 2018	**Manuel "Manolo" Sánchez Rodríguez** Strategic Initiatives & Technology Committee	Adelante Ventures LLC	Founder	Real Estate Securities Investment Firm w institutional investors
		Spring Labs Inc.	Founder	AI Tech Fincen compensating financial institutions for data sharing
	FREDDIE MAC			
May 2019	**Frank Nazzaro** CTO and Acting CIO	Travelport LLC	Chief Technology Officer	AI Technology for Recreation Facilities & Svcs
		CIT Group (purchased OneWest Bank)	Chief Technology Officer	Banking and Finance

POSSIBLE CONFLICTS OF INTEREST
One West Bank N.A., Connections
DXC Technology, Connections
Spring Labs Inc, Connections

The leadership team, like the nonbanks, operates in a world without regulation and hence poses a considerable risk for the American taxpayer.

THE PRIVATE EQUITY GROUP THAT
BOUGHT INDYMAC ASSETS

The failed US mortgage lender IndyMac sold its primary holdings to a group of private equity and hedge fund managers, including Mnuchin's investment management firm Dune Capital Management,[37] which invested some $1.3 billion in cash. The acquisition included IndyMac's thirty-three branches, mostly in Southern California, and consisted of some $6.5 billion in deposits, including loan and securities portfolios of about $23 billion. IndyMac's holding company, IMB HoldCo, acquired the mortgage servicing portfolio with unpaid principal balances of more than $175 billion.[38] IMB HoldCo (IMB) is the holding company of IndyMac and the newly created OneWest Bank.[39]

After managing it for seven years, Mnuchin and his partners sold OneWest Bank for a $1.5 billion profit in 2015. During the time in between, the group revealed a history of violations and outright fraud perpetrated on the American taxpayer. Critics say that the bank was a "Robo-signing foreclosure machine." Under Mnuchin, OneWest Bank failed to help owners modify their loans into existing government programs so they could keep their homes.[40] In one allegation, the bank foreclosed on a ninety-year-old woman and took her home due to a twenty-seven-cent error on a payment.

A complaint filed by the California Reinvestment Coalition (organized in 2011) states that OneWest—now known as CIT Bank—violated the Fair Housing Act. According to the grievance, "California neighborhoods were examined for compliance; however, the findings led to the conclusion that over seven years, OneWest lent no money to black American borrowers, and less than 0.01 percent went to Latino borrowers, and less than 0.02 percent went to Asian communities" It also claims that OneWest branches in predominantly black Los Angeles neighborhoods had been closed and only one remained open in an Asian area.[41] On July 29, 2019, as part of the FDIC consent agreement with the government, the former owners of OneWest Bank agreed to invest $7.3 million in minority communities. They also agreed to open a full-service branch serving the banking and credit needs of residents in a majority-minority low- and moderate-income neighborhood.[42]

Perhaps the most pernicious of their actions, however, is their apparent disregard for regulations when attempting to make massive profits by bending the rules. In Chapter 6, we learned that AI technology has been educated to discriminate against certain classes of people based on race, skin color, or other demographics.[43] OneWest Bank, before Steve Mnuchin took office as the secretary of the Treasury, offered $89 million to settle claims that it had abused the foreclosure process.[44]

Once the two discriminatory groups of OneWest Bank and RealPage were combined into one shadow organization, they posed a significant threat to our housing markets.

LITTON LOAN SERVICING: GOLDMAN
SACHS'S ALLEGED ROBO-SIGNERS

On June 6, 2011, Goldman Sachs sold its Litton Loan Servicing unit to the Ocwen Financial Corporation of Georgia for $263.7 million. The sale included a portfolio of $38.6 billion in mostly subprime residential mortgage loans. However, Goldman arranged to retain liability for government-regulated fines that occurred before the sale.[45]

In January 2013, the Consumer Financial Protection Bureau (CFPB) settlement agreement covered more than 220,000 borrowers whose homes were illegally sold in foreclosure between 2009 and 2010 and whose mortgages were serviced by Goldman's Litton Loan Servicing. Goldman had to pay fines totaling some $135 million to borrowers and offer $195 million worth of relief.[46]

Furthermore, in August 2014, under an agreement with the CFPB, Goldman Sachs agreed to pay $3.15 billion to repurchase mortgage-backed securities from Fannie and Freddie. The settlement included claims alleging violations of federal and state securities laws.[47] In December 2013, Ocwen Loan Servicing and former owner Goldman's Litton Loan Servicing was ordered by the CFPB to provide $2 billion in principal reduction to qualified borrowers. The consent order spoke to Ocwen's systemic misconduct, which occurred during every stage of the mortgage servicing process. The consent decree further outlined that Ocwen had to refund some $125 million to some 185,000 borrowers who had already lost their homes to foreclosure.

Ocwen provided false or misleading information to consumers about the status of their accounts. It denied loan modifications for eligible homeowners. And it sent documents through the courts after they were robo-signed during the foreclosure process. Another issue discovered was that the company illegally foreclosed on over a thousand borrowers for no apparent reason. It then failed to provide homeowners insurance payments through the escrow accounts of over 10,000 borrowers who were later charged excessive rates for forced-place insurance (a high-risk form of home insurance). After examining the potential violations, the CFPB concluded that Ocwen made troubled borrowers even more vulnerable to foreclosure.[48]

"Deceptions and shortcuts in mortgage servicing will not be tolerated," said CFPB director Richard Cordray. "Ocwen took advantage of borrowers at every stage of the process. Today's action sends a clear message that we will be vigilant about making sure that consumers are treated with the respect, dignity, and fairness they deserve."[49]

However, on September 9, 2019, under the Trump administration, a federal court rejected the 2017 ruling instigated by the CFPB. The court gave the CFPB until September 27 to file an amended complaint. The agency did not publicly comment on the ruling.[50]

CFPB WILL NO LONGER DEFEND
RECOMMENDED PENALTIES

Less than two weeks after the judge's ruling on Ocwen's dismissal bid, CFPB director Kathleen Kraninger announced that the CFPB had taken a new position regarding the unconstitutionality of the bureau, and that she intended to refrain from defending the case. The pivot came as the

CFPB joined the Trump administration and the Department of Justice to lobby the US Supreme Court to appeal the agency's Dodd-Frank Act original design.[51]

This failure to protect the American taxpayers will benefit Mnuchin, and it appears that his $1 million investment into the Trump campaign paid off handsomely. The benefit to Mnuchin's investment group is potentially more than $2 billion.[52]

Experience and knowledge of an industry is considered an essential part of responsible governing. At what point, however, does knowledge become a conflict of interest? The reports issued by the Office of Inspector General have been very critical of Mnuchin's conflicts of interest, and the additional investigation into the management and governance of the GSEs does lend credence to the OIG's reports.

In Chapter 4, we discussed that the Financial Crisis Inquiry Commission (FCIC) often pointed to the moral hazard that guided the markets before the 2008 crash. The conflicts of interest and special interests that dominated the markets then are startlingly similar to the group involved in the implementation of AI technology today. Quid pro quo is once again becoming the norm in the banking industry and its related partners.

The question remains: What do these shadow groups aim to accomplish? Those who control the AI technology will control the future of housing for the next generation of homeowners, along with the vast wealth that fuels the industry. The Occam's razor explanation would lead us to the privatization of the GSEs and the shadow groups' desire to control it. Without any threat of oversight, the ownership of the technology will be theirs.

Property managers are now near-perfect in their vertically integrated state of existence, from the builder, to the
owners and managers, to the investors, to the securitizers,
to the lenders, and all the way to ties to the Treasury.

Allowing this team to implement and control the AI technology and control the GSEs, without proper oversight,
would be a monstrous betrayal to the American taxpayers and homeowners alike. Further, the members of the
team have shown their utter blatant discrimination against
people of color and minorities, and they have a propensity
to abuse established rules. This group now has the ability
to train the technology to discriminate.

As American taxpayers, we must not allow this team to
move forward with their final plans to implement this discriminatory practice, as the results are likely to be disastrous.

CHAPTER 9

WHEN THE BOUGH BREAKS—THE RETURN OF SHADOW BANKING

I MENTIONED BEFORE that I began my career as a federal bank examiner for the Farm Credit System just as the US agriculture sector crashed. As the economic devastation spread to the rest of the economy, I transferred to general debt restructuring and liquidations. Debt restructuring is the process of reassigning more favorable rates and terms to a debt based on the premise that the bank would lose less money.

There were many bank failures in those days, including two of the nation's largest banks, Wells Fargo and Bank of America. Both were eventually acquired by other banks, and their respective names were kept for marketing and branding purposes. However, bringing the dead back to life is both a tricky and dangerous game. Death happens for a reason. In the case of Wells Fargo and Bank of America, the corrupt values of their executives had brought about their downfall. Their acquisition and reanimation were as doomed as Frankenstein and his monster.

A bank's ethical values are shaped over time. How a bank's leadership responds to situations often becomes the rule, and those rules are then passed on through policy and training to every level of employee. Thus, it is a bank's CEOs, CFOs, and other leaders who generate the expectations for behavior in-house, with customers, and with other parties outside the organization. Unfortunately, when top bank leaders are not punished for corrupt behavior, their pernicious values are allowed to permeate entire banks and, eventually, the entire banking industry. When the corrupt values of Wells Fargo and Bank of America were not allowed to die with them, it was eventually left to the American taxpayer to pay the price.

This "too big to fail" logic creates a "moral hazard" situation within the financial sector. "Moral hazard" is a common phrase in economics and insurance. Essentially, it argues that if a person or entity faces little to no consequence from a risky action, they are more likely to engage in that act. For example, an insured driver might drive more recklessly, knowing that their insurance company would cover the cost of an expensive accident.

Back in the early 2000s, financial market executives knew their governments would never let them go bust, because the ensuing chaos would be too great. Their investment discipline weakened. The most prominent financial institutions began to take excessive risks, knowing that, should things go awry, taxpayers would bail them out. Unfortunately, they were correct, and taxpayers shelled out over $700 billion.[1]

A key element of systemic risk is the evolution of industries powered by AI-driven IT networks in which specific industries become dominant by those integrated systems. Concentration tends to reflect the benefits of economies of scale and, no doubt, brings significant benefits and efficiencies as well as substantial risks.[2]

In this chapter, we will compare our findings of today's housing markets against five of the FCIC's significant findings from the 2008 investigation of the economic crash, first introduced in Chapter 4:

1. Consolidations and concentrations in the industries
2. Deregulation
3. Credit expansion and rapid growth
4. The rise of shadow banking
5. Securitization and structured financial securities

The analysis will include the market participants, including mortgage lenders, originators, GSEs, banks, nonbanks, mortgage securitizers (aggregators), and the loan servicers.

1. CONSOLIDATIONS AND CONCENTRATIONS IN THE INDUSTRIES

PRE-2008 CRASH CYCLE

Increasing concentrations at every level made failures in the financial system more likely to occur. Leading up to the 2008 financial crisis, the economy was beleaguered with concentrations increasing at every level.[3] By 2005, the ten largest US commercial banks held 55 percent of the industry's assets, more than double the level held in 1990.[4]

Today

The lenders haven't changed their behavior. In 2019, the Federal Reserve reported that large financial institutions pose the highest risk to the financial system as a result of their size, complexity, and interconnectedness. In fact, the largest, most complex bank holding companies and nonbank financial companies are the institutions posing the highest systemic risk to the US economy.[5]

The Banks: For decades banks have been merging, partnering, and expanding—so much so that the top four banks now account for 50 percent of all US banking assets.[6] In 2018, the nation's ten largest financial institutions held 54 percent of our total financial assets; in 1990, they held 20 percent. During that same time, the number of banks dropped from more than 12,500 to about 8,000.[7]

The Nonbanks: Ginnie Mae faces concentration risk, as a significant number of their issuers are susceptible to changes in economic conditions that could affect their ability to meet contractual obligations.[8] For example, in 2011, of Ginnie Mae's top five issuers, four of them were banks, including the top three issuers. In 2018, of the top five issuers, four of them were nonbanks, including the top three issuers.[9]

Nonbank servicers of loans backing enterprise mortgage-backed securities (MBS) grew from 25 percent in 2014 to 38 percent in the third quarter of 2018.

Today, the vertical trusts with their ever-increasing interconnectedness and concentrations make failures in the financial system more likely to occur. In fact, current markets are beginning to look a lot like 2007, except our investments are more significant in size, more complex, and much riskier than in 2008.

2. DEREGULATION

PRE-2008 CRASH CYCLE

Regulators argued that financial institutions with strong incentives to protect shareholders would regulate themselves by carefully managing their own risks. The supporters of deregulation were also disinclined to adopt new regulations or challenge industry on the risks of innovations.[10]

However, in May 2008, debt-to-income (DTI) ratios had risen to between 50 and 65 percent; this would later be considered a marker (a means of recognition) of subprime loans. Lower interest rates granted greater access to mortgage credit for households that had traditionally been left out—including subprime borrowers. (See Chapter 7 for a deeper exploration of deregulation.)

TODAY

THE BANKS: After the 2008 global financial crisis, the Federal Reserve announced changes that included rewriting a raft of rules introduced and reviewing the way it puts them into practice. In 2020, the Fed signaled it would take a lighter touch when supervising big banks. It was another win for the banking industry, which has long lobbied for relief and complained that the Fed's supervisory process is inflexible and applied unevenly—"moral hazard."[11] However, prudence would question such a move, given the 2019 Federal Reserve report that recognized the extreme risk the banks are carrying.

THE NONBANKS: Nonbank institutions offer essential services like access to credit and access to payment systems for many people who are unable to rely on banks or standard banking guidelines. These entities haven't typically been subject to federal supervision, and providers are often less clear about costs, terms, and penalties than better-regulated alternatives. As a result, as we've seen, hidden fees and undisclosed fines can make these services more expensive for the people who use them.

According to an FDIC study, higher leverage is associated with borrowing from a nonbank lender—a 10 percent increase. Nonbank loans are 37 percent less likely to include financial covenants,[12] which help to protect lenders from future losses by allowing them to take preemptive measures, such as minimum debt-to-income ratios or credit scores. The maintenance of covenants allows a lender to begin working with a borrower before a credit default occurs and helps to minimize losses. The share of newly issued, covenant-light, institutional leveraged loans rose from less than 10 percent in 2010 to about 85 percent in 2018, as shown in Figure 1.

Other aspects of leveraged loans have also become riskier. These factors are likely to lead to lower recoveries and a more drawn-out default cycle if borrowers begin to have difficulty servicing their debt.[13]

FIGURE 1.

The Share of Leveraged Loans Lacking Strong Protective Covenants Has Risen Sharply Since 2008

Covenant-Lite Share, Percent

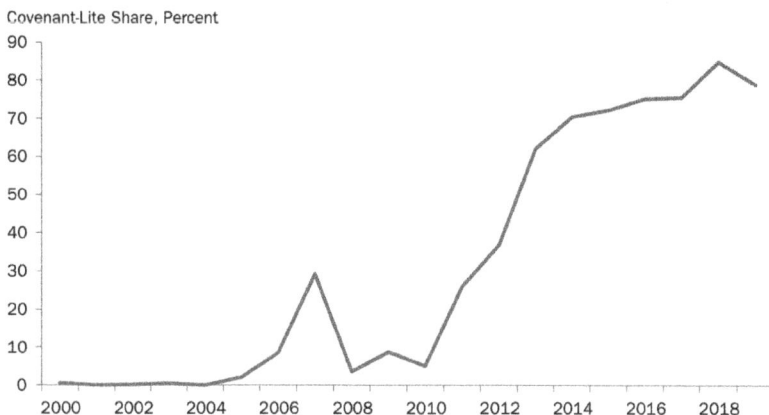

Source: S&P LCD
Note: Covenant-Lite share is of total issuance of institutional leveraged loans.

Source: "2019 Risk Review," FDIC, accessed January 2020, https://www.fdic.gov/bank/analytical/risk-review/full.pdf.

While studying the causes of the 2008 crash, the FCIC focused on how big the monthly DTI payments could be relative to a person's income. After intense debate, Richard Cordray, the interim director of the CFPB, and his aides decided they would cap the debt-to-income threshold at 43 percent.[14]

However, Fannie Mae relaxed its DTI requirements again in July 2019. It now allows borrowers to have a DTI ratio limit of 50 percent, up from 45 percent.[15] Also, nonbanks have been more willing than banks to lend to borrowers with lower credit scores.[16]

In January 2019, the *Highlights of GAO-19-239* report concluded the following:

Indicators of borrower credit risk for mortgages the
Enterprises have purchased suggest underwriting standards have loosened, which could pose an increased
risk to the Enterprises. Specifically, loan-to-value
ratios and debt-to-income ratios have increased, while
average borrower credit scores have declined. In fact,
the ratios are worse off than those before the 2008
crash.[17]

The reason for concern is that loans with high debt-to-income thresholds are particularly dangerous during a downturn, when it can be more challenging for people to come
up with payments if they lose their jobs or their obligations
grow. "It's an explosion waiting to happen," said Robert
Pozen, the former president of Fidelity Investments and a
senior lecturer at the Massachusetts Institute of Technology. "People don't seem to be worried about it, but they
weren't worried about it the last time until it all blew up."[18]

Two Freddie Mac officials told a government inspector
general that individual loans they had been pushed to buy
carried a higher risk of default, and problems could multi-
ply when the economy slows.[19] In fact, roughly 30 percent
of the loans Fannie Mae guaranteed in 2018 exceeded the
high-risk echelon, and FHA was worse, with 57 percent,
jumping from 38 percent two years earlier.[20] FHA found
that roughly 25 percent of all new mortgages it backed,
equivalent to more than $50 billion in loans, had debt-to-in-
come levels above 50 percent, the highest level since 2000.[21]

When FHFA published its *2018 Annual Housing Report*,
they reported that "the Enterprises were not involved in
subprime loans." But when the OIG reviewed the materi-

als used to clear the report for publication, they found that those materials did not contain a definition of subprime or the criteria used by FHFA to make this determination.[22]

In fact, the OIG discovered that Fannie and Freddie policy was that as long as FHFA did not issue a definition of a subprime loan, the GSEs did not have to acknowledge or report any such loan subtype. However, the details of the loans themselves contained all of the financial markers of a subprime loan, including higher DTI and lower credit scores. OIG identified loans made to ineligible borrowers with delinquent federal debt or who were subject to federal administrative offset for delinquent child support. In 2016 alone, OIG estimated that FHA, through its approved lenders, insured more than 9,500 ineligible loans worth $1.9 billion. The risk of ineligible loans faces a higher risk of default. The loans to borrowers in the Do Not Lend database had two- and three-month delinquency rates, twice as high as those of the general population.[23]

Again, the FHFA's policy was observing and taking no action, a further example of the failures in self-regulation.

On October 2, 2019, Damian Paletta of the *Washington Post* reported that the federal government has dramatically expanded its exposure to risky mortgages, as officials over the previous four years cleared the way for companies to issue loans many borrowers might not be able to repay. This article is based on interviews with twenty-four senior administration officials, regulators, former regulators, bankers, and analysts, many of whom warned that risks to taxpayers had built up in the mortgage sector with minimal scrutiny.[24]

Further, OIG reported that beginning in 2015 and continuing through today, HUD did not conduct routine or timely Management Control Reviews (MCRs) and could not ensure that its programs were operating as intended.[25]

We must conclude, then, that the poorer quality of current high-risk loans and lending is equal to or worse than before the 2008 economic crash. The numbers are much more significant in size and complexity.

"Certainly, I think we do need to be concerned overall about some of the risks that are in the mortgage market," said Mark Calabria, director of the Federal Housing Finance Agency (FHFA), which oversees Fannie Mae and Freddie Mac. "There are some patches in the housing market that are going to hit some turbulence if there's a downturn."[26]

3. CREDIT EXPANSION AND RAPID GROWTH

PRE-2008 CRASH CYCLE

By the end of 2008, the economy had grown for thirty-nine straight quarters. Large financial companies appeared to be profitable, diversified, and—executives and regulators agreed—protected from catastrophe by sophisticated new techniques of managing risk. The housing market was strong. Home prices rose at an annual rate of 5.2 percent, hitting 11.5 percent.

TODAY

The US is officially in its longest expansion, starting in June 2009. The economy has grown for forty straight quarters.[27] Between 2016 and 2019, the cumulative cost to rent increased by just 14.1 percent, compared to the cost to purchase at the aggregate three-year price of 23.8 percent.[28]

In 2019, there was also more government-backed housing debt than at any other point in US history, according to data from the Urban Institute. Now, Fannie Mae, Freddie Mac, and the Federal Housing Administration guarantee almost $7 trillion in mortgage-related debt, 33 percent more than before the housing crisis.[29]

FIGURE 2.

TOP FOUR BANKS BY ASSET HOLDINGS

Bank Name / Holding Co Name	Nat'l Rank	Assets (Mil $)
JPMORGAN CHASE BK NA/JPMORGAN CHASE & CO	1	2,292,334
BANK OF AMER NA/BANK OF AMER CORP	2	1,775,353
WELLS FARGO BK NA/WELLS FARGO & CO	3	1,667,769
CITIBANK NA/CITIGROUP	4	1,430,122

Source: "Large Commercial Banks," Federal Reserve Statistics Release, March 2019, https://www.federalreserve.gov/releases/lbr/current/.

THE BANKS: The US banking industry (Figure 2) experienced substantial growth from December 31, 1990, through December 31, 2016, and industry consolidated assets rose from about $5.5 trillion to $19.5 trillion in real terms—an increase of 256 percent or an average of slightly over 5.2 percent per year.[30]

NONBANKS: For FHA-insured mortgages, nonbank originations represented 74 percent in 2003. After declining significantly, they increased to 86 percent in the fiscal year 2017.[31] In 2016, nonbanks borrowed $3.4 trillion worldwide from the syndicated loan market, making this type of funding investment vehicle considerably more significant than the issuance of bonds and equity. The largest non-banks are outlined in Figure 3.

FIGURE 3.

THE FOUR LARGEST NONBANKS
BY PERCENTAGE OF DOLLAR VOLUME

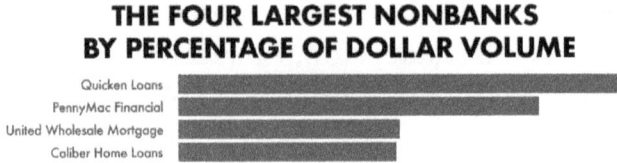

Source: Rani, Rustom M., Raymakal Iyer, Ralf R. Meisenzahl, and José-Luis Peydró (2018). "The Rise of Shadow Banking: Series 2018-039. Washington: Board of Governors of the Federal Reserve System, https://doi.org/10.17016/FEDS.2018.039 https://www.federalreserve.gov/econres/feds/files/2018039pap.pdf.

The amount of mortgage-backed securities (MBS) that Ginnie Mae guaranteed rose from $500 billion to $2 trillion in fiscal years 2007–18, exposing it to a higher risk of loss. From 2011 to 2018, the majority of institutions issuing Ginnie Mae–guaranteed MBS (issuers) shifted from banks to nonbanks, such as mortgage lenders.[32]

At the end of the day, the taxpayer now guarantees 33 percent more for billionaire investors, equaling trillions of dollars. Those funds were intended for affordable housing—contributing to that shortage of seven million units and counting.

4. THE RISE OF SHADOW BANKING

PRE-2008 CRASH CYCLE

Since the 2008 crisis, lenders have progressively walked away from mortgage lending. They are still paying for pre-

2008 offenses and feel newly imposed regulations are so strict as to be punitive. Banks made about 52 percent of all home loans in 2014, down from 74 percent in 2007, and many analysts think that share is going to go much lower.

The pre-2008 phenomenal growth of the shadow banking system—that freely operated in capital markets beyond the reach of the regulatory control—led to shadow banks greater in size and complexity than ever before.

TODAY

As we have seen, the residential mortgage market has changed dramatically in the years following the financial crisis and Great Recession due to the rise of shadow bank lenders, on the one hand, and, on the other hand, the growth of fintech lenders (high-tech online (nonbank) mortgage lenders with platform and processing completed by automation). As banks reduced their investment into government lending programs, nonbanks generally were unhampered by bank capital requirements, allowing them to quickly adapt to innovations in financial technology and profit from refinancing mortgages.[33] Once again, this shows that nonbanks have been more willing than banks to lend to borrowers with more onerous debt burdens.[34]

Nonbanks went from holding $191 billion of Ginnie Mae's outstanding balance as of September 30, 2011 (versus $1.1 trillion for banks), to $1.3 trillion as of September 30, 2018 (versus $692 billion for banks).

FIGURE 4.

CHANGING ISSUER BASE: NONBANK VS. BANK ISSUANCES (SINGLE FAMILY)

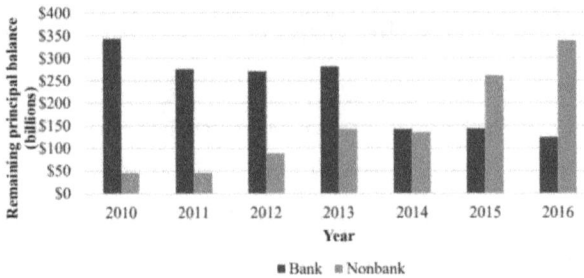

Source: Jann Swanson, "OIG Criticizes Ginnie Mae Oversight of Nonbanks," Mortgage News Daily, September 2017, http://www.mortgagenewsdaily. com/09272017_oig_audits.asp.

Ted Tozer, president of Ginnie Mae, said, "Some of the mortgage bankers have not gone through recessions when unemployment goes up, and there are delinquencies."[35]

Per Figure 4, the share of nonbank origination of FHA-insured mortgages increased from 56 percent in the fiscal year 2010 to 86 percent in 2017. The percentage of nonbank servicers of mortgages in enterprise MBS also grew from 25 percent in 2014 to 38 percent in the third quarter of 2018.[36]

Through these securitized loans, banks retain exposure to many of the loans that have shifted to nonbanks. The loans also indirectly expand the exposure of an institution to the lending activity of the nonbank. These activities include historically risky portfolio categories such as commercial real estate (CRE).[37] Banks maintained their exposure in the loans shifted to the nonbanks by issuing nonbanks lines of credit funded with banking-customer deposits.

LIQUIDITY RISKS—LACK OF
REGULATION AND OVERSIGHT:

Furthermore, some recent research suggests that nonbanks may expose Ginnie Mae to higher liquidity default and other risks in comparison with banks. More specifically, in 2018, staff from the Federal Reserve System found that nonbanks are exposed to significant liquidity risks in their funding of mortgage originations and servicing of mortgages.[38]

One consequence of these changes in the syndicated loan market is that the arranging bank now aims to distribute as much of the loan as possible to institutional investors and keep very little or nothing on their own books. Currently, the arranging banks retain, on average, only about 5 percent of a term loan.[39] The problem occurs once the economy falters and loan defaults begin. Then the nonbanks that lack the liquidity or cash on hand to make interim payments to bondholders, like Lehman Brothers in 2007, will likewise not have sufficient cash or lines of credit to do so. The results would, again, likely send the markets into a freefall.

The regulators found that nonbank issuers rely on credit lines provided mostly by banks, securitizations involving multiple players, and more frequent trading of mortgage servicing rights than banks. For instance, during times of stress, lenders to nonbanks have the right to quickly pull their lines of credit and seize and sell the underlying collateral when nonbanks do not maintain certain levels of net worth. In 2014, the FHFA Office of Inspector General found that nonbank lenders may have limited financial capacity, creating an increased risk that these counterparties could default on their financial obligations.[40]

The vulnerabilities nonbanks face are not necessarily an issue if they have the financial resources to withstand a shock, and if regulators have the information, tools, and authorities to spot problems early and resolve matters effectively.[41] However, this is not the case today.

Nonbanks have a relatively low amount of unencumbered assets—those that are not tied up as collateral for a loan and thus could be used as secondary sources of repayment on those distressed obligations or to pledge in support of lines of credit needs. In other words, nonbanks lack the financial strength to endure downturns in the economy. Most nonbanks also lack access to government institutions, such as the Federal Reserve System or the Federal Home Loan Bank System, that provide short-term credit (bailouts) to depository institutions with liquidity needs.[42]

Incomplete information on the identity of nonbanks may hinder those responsible for oversight. But FHFA does not have the authority to independently evaluate the safety and soundness of nonbank entities that conduct business with the GSEs.[43]

Beginning in the early 1990s, traditional banks funded about 90 percent of outstanding term loans, with the remaining 10 percent financed by nonbank institutional investors, as shown in the left panel of the chart in Figure 5. The exit of banks was compensated by the growth of shadow banks. As a result, by 2010, shadow banks were as crucial as banks, with each responsible for funding 45 percent of outstanding term loans.

FIGURE 5.

HOW HAVE THE PLAYERS IN THE U.S. SYNDICATED LOAN MARKET CHANGED IN THE PAST THIRTY YEARS?

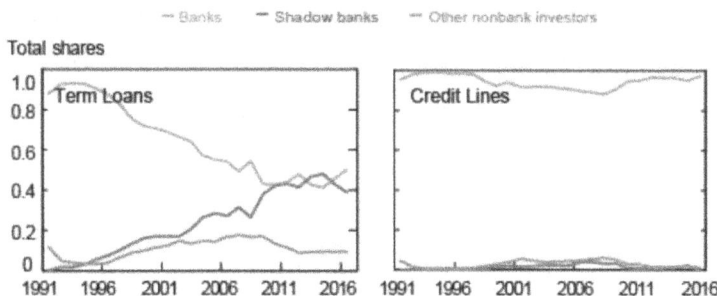

Source: Shared National Credit Program.

Notes: The left panel plots the total contributions of banks, shadow banks, and other nonbank investors in the market for term loans from 1991–2016; the right panel plots the corresponding contributions in the market for credit lines.

Source: Teodora Paligorova and João A.C. Santos, "The Side Effects of Shadow Banking on Liquidity Provision," Federal Reserve Bank of New York, Liberty Street Economics, November 2019, https://libertystreeteconomics.newyorkfed. org/2019/11/the-side-effects-of-shadow-banking-on-liquidity-provision.html.

In contrast to term loans, banks preserved their exclusive role in funding nearly all of the credit lines granted to nonbanks. In a term loan, the borrower accesses the entirety of the funding at the time of the loan closing. In contrast, in a credit line such as warehouse lending, borrowers earn the right for each drawdown of their funds. Warehouse lending is a process by which lenders extend lines of credit to nonbanks to fund mortgages until the nonbank finds a willing investor to purchase their loan portfolio.[44] However, nonbanks must meet the banks' covenants before being granted access to those credit lines.

By lending to nonbank financial institutions, banks accrue direct and indirect exposures to those institutions and to the risks inherent in the activities and markets in which they engage. FDIC analysis indicates that bank lending in the form of warehouse lines of credit to nonbank financial institutions has expanded sevenfold since 2010 and now exceeds $400 billion. The largest banks are responsible for most of this lending, as the four largest banks reported 49 percent of all loans outstanding to nonbank financial institutions as of first-quarter 2019.[45]

US Banks' Reluctance to Lend Cash— Cracks in the System

When banks don't lend directly to nonbanks to purchase loan portfolios, the Federal Reserve has the authority to place cash directly into the marketplace. Today, however, the central bank's liquidity injections include almost half a trillion dollars. Federal Chairman Jerome Powell recently said the Fed isn't trying to eliminate all volatility from markets. However, if the repo market is erratic, it signals that the Fed doesn't have reasonable control over the financial system's organization. (The repo market is a complex program, but for our purposes, it is the short-term market wherein banks invest overnight deposits that would otherwise provide no earnings into Treasury securities.)

That's something policymakers, and the broader market, can't tolerate. "We may have December in control," Lale Topcuoglu said on the Bloomberg Network. "The question is, there's January. There's February. There's March quarter-end. There's April."

This lack of clarity on the Fed's long-term objectives increases the likelihood the central bank will become more entrenched in the daily fabric of the funding markets, and that will make it more difficult for policymakers to untangle themselves.[46] In fact, the present financial picture is beginning to look a lot like 2007. The top four US banks' refusal to lend cash when combined with a burst of demand from hedge funds for secured funding could explain a recent spike in US money market rates, the Bank for International Settlements said.[47]

Bank credit lines are critical to the success of this type of nonbank funding facility. The final collapse of the likes of Lehman occurred when their credit lines were closed. The disruption in the credit line subindustry caused the massive banking disruption beginning in 2007, leading to the banking failures and the 2008 Great Recession. The credit lines had, in effect, become the load-bearing wall in their house of cards and remain its Achilles' heel even today.

The GSEs' Handling of Third Parties

In a September 2017 audit, the OIG found that Ginnie Mae was not prepared for the unintended consequences of rapid growth and shift from banks to nonbanks in its issuer base. Its staff lacked the skills necessary to immediately respond to increased risks.[48]

In its 2017 annual report, Ginnie Mae noted that the majority of nonbank issuers also involve more third parties in their MBS transactions, making its oversight of the issuers more complicated.[49] The GSEs rely heavily on counterparties, and that reliance exposes the Enterprises to several risks, including the likelihood that a counterparty will not meet its contractual obligations and that a counterparty will engage in fraudulent conduct.[50]

As we've seen, the OIG has determined that FHFA remains challenged in effectively oversee the Enterprises' management of risks related to their counterparties.[51] When working with a federally regulated bank, policies and procedures are more likely to be utilized throughout the process due to regulation and oversight. The banks also contain a knowledge base that is used to assimilate complete loan packages. However, unregulated entities have been found to skirt policies and procedures in their quest for higher profits, and Ginnie Mae doesn't have a staff sufficiently trained to review those loan packages and ascertain their completeness or legality.

The phenomenal growth of the shadow banking system that freely operates in capital markets, beyond the reach of the regulatory control, continues today in more significant numbers and greater concentrations in ownership, increasing the risk of a repeat of what occurred during 2007.

SECURITIZATION AND STRUCTURED FINANCIAL SECURITIES

Private securitizations, or structured finance securities, benefitted investors through pooling and tranching. However, today the greater drive for nonbanks and banks alike is the massive fees charged throughout the life cycle of the loans, as covered in Chapter 5.

PRE-2008 CRASH CYCLE

Before the 2008 financial crash, Wall Street labored to meet production demand. Bond salesmen earned multi-million-dollar bonuses packaging and selling new kinds of loans, offered by new types of lenders, into new kinds of investment products that were deemed safe but possessed complex and hidden risks.

However, compensation structures were skewed all along the mortgage securitization chain, from people who originated the mortgages to people on Wall Street who packaged them into securities. Regarding those mortgage brokers, often the first link in the process, FDIC chairperson Sheila Bair told the FCIC that their "standard compensation practice . . . was based on the volume of loans originated rather than the performance and quality of the loans made." She concluded, "The crisis has shown that most financial institution compensation systems were not properly linked to risk management. Formula-driven compensation allows high short-term profits to be translated into generous bonus payments, without regard to any longer-term risks."[52]

In 2008, securitization "was diversifying the risk," said Lawrence Lindsey, the former Fed governor. "But it wasn't reducing the risk . . . You, as an individual, can diversify your risk. The system as a whole, though, cannot reduce the risk. And that's where the confusion lies."[53]

TODAY

Ginnie Mae's highest potential off-balance sheet exposure to credit losses is related to the outstanding principal balance of MBS held by third parties, which was $2 trillion on September 30, 2018.[54] The reemergence of demand for commercial mortgage-backed securities (CMBS) after the financial crisis is also reflected in an increase in issue size.

The median issue amount of CMBS issue sold since 2015 saw an increase in size and complexity of approximately 111.7 percent from 2009.[55]

"We are starting to see different kinds of capital coming into the multifamily market," said Josh Grossman with money management firm LEM Capital LLC. In September 2018, the global investment company GIC invested in a new multifamily real estate investment firm, Greystar Real Estate Partners' perpetual life fund, Greystar Growth & Income Fund, and the Dutch financial management firm PGGM. "There's more capital allocated to multifamily, with a significant amount from overseas," said Steven DeFrancis, Atlanta-based CEO of Cortland.[56]

The 2008 Financial Crisis Inquiry Commission concluded that the monetary policy of the Federal Reserve, including the lowering of interest rates, and along with capital flows from abroad, created conditions in which a housing bubble could develop. However, these conditions need not have led to a crisis. The Federal Reserve and other regulators did not take actions necessary to constrain the credit bubble. In addition, the Fed's policies and pronouncements encouraged rather than inhibited the growth of mortgage debt and the housing bubble.

On November 28, 2018, J. P. Morgan Chase, in a new study for the firm's wealthiest clients, emphasized that the largest firms are most at risk of not being able to sell credit, such as high-yield bonds. That's because the larger, more sophisticated investors will likely have more private assets in their portfolios that are hard to sell. "The conventional wisdom is that if you are big and sophisticated, you'll be okay," said John Bilton, head of global multi-asset strategy at J. P. Morgan Asset Management. "But the reverse is true."[57]

SUMMARY: WHEN THE BOUGH BREAKS

Will we see a repeat of HUD's role in another pending economic crash, or has HUD and the housing market been tamed?

Before 2008, the regulators argued that financial institutions, with strong incentives to protect shareholders, would regulate themselves by carefully managing their own risks. However, in the end, this was not the case, leading to the conclusion that self-regulation is a failed policy.

On May 9, 2019, one of the investing groups suing J. P. Morgan Chase and other Wall Street banks over a loan that went sour in 2014 alleged that the underwriters engaged in securities fraud. If successful, the lawsuit could radically transform the $1.2 trillion leveraged lending market.[58] On the other hand, so much for protecting shareholder value.

In early 2014, just weeks after Jamie Dimon, CEO of J. P. Morgan Chase, settled out of court with the Justice Department over the alleged fraud and corruption charges, the bank's board of directors gave him a 74 percent raise, bringing his salary to $20 million.[59] How a bank's leadership responds to various situations often becomes the rule, and these rules are then passed on through policy and training to every subsequent level of employee. Moral hazard and the too-big-to-fail mentality continue to spread through the banking industry.

"When you have a big loss in the marketplace, there are only three people that can take the loss—the bondholders, the shareholders, or the taxpayers," said William Seidman, who led the Resolution Trust Corporation (RTC) from 1989 to 1991. "That's the dance we see right now. Are we going to shove this loss into the hands of the taxpayers?"[60]

Millions of homeowners lost their homes to foreclosure sales in the US between 2006 and 2014. The effects of the subprime mortgage crisis are still being felt today. The National Association of Realtors says that the experience damaged credit ratings and psyches. There is even a term for the mental toll the crisis took: "post-foreclosure stress disorder."[61]

The housing market has not been tamed. In fact, asset managers and institutional investors are raising concerns about what will happen during the next period of extreme market stress, now that banks are no longer big players in the markets and trading fixed income in the decade since the financial crisis. As in 2008, once the crisis begins and vacancies begin to escalate due to income inequality, those bonds will fail in their value.

In Chapter 4, we found that the rents supporting those loans and investments are not sustainable, and thus, the values based on those rents cannot be supported—and "when the bough breaks," the long winter will follow. We've been here before, and we've seen it before.

Winter is coming.

CHAPTER 10

HUD IS CHANGING THE RULE ON DISCRIMINATION

On November 11, 1620, the Pilgrims came ashore on land that is now in Provincetown, Massachusetts, on Cape Cod. It was the year that English settlers, seeking religious freedom, boarded a merchant ship, the *Mayflower*, and braved a hazardous trip across the Atlantic Ocean to establish a new home.

Since then, we have set in place a Constitution upon which the United States of America was founded. We, as human beings with different needs and wants, could not form a perfect union if we wanted to, yet our Founding Fathers brought us together "e pluribus unum: out of many, one." We came together, "we the people."

However, there were apparently some at the table who secretly crossed their fingers when they signed, because there has been a battle ever since over who has the right to decide our freedoms. Democracy in this country moves very slowly, and for some, not at all.

Perhaps George Orwell, in his novel *Animal Farm*, best sums up our current controversy regarding equality: "All animals are equal, but some animals are more equal than others. A proclamation by the pigs who control the government."[1]

After millennia of dictatorial rule throughout the world, new laws came from the United States regarding free thought, personal freedoms, the right to choose, and personal accountability. These were a technical part of the framework our forefathers used in crafting an American constitutional democracy. The Pledge of Allegiance, after all, includes "liberty and justice for all."

After the Civil War, however, black Americans would struggle for almost one hundred more years under the inhumane treatment in the Jim Crow era. However, in 1963, as the civil rights movement was emerging, the Reverend Martin Luther King, Jr. rose up to defend the freedoms they had been promised:

> I have a dream that one day this nation will rise up, live out the true meaning of its creed: "We hold these truths to be self-evident, that all men are created equal." I have a dream that my four little children will one day live in a nation where they will not be judged by the color of their skin but by the content of their character. Darkness cannot drive out darkness; only light can do that. Hate cannot drive out hate; only love can do that.[2]

THE MISSISSIPPI SOVEREIGNTY COMMISSION

"I have not the smallest amount of fear," said Mississippi governor James Coleman all through his 1956 swearing-in, "that four years hence when my successor stands here on this same spot to assume his official oath, the separation of the races in Mississippi will be left intact and will still be in full force and effect in exactly the same manner and form as we know it today."[3]

Underneath Coleman's governance, the state legislature fashioned the Mississippi Sovereignty Commission (MSC), a twelve-member supervisory body devised to oversee any perceived threat to the racist way of life. The commission's actions encompassed upholding the state's segregation and Jim Crow laws, opposing, among other things, school integration.[4]

The agency was given authority to investigate residents (mostly black Americans) of the state, issue subpoenas, and even exercise police powers, which often led to police brutality. During its existence, the commission profiled more than 87,000 persons associated with or alleged to be associated with the civil rights movement.[5]

The responsibilities of the MSC were wide-ranging. Sarah Rowe-Sims, a specialist on the Sovereignty files, writes, "From 1956 to 1973, the commission spied on civil rights workers, acted as a clearinghouse for information on civil rights activities and legislation from around the nation, funneled money to pro-segregation causes, and distributed right-wing propaganda."[6]

Furthermore, historian Robby Luckett says the MSC sometimes hired black informants: "They paid money to black Mississippians to infiltrate the meetings of civil rights activists." The records reflect that the process at times included placing the black participants' family members into detention centers until their prescribed tasks were completed.[7]

The commission was implicated in the 1964 deaths of three civil rights workers, including two young men from northern states. The men were traveling through small Mississippi towns when they were pulled over for speeding. They were jailed for no apparent reason, then released covertly, followed, abducted, and murdered. The Ku Klux Klan and two Mississippi police departments were implicated in the plot to murder them. The ACLU officially filed a lawsuit against the MSC in 1977 and waged a twenty-one-year struggle to have the agency's files unsealed. That finally happened in 1998.[8]

Speaking of the MSC's tactics, in 2017, Horace Harned, a commission member, told a reporter, "Whether it was legal or not . . . never bothered me . . . We kept the radicals and communist-led marchers from taking over Mississippi."[9]

The Mississippi Sovereignty Commission epitomizes the convergence of white fears—including change, civil rights, nonwhite upward mobility—and it stands as a stark example of a kind of state-sanctioned vigilantism.

THE VOTING AND CIVIL RIGHTS ACTS

By the 1960 presidential campaign, civil rights had emerged as a crucial issue. Kennedy may have been hesitant to move forward with civil rights legislation, but millions of African Americans were not going wait, not any longer. During the 1960s, President Lyndon B. Johnson passed a series of voting rights acts, finally correcting an unfortunate ruling by the Supreme Court—and showing that "we the people" means all of us. At this same time, the deaths of American soldiers in Vietnam fell heaviest upon young, poor black Americans and Hispanics.[10] However, on the home front, these men's families could not purchase or rent homes in certain residential developments on account of their race or national origin.

The Civil Rights Act of 1964 included labor-law legislation that outlawed discrimination based on race, color, religion, sex, or national origin, and ended unequal application of voter registration requirements and racial segregation in schools, at the workplace, and by facilities that served the general public (public accommodations).[11]

On April 11, 1968, President Johnson signed the Civil Rights Act of 1968, which was meant as a follow-up to the 1964 act. Congress passed Title VIII of the Civil Rights Act of 1968, called the Fair Housing Act, four days after the assassination of Martin Luther King, Jr. This legislation prohibits discrimination by direct providers of housing (landlords and real estate companies) as well as other entities (such as municipalities, banks and other lending institutions, and homeowners insurance companies) and in housing-related activities such as advertising, zoning practices, and new construction design. As a result of this legislation, the practices of redlining and the writing of racially restrictive covenants into deeds were deemed illegal.[12]

THE OPPOSITION TO EQUALITY

However, in Chapter 1, we discussed that discrimination continued in the housing markets for minorities through the Nixon administration. From the beginning, the cards were stacked through various schemes by the National Association of Realtors and lenders alike.

Realtors, as we saw in Chapter 1, developed a process designed to seek "people who are a better fit" for their communities and to keep "undesirables" out of the community. Lenders, on the other hand, chose to use redlining, the practice of denying a creditworthy applicant, typically a person of color or other minority, a loan for housing in a certain neighborhood even though the applicant may have been eligible. Both of these processes are an important part of the housing delivery system.

In the United States, purchasing a home is fundamental to achieving the American dream. Forty-two percent of the net worth of the average households comes from equity in their homes—most people's single largest asset. When the 1933 Home Owners' Loan Corporation (HOLC) made it possible for most Americans to fund the acquisition of their own homes, they fundamentally paved the way for millions of white Americans to start their own wealth-building.

THE RESULTS OF DISCRIMINATION

In 1995, the median white family had over eight times the net worth of the median black family. The gap is even greater for Latinos—the median white household has more than twelve times the wealth of the median Latino family.[13]

In 2019, the Department of Housing and Urban Development (HUD) proposed changes to the nation's fair housing rules, a move that fair housing advocates claim is part of a Trump administration effort to gut federal protections against housing discrimination.[14]

Disparate impact occurs when policies, practices, rules, or other systems that appear to be neutral, in reality result in a disproportionate impact on a protected group.[15]

Lisa Rice, president of the National Fair Housing Alliance, says, "These types of Fair Housing Act cases go back more than forty to fifty years. In 2015, the Supreme Court upheld the use of disparate impact while imposing some limitations. But many corporations and conservatives don't like this legal approach."[16]

HUD'S IMPLEMENTATION OF THE FAIR HOUSING ACT'S DISPARATE IMPACT STANDARD

Title VIII of the Civil Rights Act of 1968 prohibits discrimination in the sale, rental, or financing of dwellings and in other housing-related activities on the basis of race, color, religion, sex, disability, familial status, or national origin.

Congress gave the authority and responsibility for administering the Fair Housing Act and the power to make rules to carry out the act to HUD.

In 2015, in the case of *Texas Department of Housing and Community Affairs v. Inclusive Communities Project, Inc.*, the Texas Supreme Court undertook its own analysis of the Fair Housing Act and discussed the standards for constitutional questions and necessary limitations regarding disparate impact claims. Later, HUD secretary Ben Carson decided to use these amendments to bring HUD's disparate impact rule into closer alignment with the analysis and guidance provided in *Texas v. Inclusive Communities* as understood by HUD, to codify HUD's position that its rule is not intended to infringe upon any state law.

In discussing disparate impact liability, the court had noted that "disparate-impact liability must be limited, so employers and other regulated entities can make the practical business choices and profit-related decisions that sustain a vibrant and dynamic free-enterprise system." The Court also prohibited disparate impact suits that would displace "valid governmental and private priorities."[17]

The HUD rule goes on to establish unprecedented guidance for Artificial Intelligence–driven technology that powers the housing market by delivering reports on credit risk, home insurance, mortgage interest rates, and much more. Under the new rules, lenders would not be responsible for the effects of an algorithm provided by a third party—a policy that would create an industry back door to discrimination.

"This is a proposal to very dramatically revise and effectively destroy an existing 2013 civil rights regulation," says Megan Haberle, deputy director for the Poverty & Race Research Action Council. "This is a core part of the Fair Housing Act, and very early fair housing cases across the country have recognized the discriminatory effects standard."[18]

Kriston Capps, a staff writer for CityLab, said that "in addition, the new HUD rule would establish three new defenses for landlords, lenders, and others accused of discrimination based on models and algorithms. The first defense would enable defendants to indicate that an algorithm model isn't the cause of the harm. The second would allow the defendant to show that a model or algorithm is being used as intended, and is the responsibility of a third party. Finally, the new rule would allow the defendant to call on a qualified expert to show that the alleged harm isn't an algorithm model's fault."[19]

Natalie Moore reported through NPR that "the Fair Housing Act recognizes disparate impact. The US Supreme Court upheld it. Now the US Department of Housing and Urban Development (HUD) wants to replace an Obama-era rule that codified disparate impact when dealing with housing discrimination cases."[20]

HUD argues that disparate impact is vague, and the proposed rule puts in a five-step process raising the burden of proof on the complaining party. "I would argue it's impossible to prove discrimination," said John Petruszak of the South Suburban Housing Center.[21]

HUD proposed the rule in August 2019. There's no timeline for when it would be implemented, and Congress doesn't have to approve it, as Congress has granted HUD this authority.[22]

THE CONSEQUENCES OF DISCRIMINATION IN THE HOUSING MARKETS

On February 2, 2016, David Grusky and Clifton B. Parker published a study in the *Stanford News* that concludes we live in a society that is racially and economically divided. "In fact, the US ranks at the bottom when it comes to comparative data on poverty, employment, income and wealth inequality, education, health inequality, and residential segregation. Current policies and practices reinforce and perpetuate segregation and inequality. We simply cannot prosper as a nation with this level of inequality and division. Housing lies at the very center of this phenomenon. What we do about access to housing opportunity and the dismantling of segregation affects the entire fabric of our nation."[23]

In America today, just about half of all black Americans and 40 percent of all Latinos live in neighborhoods without a white presence. The average white person resides in a community that is nearly 80 percent white. To exacerbate the problems, there were 28,181 registered complaints of housing discrimination in 2016, all left unanswered by the now-defunct CFPB. Also, some 91.5 percent of all acts of housing discrimination reported in 2016 occurred during the rental prescreening process.[24]

The likelihood of discrimination against people of color and other minorities from abuse and misuse of the AI technology remains relatively high, as the Trump administration continues its use of automated programs and processes. Historically, this administration tends to provide outcomes that best benefit itself, and discrimination can be relatively hidden within the algorithms.

In the case of the disparate impact rule, the AI-technology networks would profoundly influence or manipulate the learning insights and assumptions within the algorithms, causing grave concern for how data is used in cases in which transparency may be essential for regulatory purposes. At the end of the day, should HUD implement AI-driven technology into its mainframe, this system of governance without the proper oversight would allow discrimination to destroy the housing markets for the next generation of homeowners.

In effect, allowing AI-driven technology to be placed within HUD would eliminate the entire housing market as established within the New Deal under the program of HOLC. However, it appears this is precisely the goal of the Trump administration and its supporters.

The time has come for Americans to take a stand, acknowledging our sullied past and our hand in discrimination, and to make things right. Sometimes as a society, in order to move forward, we must first clean up our past.

We can no longer hide behind our ancestors' discrimination; this one is on us.

CHAPTER 11

THE FACE DANCERS, THE AMICUS BRIEFS, AND THE LEGAL CHALLENGE BEFORE THE US SUPREME COURT

LET'S RETURN AGAIN to Ferdinand Pecora, the head of the special counsel appointed to investigate the causes of the 1929 financial crashes, who memorably observed "how men of might . . . have by the waving of a hand and adoption of a resolution taken millions and millions of the hard-earned pennies of the people and turned them into gold for themselves."[1]

Understanding "the waving of a hand and adoption of a resolution" is critical to understanding how political coalitions or alliances operate. The members of an alliance rarely break the rules, as this would open them up to legal wrangling. However, their compliance does not extend to their face dancers.

In the futuristic world of Frank Herbert's series *Dune*, "face dancers" are a servant caste of genetically modified humanoid shapeshifters, modified over many millennia to be loyal to their wealthy masters, who consider them expendable. Face dancers can also physiologically change their appearance to impersonate other people, and they will ignore the laws on behalf of their masters and change the rules and regulations to suit their needs.[2] Today the role of face dancers is played by lobbyists and deployed by the elites.

You see, in ancient days, the wealthy caste learned that indifference breeds wealth, and wealth breeds power, and power breeds freedoms.

Once a coalition is in power and its preferred lawmakers in place, the alliance's new laws are offered for votes, either in legislatures or in boardrooms. Voting members need only to approve. Wealthy elites continue to win because when they are in power, they craft legislation to their benefit, and then they craft the vote to get their designated outcome.

The Trump administration has told the US Supreme Court that the Consumer Financial Protection Bureau (CFPB) is unconstitutional because Congress limited presidential power by limiting presidential appointments to the bureau to five-year terms except for "just cause."

However, not everyone agrees with that assessment. "This case strikes at the heart of the CFPB's legitimacy and authority to protect consumers, specifically concerning mortgage lending practices," according to the opening statement by the American Association of Retired Persons (AARP). "AARP's brief addressed the importance of CFPB's broad authority to enforce consumer protection laws in protecting older people."[3]

In Chapter 7, we outlined the purpose and role of the CFPB, the broad authority they need to enforce and protect consumers, and the work they completed in order to defend the American taxpayers. However, the Trump administration and their GOP operatives have likewise laid out reasonings to support the destruction of the CFPB. Their view put simply, the CFPB is a hindrance to unfettered access to profits (cumbersome regulations).

This chapter will continue that discussion by defining who the players are and what they aim to accomplish. We will look first at the legal case that stands before the US Supreme Court in 2020, seeking the destruction of the CFPB. Then we will look at three of the special interest groups that support this administration by paying for the war on the CFPB. We will study their motives, why they want the regulator removed, and what they stand to gain from the billions they have thus far invested into the war against the CFPB.

Through the course of this book, we have established two facts: First, the Trump administration's intent is to destroy the CFPB, and they have instructed the Justice Department, the White House, and the CFPB itself to use all resources available to accomplish that goal. Second, the CFPB is the only regulator designed to protect the taxpayers from the harmful effects of the AI technology abuses.

PART I: THE LEGAL CHALLENGES BEFORE
THE US SUPREME COURT

At the time of this writing in March 2020, there is a case before the Supreme Court that is intended to destroy the only regulator between AI technology and the consumer. A second case was headed to the Supreme Court, pitting the taxpayers of the United States against mortgage lender PHH Corporation, but once CFPB director Kathy Kraninger gave notice to the courts that she will no longer support or defend the American people in the case, neither side filed the paperwork to make the request be heard.

The details of the cases themselves are unimportant to this administration; in fact, there's reason to believe the cases are merely pawns to further the destruction of the CFPB via the Supreme Court.

What changed or was changing that gave the administration hope of a victory after they failed their initial court case in 2017 (*PHH v. CFPB*, heard by the US Court of Appeals, District of Columbia)? Are they aware of facts or circumstances while the taxpayers and consumers are purposely kept in the dark? We know that Wall Street is making massive bets on what the court will do and the taxpayers bear all the risks and none of the benefits.

In the first, abandoned case, New Jersey–based PHH Corp. was found guilty of their actions, discussed below; however, on appeal, the fines as ordered by the CFPB were canceled. The same issues were litigated in another legal challenge (*PHH v. CFPB*), discussed below. The company, PHH, lost that case against forty-nine state attorneys general and the District of Columbia, agreeing to pay a $45 million settlement that resolved allegations that PHH—the nation's ninth-largest shadow bank residential mortgage originator and servicer—improperly serviced mortgages.[4]

The CFPB alleged that PHH operated a fraudulent scheme beginning in about 2000 and continuing for approximately fifteen years, whereby it received as much as 40 percent of the Private Mortgage Insurance (PMI) premiums that consumers paid to mortgage insurers, totaling hundreds of millions of dollars in kickbacks. Along with overcharging loans in some cases, PHH charged more money to consumers who did not buy mortgage insurance from one of its kickback partners.

Furthermore, PHH created higher-priced insurance by pressuring mortgage insurers to "purchase" its reinsurance, with the understanding that insurers would receive borrower referrals in exchange. PHH continued to steer business to its mortgage insurance partners even when it knew the prices they charged were higher than those of competitors.[5]

In the second case, the debt settlement company Morgan Drexen "charged more than 22,000 customers hundreds of millions of dollars in illegal upfront fees to help them resolve outstanding debts," according to the CFPB. The lawsuit alleged that the company "illegally deceived consumers into signing up for costly bankruptcy-related services by telling them they would be 'debt-free in months,'"[6] then failed to provide those services.

The CFPB's forensic accountant Tim Hanson stated that Morgan Drexen "charged or received a total of $132,882,488 in upfront fees and subsequent fees from the two groups of affected consumers" during the period between October 27, 2010, and June 18, 2015. The court found Hanson's methodology sound and his conclusions persuasive. Accordingly, the court awarded restitution for $132.9 million, the amount the CFPB proved Morgan Drexen had taken "up front" from the designated consumers. The court would go on to conclude that Drexen was guilty of "reckless violations."[7]

However, once the first case (*PHH v. CFPB*) laid out their appeal, the objectives of the Trump administration became clear. They sought to determine whether the CFPB meets the means of independence and/or impedes the president's ability under Article Two of the Constitution to "take Care that the Laws be faithfully executed."[8]

In the opinion of "all the president's men," the Trump administration should have absolute power and authority over the entirety of government. Therefore, their case depends on proving the following: First, is the means of independence permissible? Second, does "the nature of the function that Congress vested in" the agency call for that means of independence?[9]

Broad margins separate the legality of an independent CFPB from any unconstitutional effort to lessen presidential control over primary executive responsibilities. The threat that PHH's challenge poses to the recognized validity of other independent agencies, meanwhile, is very real.[10] Should the court find the CFPB to be illegal in its design, then agencies such as the Federal Reserve itself could also be found illegal in their designs.

On January 1, 2018, the appellate court ruled the structure of the CFPB to be constitutional but also provided a victory for PHH in having the penalties dismissed, with the fine pending a further review.[11] US Circuit Judge Brett Kavanaugh, with whom Senior Circuit Judge A. Raymond Randolph joins, delivered the dissenting opinion.

> (4) Judge Kavanaugh makes much of the fact that the CFPB Director's five-year term could result in a one-term President being unable to remake the agency by

naming a CFPB Director during his or her tenure. Kavanaugh Dissenting OP. 190-91. However, the same can be said of the Federal Reserve, where, absent the circumstance of a Board Member's early retirement, a President can never appoint a majority of the Board. See 12 USC. 241,242.[12]

Similar to the first case, in July 2013 Nevada company Morgan Drexen filed a lawsuit against the CFPB in a Washington, DC, federal district court, alleging the CFPB's structure was unconstitutional because it violated the Constitution's separation of powers.[13]

On a 2–1 vote, a three-judge panel of the US Court of Appeals for the District of Columbia Circuit said Morgan Drexen Inc. and an attorney who contracts with the firm, Kimberly Pisinski, had no legal grounds to make a claim.[14]

In this dissent, Kavanaugh refers to the PHH case currently pending before the US Supreme Court as follows:

> KAVANAUGH, Circuit Judge, dissenting: "I would grant the motion for an injunction pending appeal. In my view, the Company has shown a likelihood of success on the merits of its constitutional claim, for reasons fully explained in this Court's opinion in *PHH Corp. v. CFPB*, 839 F.3d 1 (D.C. Cir. 2016)."[15]

Kavanaugh continues, "To be sure, the PHH case will soon be reheard by this court en banc. But in my view, the CFPB's structure is unconstitutional. I believe that the CFPB's structure is likely to be ruled unconstitutional, whether by this Court sitting en banc or by the Supreme

Court. The Company has shown a likelihood of success on the merits. I respectfully dissent from the Court's denial of the motion for an injunction pending appeal."[16]

Judge Kavanaugh was sure that this issue was going to be heard by the Supreme Court, and he was right, in the case *Seila Law LLC, Petitioner v. Consumer Financial Protection Bureau.*[17]

KAVANAUGH ON THE EXECUTIVE BRANCH

There have been several instances throughout the Trump administration wherein individuals appeared to have "auditioned" for certain high-level cabinet positions or political appointments. Even in a position of such responsibility, those individuals do not declare their obvious conflict of interest.

Commenters on the left see in Kavanaugh's PHH opinions a hostility to the CFPB's mission more than to its structure, detecting an anti-consumer bias and general hostility to financial regulation.[18] Yet Kavanaugh's views were lauded by the White House, which praised his record of "protecting American businesses from illegal job-killing regulation."

Andrew Nolan, coordinator section research manager of the *Congressional Resource Service* reported the following:

On July 9, 2018, Donald J. Trump announced the nomination of Judge Brett M. Kavanaugh of the US Court of Appeals for the District of Columbia Circuit (DC Circuit). In his role as a Circuit Judge, the nominee has authored roughly three hundred opinions (including majority opinions, concurrences, and dissents) and adjudicated numerous high-profile cases concerning, among other things, the constitutionality of the current structure of the Consumer Financial Protection Bureau, the validity of rules issued by the Environmental Protection Agency under the Clean Air Act, and the legality of the Federal Communications Commission's net neutrality rule.[19]

Before Kavanaugh's service in the Bush administration, he worked for three years in private practice at the law firm of Kirkland & Ellis, LLP, the largest law firm in the world, with an annual revenue of $3.17 billion. He also served in the Office of the Independent Counsel and the Office of the Solicitor General.[20]

A critical question now is how Justice Kavanaugh may view the types of legal issues in which moderate Justice Kennedy's vote was often determinative.

It is a rare occurrence when a judge writing the dissenting opinion in a case is promoted to the US Supreme Court before that case is presented there, and now is likely to provide the swing vote.

Historically, judges, and especially Supreme Court justices, who were nominated by the US president were first recommended by the American Bar Association.[21] As we discovered in Chapter 8, the leadership chain of command is in control of the implementation of the AI technology, utilizing a "group cloaked in secrecy and shadows." It now appears that the appointments to the US Supreme Court, as well as hundreds of federal judges, also come from the shadow groups.[22]

CONFLICTS OF INTEREST AND INTERCONNECTEDNESS

In Chapter 5, we discovered that Bob Faith, owner and CEO of Greystar, the largest property manager in the country, controls the AI technology utilized in the housing industry. Faith spent years with Texas-based developer Trammell Crow, then continued to South Carolina, where he launched Greystar Real Estate Partners in 1993. Faith also served as South Carolina governor Mark Sanford's economic development director from 2002 to 2006.[23]

South Carolina's Republican senator Lindsey Graham called Supreme Court nominee Brett Kavanaugh "the single best legal mind of his generation," adding that he was confident the judge "is going to be on the Supreme Court."[24] On September 27, 2018, Jen Kirby reported on news site Vox.com that Graham delivered a shockingly fiery speech in support of the nominee during the questioning of Kavanaugh about allegations that he sexually assaulted Christine Blasey Ford.[25]

In Chapter 5, we discussed that interrelationship develops once two or more businesses begin "sharing" aspects of business, such as cash, liabilities, management, labor, and technology, and segments of their business begin to become blurred with other entities. To this end, it's important to note that Greystar's Brittany Jones, External Communications, also worked for Senator Graham as part of his re-election campaign.

FIGURE 1: EMPLOYMENT VERIFIED AT GREYSTAR
AND FOR SENATOR LINDSEY GRAHAM

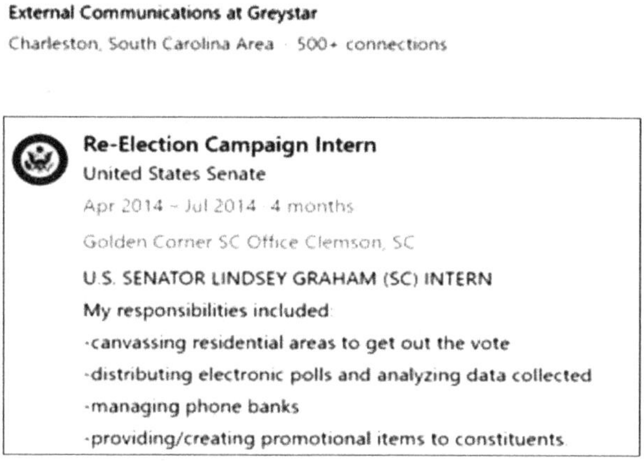

External Communications at Greystar
Charleston, South Carolina Area · 500+ connections

Re-Election Campaign Intern
United States Senate
Apr 2014 – Jul 2014 · 4 months
Golden Corner SC Office Clemson, SC
U.S. SENATOR LINDSEY GRAHAM (SC) INTERN
My responsibilities included:
· canvassing residential areas to get out the vote
· distributing electronic polls and analyzing data collected
· managing phone banks
· providing/creating promotional items to constituents

Source: Brittany Jones's LinkedIn profile, accessed January 2020, https://www. linkedin.com/in/brittanylillianjones.

The mere appearance of this conflict should be setting off alarm bells throughout this country.

PART II, THE AMICUS BRIEFS: SUPPORTING THE DESTRUCTION OF THE CFPB AND THE CONVERGING OF SPECIAL INTERESTS

Since the beginning, there has been significant conflict as to how the US housing market should work. The opposing sides come down to a debate about who gets to control the housing markets, big government (public utility) or the free-market system.

In Chapter 1, the opposition party to the New Deal program on housing was known initially as the American Liberty League, formed in 1934, and later as the Hoover Coalition. The League consisted of Republicans, Democrats, lobbyists, and business leaders who opposed the New Deal. The group was unorganized, yet vocal, and included congressional representatives known as the Conservative Coalition.[26]

We'll now look at three of the special interest groups who are waging war today against the CFPB as regulator; in fact, each of these lobbying groups has been active in politics since the days of Hoover. This group of lobbyists, the face dancers, include the American Bankers Association, the National Association of Realtors, and the US Chamber of Commerce, which have all worked diligently to undo the various aspects of the New Deal, including the destruction of the housing markets. These face dancers have wreaked havoc against minorities for decades, while presenting themselves as upstanding leaders. However, as we dig deep into the actions of these special interest groups, their reality of evil deeds and corruption becomes evident.

Matt Taibbi, a contributing editor for *Rolling Stone*, said the Dodd-Frank legislation is a lesson in the government's inability to craft the most straightforward and most critical reforms, especially if those reforms happen to clash with powerful financial interests. From the moment it was signed into law, lobbyists and lawyers have fought regulators over every line in the rulemaking process, funded by endless piles of cash.[27]

Lobbyists are professional promoters who labor to influence political decisions on behalf of people and corporations. Their advocacy leads to the proposal of new legislation or the amendment of existing laws and regulations.

I have met many lobbyists during my career, and I have, on occasion, questioned their motives or their truth. Interestingly, they usually answered with "truth is a matter of perspective," adding that their perspective is the only one that matters. They will say anything, do anything, for their masters, the wealthy caste. In the *Dune* series, face dancers commit acts of barbarism, murder, and mayhem, bring periods of famine and death, and topple governments—anything for their masters. No moral price is too high.

What do the special interests want for the vast sums of money they are spending, what do they aim to achieve, and what are their real motives?

THE AMERICAN BANKERS ASSOCIATION

According to their website, the American Bankers Association (ABA) is the united voice of America's banks—small, regional, and large—that together employ more than two million women and men, hold nearly $17 trillion in assets, safeguard $13 trillion in deposits, and extend more than $10 trillion in loans.[28]

In the 2018 election cycle, Wall Street banks and financial special interest groups reported spending almost $2 billion to influence lawmakers—more than $2.5 million per day. In addition, a total of 443 financial sector companies and trade associations spent at least $500,000 each day during this period.[29] Their vast level of spending exposes the constant battle to restructure the financial system and the industry's dogged efforts to either repeal or acquire privileged exemptions from all or part of the Dodd-Frank financial reform law.

Rob Nichols, president of the ABA, said, "[Office of Management and Budget Director Mick] Mulvaney expressed willingness to review the CFPB's policies," and that he hoped that Kathy Kraninger would "build on that foundation." Nichols added, "We look forward to learning more about her views on specific regulatory issues during the confirmation process."[30]

In 2018, payday lenders got regulators to change the rules on basic underwriting standards for borrowers. The federal regulators wanted to ensure that borrowers of payday loans would be able to make their payments, a sound lending policy. However, the lenders prevailed and a law was passed that would make it harder for consumers to join together to sue their lenders.[31]

On February 22, 2018, CBS News published a story that revealed hedge fund managers, payday lenders, and all types of banking personnel met with Trump at his properties, paying high prices for the access. For example, bank executives met for a convention sponsored by a trade magazine at the Trump National Doral in Miami. Its panel discussions included one titled "The Trump Presidency and What It Means for Banking."[32]

In Chapter 5, we discussed ancillary income in fees and related services, and how the fee income has skyrocketed over the past few years. Bank income today is generated by non-interest-related activities as a percentage of total income (net-interest income plus non-interest income). We have become an economy built on fees and fee income, with nearly half of all banking income now derived from fee income and not earnings. That means the billions of dollars the financial industry spent to wage war against the CFPB was actually funded by consumer fees and not bank earnings. We are paying for our own demise.

Figure 2 lists the fee income of the top four banks.[33]

FIGURE 2:

TOP FOUR BANKS 2017 OVERDRAFT/NSF FEE INCOME

Rank	Bank Name	Total Income	Interest Income	Non-Interest Income (NII)	% NII to Income
1	JPMORGAN CHASE BANK	2,140,778,000	48,270,000	41,943,000	46%
2	WELLS FARGO BANK	1,747,354,000	80,083,000	25,498,000	32%
3	BANK OF AMERICA	1,751,524,000	49,884,000	25,660,000	34%
4	CITIBANK, N.A.	1,385,697,000	49,981,000	14,623,000	23%

Fee income is of such magnitude that the very system that enables such wealth to be created also enables massive corruption. The access to vast sums is just too tempting, and the industry resides in a world without consequences. Moral hazard comes into play; the bigger the bets, the better. Without a regulator, the risks to be taken will be limitless.

In Chapter 7, we discussed the industry's evil deeds and the hundreds of billions of dollars in fines they have paid. Furthermore, in 2018, forty-nine states' attorneys general found the banking system to be as corrupt as the banking system of 1929.[34] Now, with the destruction of the regulator, who will be left to protect the consumers?

It's about regulation and unfettered access to profits.

THE US CHAMBER OF COMMERCE

According to its website, the US Chamber of Commerce, organized in 1912, is the world's largest business organization, representing the interests of more than three million businesses of all sizes, sectors, and regions.[35]

Corynne Cirilli reported via the website Racked.com that the US Chamber of Commerce might not be what you think. The group, which accepts funding from companies such as Gap Inc. and Target, is a powerful lobbying force in Washington.[36] In 2001, the *Wall Street Journal* outed Walmart, Daimler Chrysler, and Merck as secret Chamber clients. The Chamber has long refused to name any of its members,[37] but Bruce Freed, president of the Center for Political Accountability, was told that the Chamber has been known to set up a campaign promoting a company's pet cause if it donates at least $1 million annually.[38]

"It's surprising for many people to learn what the Chamber of Commerce does," explains Dan Dudis, the director of Chamber Watch at Public Citizen, in an article on Racked.com. The report goes on to share that according to the *Washington Post* and the Center for Responsive Politics, the Chamber and its affiliates spent more on lobbying than any other group in the country, nearly $104 million in 2016."[39]

In 2010, Josh Harkinson, a reporter with *Mother Jones*, stated "that with a name that evokes Main Street and Little League teams, and with millions of dollars to spend on lobbying, the US Chamber of Commerce has long been a powerful force on Capitol Hill."[40]

The change in purpose can be traced to former Chamber CEO Tom Donohue, who said he wanted "to build the biggest gorilla in this town—the most aggressive and vigorous business advocate our nation has ever seen."[41] Donohue received a lot of attention for his $3.7 million salary, making him the sixth-highest-paid lobbyist in the country.[42]

Shortly after the Supreme Court's 2010 Citizens United ruling, Donohue announced that the Chamber would raise $40 million to spend on electing politicians who would support the interests of big businesses. The budget later increased to $75 million.[43]

Despite the claims that the Chamber represents its core business members, the *New York Times* reported in October 2010 that more than half of the Chamber's contributions—some $140 million in 2008—came from just forty-five donors.[44]

Alyssa Katz, the author of *The Influence Machine*, says, "The Chamber, through its secret corporate donors, are responsible for the reversal of environmental protections, the destruction of unions and worker protections, the rise of anti-government dogma, the cover for a corporate agenda. Through its propaganda, lobbying, and campaign cash, the Chamber has created a right-wing monster that even *it* struggles to control, a conservative movement that is destabilizing American democracy as never before."[45]

On March 16, 2017, Dudis, of Public Citizen's Chamber Watch project, and Lisa Gilbert, director of Public Citizen's Congress Watch, reported the following:

- The Chamber of Commerce sided with British Petroleum over thousands of American small businesses in litigation related to the Deepwater Horizon oil spill in the Gulf of Mexico.

- The Chamber of Commerce filed an amicus brief in support of for-profit Corinthian College's efforts to prevent students it had fraudulently misled from suing in court. The Chamber supported Corinthian despite the mountain of evidence supporting the claims of fraud.

- The Chamber of Commerce supported the Canadian energy giant TransCanada, of the Keystone XL pipeline, over American landowners and farmers who didn't want the pipeline being channeled through their land.

- The Chamber of Commerce filed an amicus brief in favor of removing Seattle's $15-an-hour minimum wage, claiming that it would be bad for workers.

"By looking at just who the Chamber supports via its litigation, it quickly becomes apparent that the Chamber is not a voice for small business, but rather a force to defend the interests of big business, no matter the cost," said Gilbert.[46]

The cases cited stand out as some of the most egregious examples of the US Chamber's loyalty to pro-corporate influence and return on investment (ROI) at any cost.

It's about political power.

National Association of Realtors

The National Association of Realtors (NAR), organized in 1908, is America's largest trade association, representing 1.3 million members. The core purpose of NAR is to help its members become more profitable and successful.[47]

NAR also lobbies federal lawmakers and presidential administrations on the issues facing the business sector, including health care, bankruptcy legislation, and tax rates. The group has fought for the deregulation of the financial services industry. Organizations themselves cannot contribute to candidates and party committees.

FIGURE 3. CONTRIBUTIONS AND SPENDING BY
AFFILIATES OF THIS ORGANIZATION

Profile for 2012 Election Cycle

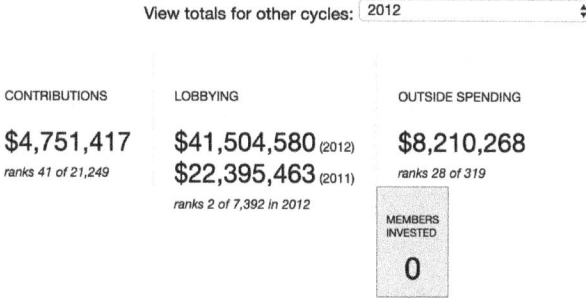

View totals for other cycles: 2012 ⬍

CONTRIBUTIONS	LOBBYING	OUTSIDE SPENDING
$4,751,417	**$41,504,580** (2012)	**$8,210,268**
ranks 41 of 21,249	**$22,395,463** (2011)	*ranks 28 of 319*
	ranks 2 of 7,392 in 2012	

MEMBERS
INVESTED

0

*Source: "National Assn of Realtors," OpenSecrets.org, accessed January 2020,
https://www.opensecrets.org/orgs/summary.php?id=d000000062&cycle=2012.*

Ten of sixty-two National Association of Realtors lobbyists in 2012 previously held government jobs.[48] Richard Mendenhall, a former president of NAR, said, "the National Association of Realtors has been recognized by *Fortune* magazine's listing of America's twenty-five most powerful lobbying organizations for four consecutive years. Something to brag about? You bet."

Based on a survey, NAR ranked ninth in the magazine's "Washington Power 25" list in 2001. This was up from number eleven in 1997, seventeen in 1998, and fifteen in 1999.[49]

Since 2004, the organization has spent some $440 million lobbying on issues like tax reform, flood insurance, and privatizing Fannie Mae and Freddie Mac. During 2018's first half, NAR spent $27.3 million on federal lobbying, second only to the US Chamber of Commerce, which shelled out $43.7 million.[50]

The NAR is also the sole funder of the National Association of Realtors Congressional Fund, a super PAC, which has spent about $313,000 so far on candidates in their bid to support the Supreme Court's ruling in Citizens United.[51]

Not only that, but we can't forget the conflicts of interest wherein property managers use their real estate broker's license, which requires them to be deemed a fiduciary. And yet, NAR's largest donors come from this group. What could go wrong from all the conflicts of interest?

During the 1950s and 1960s, NAR opposed fair housing legislation nationally.[52] They amassed their face dancers and spun their webs of deceit, spreading discriminatory hate and contention. Even after the passage of the Fair Housing Act, many local boards continued to prevent or discourage black real estate brokers from becoming Realtor members.[53]

According to NAR, after 1939, it was cheaper to purchase with a federally insured mortgage than to rent. Of course, this was only true for some Americans, because only white communities held property values, according to NAR, and too many of their Realtors accepted that segregation by race was necessary.

The NAR pushed restrictive covenants against people of color and minorities, which led to official redlining practices that began in the 1930s.[54] One such NAR policy read, "At no time shall said premises . . . be sold, occupied, let or leased . . . to anyone of any race other than the Caucasian, except that this covenant shall not prevent occupancy by domestic servants of a different race domiciled with an owner or tenant."[55]

Has NAR ever changed its discriminatory practices? Their response to these court cases suggests they haven't. They will do anything, say anything, or be anyone to make their profits. In fact, their very purpose "is to help its members become more profitable and successful." Of course, with this amount of political spending, who really are their members? Always, the face dancers of modern society and their webs of deceit.

It's about political power.

DOES TRUTH MATTER?

Various audits by OIG found rampant conflicts of interest throughout the entire process of implementing the AI technology, including administrative conflicts of interest with senior executive officers. They've reported the abdication of responsibility by FHFA to the GSEs, which substantiates the claim of shadow operations within the leadership chain of command as outlined in Chapter 8.

On June 6, 2017, policy and communications strategist Charlotte Hill reported in *HuffPost* that corporations get $4.4 trillion in federal contracts and subsidies annually. A 2014 Sunlight Foundation report found that lobbying earns corporations a huge return on investment: "For every dollar spent on influencing politics, the nation's most politically active corporations received $760 from the government." Also, the study found that for every dollar spent by unions and public interest groups on direct lobbying, business interests spent $34.[56]

Companies can't purchase votes in a democracy; nevertheless, our democracy is operated through a bureaucracy. Taxpayers can cast a vote or attend rallies and protests, but real people—even committed professionals—have limited time and energy.[57]

Regardless of how the Supreme Court rules on the CFPB, their decisions will forever remain suspect, leaving little room for legitimacy. In fact, my study finds that, like in the days of Pecora, the length and breadth of the conflicts of interest and the shadow operations supporting special interests are not limited to just a few bad actors, but permeate the entire legal process and nearly everyone they appointed to it. The day of the special interests has arrived.

Will there ever be a price too high for the consequences of power, wealth, and greed? What can the middle class do against such reckless greed . . . and endless troves of dark money, and countless armies of face dancers?

The question remains, how will the US Supreme Court rule on the CFPB, the one tin soldier? They will lock him up!

In the age of digital data, which gives access to such vast troves of knowledge, how is it possible to become beleaguered with fake news? Pontius Pilate once asked, "What is truth?" (John 18:38, KJV). Much is said today regarding morality; however, in recent years, the definition seems to be evolving toward a particular perspective.

But can we not all agree that truth is also an essential part of morality? After all, not bearing false witness is one of the Ten Commandments.

It has been said that the three keystones of democracy are truth, honesty, and integrity. Lying will destroy a democracy faster than any military power on earth. Nazi Germany proved that. The loss of truth is a cancer that eats away at our democracy from within, a long and painful ordeal, regardless of the outcome.

Today, America stands at the crossroads in a land devoid of truth. Truth has become a matter of perspective, and we no longer recognize friend from foe. The one tin soldier is now bound in chains, judged in the jackals' court of the face dancers. The jackals demand justice, the face dancers begin their dance, and what is their price? There is no moral price too high for their wealth and power. First, a favor, then the head of the one tin soldier will be delivered to their king. In the end, there won't be any choirs singing, there won't be any military parades, and there will be no safe space for the children, no crib for their bed on the day after our one tin soldier is locked away.

What is the value of truth, anyway? It's just a matter of perspective.

CHAPTER 12

THE WISDOM OF SOLOMON

AFTER WORLD WAR II, once soldiers began returning home, a severe housing shortage occurred. This also happened in 1968, where Congress found "that the supply of the Nation's housing was not increasing rapidly enough to meet the national housing goal." As their predecessors did in the 1950s, Congress used the Housing Act of 1949—which grants Congress the power to intervene in the markets—to achieve as soon as feasible the goal of a decent home and a suitable living environment for every American family.

Today, as we've seen, we face another housing shortage. Thus, the obvious question remains: Why hasn't Congress enacted similar legislation to what was successful in our recent past? What has changed in policy and procedure that might be hindering such action?

THE HOUSING ACT OF 1949

In Chapter 4, we discussed HUD's second period, the years since the Nixon administration sought to engage the free (for-profit) market in the production of low-income and affordable housing.[1]

In his 1934 speech, Frederic C. Howe shared the beginning framework of what would become HUD's mission statement (its *Federalist Papers*, if you will):

> We want, and we must have, attractive low-cost housing for those in the lower-income groups. The need for proper low-cost housing is not confined to the cities. But we do have a right to require that every child born into the world shall have an equal opportunity under the law with every other child. Every child is entitled to protection from the influence of vice and crime and physical degeneration."[2] This is the very purpose of HUD's existence, or at least, its original design—a benefit for taxpayers and consumers.

It matters who writes bills and who oversees the crafting of legislation. One example is the Home Owners' Loan Corporation, the agency created to solve the housing crisis. The Great Depression had seen home mortgage delinquency rates exceed 50 percent and remain delinquent for more than fifteen months, with catastrophic effects. In 2008, for comparison, the delinquency rates only hit about 4.2 percent.

The crafting of this section of the New Deal was incredible in and of itself. Multiple opposing factions had to be brought to the bargaining table, and each faction had very different needs. First, the lenders had mountains of defaulted loans, threatening the banks' remaining capital, which they needed to keep their doors open. Included in those defaulted loans were years of back taxes that local communities needed to keep their doors open and to provide much-needed services. Second, the homeowners were experiencing the Depression and all its intertwined consequences, including the lack of funds to make payments. From where would come the needed funds to fix this tragic problem?

Effective legislation needed to include all the parties to ensure all were made whole. In the end, the agencies were granted the authority to issue tax-exempt and government-guaranteed bonds, then sold those bonds into the marketplace. The plan worked beautifully.

This process married the homeowner to the activity of paying off the old loan in full, along with delinquent taxes, by replacing the old debt with a new mortgage designed to be repaid over an extended period while owners retained their homes. Under Roosevelt's New Deal HOLC program, over 80 percent of those defaulted homeowners paid off their mortgages. The benefit was to be given to the taxpayers, not the greedy investment bankers.

In the end, the government did not sustain any losses in the HOLC Program—unlike the 2008 bailout when millions of homeowners lost their homes. The Bush administration turned the 2008 bailout decision-making authority over to the likes of Goldman Sachs. However, according to a March 7, 2019, article in *National Review*, by the time the Federal Reserve ended its 2008 buying spree to stabilize the markets, the bond purchases had reached $4.5 trillion. By 2019, that bond debt sits at $8.5 trillion, the effect of a 131 percent increase.[3]

To borrow a phrase from President Ronald Reagan, who became popular for asking the simple question, "Are we better off than we were before?" Are we better off before or after the Nixon administration's changes to the HUD housing market?

THE HOUSING CRISIS TODAY

According to the National Low Income Housing Coalition, America has a crippling shortage of about seven million affordable rental units available to low-income renters or the severely rent-burdened.[4] Low-income housing is vanishing from the marketplace.

Rents all across America are skyrocketing in the metropolitan areas, by as much as 52 percent since 2012.[5] In California in 2017, 134,000 people were homeless during HUD's annual census, a 14 percent jump from 2016. Nationally, the homeless population is skyrocketing, up 47 percent from 2012. Children are twice as likely to be homeless as adults.[6]

This is a crisis.

HOW HOUSING COSTS AFFECT YOUR BUDGET

In Chapter 1, we discussed the story set in Rome regarding the first private utility, fire departments that existed some 2,000 years ago. At first, the price was reasonable. As time went on, however, Croesus (Crassus) charged what the traffic would bear. In the end, the price for extinguishing the fire was fixed at such a high rate that the homeowner accepted a small sum for the home and turned over the property to the fire department.

In the beginning (1933), HOLC estimated that the homeowner should not pay more than 20 percent of their income toward housing. They compared the percentage to area median income (AMI), which at the time was $1,480 (annual), as a means of calculating rent burdening.[7]

Today, rent burdening of 30 percent of income toward housing costs has been determined to be the high price homeowners can bear. Yet over 43 percent of taxpayers are paying more than 50 percent of their income toward housing, and if something goes wrong, they just hand over their homes and move into the streets—into homelessness.[8]

The following examples represent typical lower-income family budgets, where both spouses work outside of the home and still have to make tough choices, including eating poor-quality food and forgoing important expenditures such as health care.

We will look at three examples.

- Example 1 is the typical proposed budget a borrower would have to submit for loan approval today, where they can only cover 81 percent of total budget costs.

- Example 2 examines what that budget would look like should the borrower only spend 20 percent of their income on housing; in this example, the lower-income borrower can afford their home and cover all needed household expenditures.

- Example 3 reveals what that budget would look like at 30 percent debt-to-income ratio (DTI), HUD's original budget marker.

Even at 30 percent DTI, the homeowner can only cover 90 percent of their household budget.

FIGURE 1.

FAMILY OF FOUR BUDGETS BASED ON HOUSING COSTS (DEBT TO INCOME)

Borrower Purchase Price	200,000
Down Payment 3%	0
Down Payment $	6,000
Loan Amount	194,000
Payment	1,950

Annual Income	60,000			Annual Income	60,000			Annual Income	60,000		
Typical Family Budget			Example 1	Family Budget 20% DTI			Example 2	Family Budget 30% DTI			Example 3
	Monthly Expenses	Annual Expenses	% of Income		Monthly Expenses	Annual Expenses	% of Income		Monthly Expenses	Annual Expenses	% of Income
Housing	1,950	23,400	39%	Housing	1,000	12,000	20%	Housing	1,500	18,000	30%
Transportation	550	6,600	11%	Transportation	550	6,600	11%	Transportation	550	6,600	11%
Food	880	10,560	18%	Food	880	10,560	18%	Food	880	10,560	18%
Utility bills	344	4,128	7%	Utility bills	344	4,128	7%	Utility bills	344	4,128	7%
Phone	120	1,440	2%	Phone	120	1,440	2%	Phone	120	1,440	2%
Child care	280	3,360	6%	Child care	280	3,360	6%	Child care	280	3,360	6%
Ongoing Education	75	900	2%	Ongoing Education	75	900	2%	Ongoing Education	75	900	2%
Clothing	125	1,500	3%	Clothing	125	1,500	3%	Clothing	125	1,500	3%
Health insurance	800	9,600	16%	Health insurance	800	9,600	16%	Health insurance	800	9,600	16%
Other Insurance	175	2,100	4%	Other Insurance	175	2,100	4%	Other Insurance	175	2,100	4%
Student Loans	350	4,200	7%	Student Loans	350	4,200	7%	Student Loans	350	4,200	7%
Health and fitnss	58	696	1%	Health and fitnss	58	696	1%	Health and fitnss	58	696	1%
Term Debts/Cards	250	3,000	5%	Term Debts/Cards	250	3,000	5%	Term Debts/Cards	250	3,000	5%
Totals	5,957	71,484	119%	Totals	5,007	60,084	100%	Totals	5,507	66,084	110%

In the second family budget example, which allocates 20 percent of income towards housing costs, allows for the tenant to provide for all household needs, including health care and education. The budget works under the original housing program as established by HOLC. Conversely, though, those paying 30 percent or more on housing are left vulnerable to unexpected costs. In this group, nearly 44 percent of respondents said they could not cover an unexpected $400 emergency expense or would have to rely on borrowing or selling something to do so—just one hospital bill away from the streets.

Today, we know that health insurance is unaffordable for tens of millions of families in the US. What we fail to recognize is that the real culprit within the family budget has been the cost of housing, which has skyrocketed 61 percent since 1980, while income has only increased 5 percent. Historically, families pay their housing expenses first, and the spike in housing costs has left insufficient income to cover the remainder of household expenses, including insurance.

Furthermore, as can be seen in Figure 2, household debt has increased steadily since the Nixon changes to HUD. Most of the debt is the home mortgage. The sheer dollar volumes and accumulation over such a short period are concerning, especially given the fact that the world has never before seen this volume of debt.

FIGURE 2.

HOUSEHOLD DEBT IN HISTORICAL CONTEXT

- Total Debt (Estimated) Pre-1999
- Mortgage · HE Revolving · Auto Loan · Credit Card · Student Loan · Other

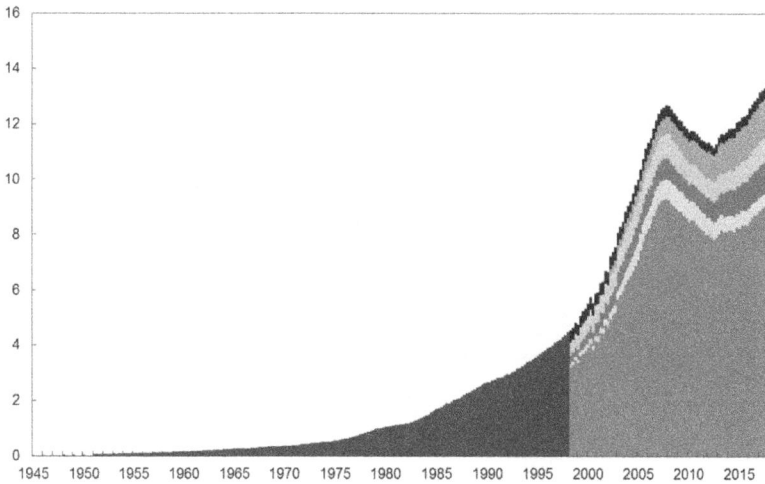

Source: New York Fed Consumer Credit Panel / Equifax; Federal Reserve Board;
Note: For comparability, we applied the pre-1999 quarterly growth rate from the Flow of Funds to splice the two series in 1999.

Source: "Trends in Household Debt and Credit," Federal Reserve Bank of New York, Staff Report No. 882, March 2019, https://www.newyorkfed.org/medialibrary/media/research/staff_reports/sr882.pdf.

The escalation in prices beginning in 2006 correlates with the sudden rise of AI technology that was introduced into the model. The market continues to roil out of control—the consequences of industry consolidations and price-fixing.

In the following example, we can see the OIG's concerns about the rising costs of housing and whether we should move the housing cost to 50 percent of the budget.

In Figure 3, you will find an example of predatory leasing to tenants (see Chapter 7, under Predatory Leasing and Ten Steps to Homelessness) with limited budgets fighting to make ends meet, who have to make choices between running water or living in the streets. However, at 50 percent DTI, the homeowner can still only cover 70 percent of their household budgeted needs.

FIGURE 3.

FAMILY OF FOUR BUDGETS BASED ON HOUSING COSTS DEBT TO INCOME 50% - SUBPRIME LOAN

Borrower Purchase Price	200,000
Down Payment 3%	0
Down Payment $	6,000
Loan Amount	194,000
Payment	1,950

Annual Income	60,000		
Typical Family Budget			Example 4
	Monthly Expenses	Annual Expenses	% of Income
Housing	2,500	30,000	50%
Transportation	550	6,600	11%
Food	880	10,560	18%
Utility bills	344	4,128	7%
Phone	120	1,440	2%
Child care	280	3,360	6%
Ongoing Education	75	900	2%
Clothing	125	1,500	3%
Health insurance	800	9,600	16%
Other Insurance	175	2,100	4%
Student Loans	350	4,200	7%
Health and fitenss	58	696	1%
Term Debts/Cards	250	3,000	5%
Totals	6,507	78,084	130%

This segment of the population is proliferating as income inequality continues to escalate. Ever-shrinking paychecks become ever less likely to meet monthly obligations, leaving these families exposed and vulnerable to predation. These are desperate circumstances in which to care for and raise a family.

Everything has a beginning, and everything ends. From the loss of loved ones to the communities we live in and the economies that sustain us, all things follow a natural order. What happens in between the beginning and the end tends to be overlooked, especially in the age of sound bites. The devil's in those details, though. In the words of an old colleague, "Figures don't lie, but liars can figure."

HOW WE GOT HERE

What ties all of the events of this book together? Artificial Intelligence–driven technology. With the CFPB dead, who would be left to regulate this powerful technology? The Federal Trade Commission (FTC) has some authority, as its specialty division handled the legal case with Real-Page in the Texas discrimination suit. However, the head of that FTC bureau, Bruce Hoffman, resigned effectively on October 11, 2019. Apparently, the group has been reassigned to other duties.[9]

In Chapter 8, we discussed the leadership chain of command that operates in the shadows, beyond the reach of regulators. Without any threat of oversight, the ownership of the technology will be theirs. As the OIG has pointed out repeatedly, many conflicts of interest exist. The shadow banking world is now near-perfect in its vertically integrated state of existence, from the builder, to the lenders, to ties right to the Treasury. Vast sums of wealth are at stake.

A REMINDER OF OUR HISTORICAL PERSPECTIVE

During the 1920s, the wealthy industrial elites who controlled Congress handpicked a Supreme Court that maintained strongly pro-business, anti-labor positions and embodied outright judicial hostility toward labor and the working class. The court struck down any state-adopted economic regulations and passed numerous laws in defense of laissez-faire policies. If the wealthy elites decided any legislation infringed upon their rights to economic sovereignty or hindered their ability to make unfettered private contracts, they called upon the Supreme Court to overturn it. This concept of government became linked to the idea of originalism.

During the late 1930s, after the Republican Party essentially collapsed, having been blamed for the Great Depression and their lack of response, President Hoover helped to organize a new breed of Republican, known as the Young Republicans. The basis of the Hoover Doctrine is the trickle-down economics theory—unfettered access to profits, without regulation or oversight. Then 1978 happened.

The beginning of a new movement, Reaganomics, brought about the rebirth of the Hoover Doctrine: the perspective that mine is the only one that matters—in other words, greed. Trickle-down economics was reborn and repackaged. Big is better, and the winner takes all, damn the consequences. The American taxpayers will bail them out if needed—and we have, many times over. The age of the aristocracy returned along with all its consequences, as always driven by income inequality.

ORIGINALISM

As we have seen, originalism is a theory centered on the interpretation that the Constitution can only be interpreted based on the original understanding of the authors or the people at the time it was ratified. This concept views the Constitution as stable from the time of enactment, and the meaning of its contents able to be changed only by the steps set out in Article Five.[10]

At its center is the conviction that legislation such as President Franklin Roosevelt's New Deal programs and later the 1968 Fair Housing Act is unconstitutional, because the laws did not follow the steps outlined in Article Five. The same argument is utilized against the constitutionality of the CFPB.

THE FEDERALIST SOCIETY

The Federalist Society was started in 1982, during the Reagan years, by conservative law students at Yale and the University of Chicago who desired to create a balance for what they saw as the liberal dogma of law faculties around the country. Its first faculty advisor was Robert H. Bork,[11] whom we'll discuss later.

One of the guiding principles of this group, according to Executive Vice President Leonard Leo, is that "[freedom of religion] protects the right of conscience, not just in houses of worship but in workplaces, schools, hospitals, government offices, and anywhere else we go in this world."[12]

"It may take ten years, it may take twenty years for the second wave to crest, but crest it will, and it will sweep the

elegant, erudite, pretentious and toxic detritus of non-originalism out to sea," Judge Bork said in a fiery 1987 speech.
At the time, Bork co-chaired the society's board with Senator
Orrin Hatch of Utah.[13]

On August 31, 2019, Amanda Hollis-Brusky and Calvin
TerBeek reported on Politico.com about a recently unearthed
1984 grant proposal that provided evidence that the Federalist Society members were, in fact, "advocates for specific
outcomes on legal or political issues." Given the importance
of active federal judges to the long-term goal of reshaping
the law, the society not only has held explicit ideological
goals since its infancy in the early 1980s but has sought
to apply those ideological goals to legal policy and political issues.[14]

The Federalist Society now has a 5–4 stranglehold on
the Supreme Court.[15]

Since the Great Depression, this group has worked behind
the scenes to take political power back from the working
class and give it to the wealthy. These are the face dancers—
say anything, do anything, be anything for their masters,
the wealthy five percent.

However, also in the 1970s, the country was tearing itself
apart. With massive demonstrations and government-sponsored retaliations, the war in Vietnam was taking its toll on
America, as was the corruption in government.

The Nixon coalition was in shambles. They had made
progress in moving the cause of originalism forward. It was
just within their grasp when Watergate happened, followed
by the tragedy at Kent State. After that, the propaganda
machine began. Citizens United followed with vast pipelines
of wealth. The rebirth of originalism was the rallying call.

In 1978, Robert Bork, an influential antitrust scholar, wrote a notable book, *The Antitrust Paradox*.[16] Bork was concerned that the followers of the New Deal would take over the country through antitrust legislation that protected small businesses, and he said that antitrust laws were protecting inefficient businesses.

On December 20, 2012, Barak Orbach, a professor of the law, reported that Bork wrote, "Congress enacted the Sherman Antitrust Act as a consumer welfare prescription." The Supreme Court adopted that sentence in 1979 as the stated goal in antitrust today. [17] That is the stated goal in antitrust today. It is a big deal. A huge deal.

CARTELS AND PRICE-FIXING

In his book, Bork wrote, "While it was appropriate to prohibit cartels that fix prices and divide industries and mergers that produce monopolies, supposedly exclusionary practices, such as vertical trust agreements and price discrimination, did not harm consumers and so should not be prohibited."[18]

Under this definition, the multifamily housing cartel discussed in Chapter 6 would be deemed beneficial for the consumer, along with the allegedly excessive rents of some $4.8 billion annually. This is true even though we've seen the results of escalating rents and know that those ever-rising rents are not sustainable. We see the ballooning homelessness, and we now know it's a process that, in many cases, is being done to families.

How far will this group push their agenda? The last time they took control of the three branches of government was

1920. The 1929 economic crash that followed has the distinction of being known as the Great Depression because, for two years, the American people were left to fight over the crumbs that fell from the tables of the most corrupt government, judicial system, and monetary system this country had ever witnessed; we know this because of the 1934 Pecora Report. Ordinary Americans lost confidence in the institutions of their government, including the financial system.

The Pecora Report revealed the massive conflicts of interest between government officials including presidents, judges (even US Supreme Court judges), and the titans of Wall Street. The conflicts allowed a massive campaign of fraud to be perpetrated on the working class and working poor, resulting in the demise of the entire housing market.

Below are a few of the findings upon a review of the 1934 Pecora Report:

1. STOCK MANIPULATION

Pecora found that Wall Street packaged and sold stocks that had been manipulated in value. Bankers knowingly sold overvalued stock to certain investors and then pocketed the massive profits, while the non-preferred investors suffered enormous losses. For example, under CEO Charles Mitchell, National City Bank (which later became Citi Bank) conspired with the Anaconda Copper Company to defraud the public out of more than $150 million. The scheme set up a joint account of nearly 1.5 million shares of Anaconda Copper stock, which was valued at only $4 per share because of the company's near-bankrupt status.

The bank then repackaged, aggressively advertised, and sold the stock through its National City affiliate. National City then pushed the newly repackaged stock to $128 per share for three months, and then dumped it. In the end, the stock was once again only worth $4, and the working-class clients of National City Bank absorbed the massive losses.[19]

2. INSIDER TRADING AND CONFLICTS OF INTEREST

Chase National Bank CEO Albert Wiggin accepted millions of dollars in stock from clients at discounted values. When questioned, Wiggin responded, "I assumed it was a favor, and I was very glad to take it."[20] Pecora also uncovered J. P. Morgan's preferred list of influential friends, which included former US presidents and Supreme Court justices. These select few participated in stock offerings at steeply discounted rates and were granted access to untold wealth, so long as they colluded with the corporation's unfettered access to profits.[21]

3. FAILURE TO DISCLOSE RISKS

Failure to disclose risks was one of the most pervasive findings. Pecora saw that Wall Street bankers went to great lengths to hide or exaggerate actual stock values. They concealed what investments actually contained, especially considering pending risks such as litigation or loss of value. Specifically, Pecora found that under CEO Charles Mitchell, executives at National City Bank committed outright fraud in preparing stock release information.[22]

4. PREFERENTIAL INTEREST-FREE LOANS

Pecora discovered another pernicious practice—the interest-free loans to which bank managers helped themselves. Wall Street bankers lent themselves millions of dollars of money from the savings accounts of its clients, and then used that money to gamble in the stock market, essentially stealing millions without any repercussions.[23]

By the time Franklin D. Roosevelt was elected to the presidency, many Americans were unable to meet their mortgage payments. The average value of homes fell as much as 40 percent, the default rate jumped to about 50 percent of all households that had mortgages, and the average delinquency was fifteen to eighteen months.

This is where Americans felt the full effects of the Depression. It was one thing to lose your job, which 25 percent of all American families did, but no one was prepared for the brutal reality that the banks were prepared to throw nearly one million families into the streets—children, the elderly, babies, and all. Nothing drained national hope faster than a million homeless, freezing, huddling masses across America.

This is how far this group is willing to go. In the ancient days, they learned that indifference breeds wealth, and wealth breeds power, and power breeds freedoms. No price is too high for their power and freedoms.

THE UNINTENDED CONSEQUENCES OF ORIGINALISM

Is Howe's story of the Roman Crassus relevant today? Is the American working class treated fairly in this economy? Do we all have a fair shot at the American Dream? Or have our housing markets destroyed our way of life? Consider the following examples:

HEALTH CARE SYSTEM: Almost 20 percent of Americans, or more than 40 million adults, can't afford or access needed health care, according to a US government report. More than 3.6 million US children don't have affordable health care.[24]

America was on pace with other countries until the 1980s, when its health spending grew at a much faster rate compared to its GDP. In 2017, Americans spent 17 percent of their GDP on health care, whereas the next-highest comparable country (Switzerland) spent 12 percent of its GDP.[25]

Imagine, if you will, a mother rushing to the hospital with her unconscious daughter, pleading, "Please, doctor, please save my child's life." The insurance company then steps in and states, "Let's now bargain for your child's life. What price will the market bear?" The mother responds, "Please, insurance agent, take my house, just let the doctor save my child's life." In America today, you get the health care you can afford.

EDUCATION SYSTEM: There are more than 44 million American student borrowers who collectively owe $1.5 trillion in student loan debt.[26] The cost of tuition is reaching all-time highs, while interest rates on student debt are also climbing to all-time highs. Students are spending more time working than studying—85 percent of students now work paid jobs while enrolled.[27]

Imagine, if you will, a young mother from an impoverished background wanting to improve her lot in life and provide a better life for her children. She works long hours at Walmart, making less than $14 per hour. Her only hope of improving her life is through education; however, she hasn't the money to cover the cost. "Please, Uncle Sam," she pleads. "Lend me some money so that I may improve myself. I'll surrender my financial freedom for payment. Just don't burn down my hopes and my dreams—my shot at the American Dream." In America today, you get the education you can afford.

How long can we, as free people, accept this behavior? What life will be left for our children and grandchildren? If we liken it to the Roaring Twenties, life at the top was good, but not so much for the working class. We now once again live in a world where the working class has no rights, except the right to quit.

In 1978, *The Antitrust Paradox* set off a firestorm of controversy. However, what this book and the ideology it represents would really do was strike at the heart of the principles of the New Deal. In fact, this event struck a dagger straight through its heart, a mortal wound. The scales of justice have been sliding conservatively right ever since, and this isn't good for consumers or small businesses, regardless of your religious or political views.

The Federalist Society, along with those filing amicus briefs, are the descendants of this coalition. Their goal is to place the power of the government back into the hands of corporate America. This same coalition of investors, bankers, and lobbying groups existed before the Great Depression as the party responsible for that massive collapse, and they gained political power again in the 1980s, causing the economic crash of the Savings and Loan Associations by the 1990s. This coalition is now made up of the industries that can be tied to the 2008 economic crash, and it supports the destruction of the Consumer Financial Protection Bureau.

SHIFTING PUBLIC POLICY TO ORIGINALISM

It is possible that the Roberts US Supreme Court (2005–present) will enforce the concept of originalism, and the monopolies and price-fixing will be ruled as legal and beneficial. According to Nancy LeTourneau, a contributing writer for the *Washington Monthly*, this also has been a process. Other than passing massive tax cuts, Senate Majority Leader Mitch McConnell has made it clear he is not interested in passing legislation. Instead, the Senate leader is focused solely on confirming conservative justices to federal courts. That's why he referred to his decision to block President Barack Obama's Supreme Court nominee, Merrick Garland, as his most significant political accomplishment.[28]

After almost one hundred years, our court system has nearly returned to the draconian conservatism of the 1920s. Again, the US government is drowning in unsustainable corruption. Taxpayers are sacrificing their earned benefits, such as infrastructure, health care, and education, to pay the corruption debt. In addition, the working class is being crushed by the weight of their obligations and their lack of wages to cover them.

The court cases discussed in this book were designed to destroy the regulator—the CFPB—and to allow corporate America and the housing markets to discriminate and remain unchecked and unchallenged as they unleash this terror of corrupted technology upon the country. They are originalism in action.

These court cases are the culmination of eighty-five years of plotting and scheming to strip freedoms away from the working class. If the 2020 Supreme Court issues its ruling and writ of execution against the CFPB, the New Deal will die. The belief that the Constitution was, in fact, written of the people, by the people, for the people, will die.

ARE WE BETTER OFF THAN BEFORE?

At first, Crassus's price for firefighting was reasonable. As time went on, however, he charged what the traffic would bear until, in the end, the price was the house itself. Similarly, at first, the HOLC price of housing was reasonable. As time went on, rents skyrocketed. HUD allowed property managers to charge what the traffic would bear. Today, the price for housing has been fixed at such a high point that homelessness is skyrocketing, and properties are being turned over to the investors of HUD.

Crassus became the biggest landlord in Rome. He took possession of a great part of the city and became Rome's greatest money lender. Since Robert Bork's 1978 antitrust legislation, according to *Forbes* magazine, over the past ten years the number of billionaires in the world has increased nearly threefold, from 793 to around 2,200. Their combined net worth more than tripled, from $2.6 trillion in 2006 to $9.1 trillion in 2018. Billionaires grow $2.5 billion wealthier every day.[29]

The vast sums of wealth moving through ever more efficient pipelines is no accident. This is a process that is being done to the middle-class taxpayers by the face dancers of our society. This process, like the predatory leasing and Ten Steps to Homelessness, is designed to shift wealth to the top. The aggressive debt collection campaigns and the excessive fees garnered by the banking industry are all part of the process. Greed is good and now on steroids—supported by the endless possibilities of AI technology.

It was hinted by historians that Crassus's workers started fires so that their master might put them out. In the same manner, it is possible that the property managers are engaged in price-fixing and discrimination to increase their own profits. The multifamily housing cartel has become rich and powerful enough to be America's greatest shadow bank money lenders and to share the bounty with the first cartel—a group of men holding political power.

To answer Ronald Reagan's simple question, we only have to look at Figure 2, the accumulation of the housing debt, and the skyrocketing number of taxpayers who can no longer afford their housing according to our family budgets discussed earlier. No, we are not better off.

It is time for taxpayers to readdress the failed Nixon experiment on our housing markets. Self-regulation, also known as unfettered access to profits, has never been proven to work at protecting the taxpayers from abuse.

THE PROBLEM: FEE INCOME AND PIPELINES

The 2008 Inquiry Commission found that concentrations led to efficiencies; however, it was the pipelines that made the entire massive process possible. Without them, the large tranches could not be fulfilled.

The concentrations also created significant risk, as fewer industry participants fought for fewer available opportunities. They had to promise more profits to secure business. These promised profit increases generally come at the expense of the tenant, who has to pay more rent and fees to satisfy those contracts and management agreements.

Why do lenders take excessive risks? The answer may not surprise you; however, the sheer volume of fee income just might.

Fee income, as discussed in Chapter 5, is of such magnitude that the system that enables such wealth to be created also enables massive corruption—in fact, it thrives on corrupt practices. The term "moral hazard" comes into play; this industry resides in a world without consequences. Without a regulator, the risks that will be taken in search of more reward will be limitless, as will the bailout bequeathed to the taxpayers.

In the case of the HUD changes enacted by Nixon, the corrupt values of the executives in the housing markets and in government brought about the inevitable crisis in affordable housing.

THE ERA OF THE NEW DEAL FROM 1932 TO 2020

So where do we go from here? We have come full circle. We find ourselves at the end of an age—the age of the New Deal, when the working class was granted access to education, safe and secure housing, and a place at the table. In 1932, when Roosevelt began the New Deal programs, less than 10 percent of rural America had electricity. By the time FDR died in 1945, an estimated 90 percent of rural America was electrified.

What does the end of an age look like? We can see the effects in the crumbling transportation infrastructure; trillions of dollars are needed for repairs and improvements in roads and bridges, and yet no money exists to cover such needed investments. Furthermore, massive corporations financially and politically control entire regions of the country, and the propaganda wars are all signs of a changing age.

THE NEW AGE

At the end of the day, this book is about the implementation of and control over the Artificial Intelligence–driven technology. The fight is over the future control of the technology and who will benefit: corporate America or the American taxpayers. We've witnessed what corporate America will do if faced with financial decisions; they will engineer evermore creative ways to bilk the taxpayers.

A correlation was found to exist between the use of AI technology and the skyrocketing rental rates and ballooning homelessness in metropolitan markets. A correlation was discovered between the Trump administration's role in the destruction of the CFPB—the only regulator between AI technology and the consumer—and their drive to privatize the Enterprises.

The greatest threat America faces today lies with the convergence of special interests and who gets to control the AI technology, not only in the marketplace but in the housing markets as well.

However, even more terrifying is the HUD rule change, which establishes unprecedented guidance for the AI technology that powers the housing market. Landlords would not be responsible for the effects of an algorithm provided by a third party—an industry back door to discrimination.

The Trump administration's converging of special interest groups is gutting the Treasury, and they are making the middle class pay them to do it. They are burning our house to the ground, and they own the fire department.

This is not a problem just for Democrats, and not just for Republicans; this is an *everyone* problem. This is our circus, and these are our monkeys. Will we choose to work together before the economic crash occurs, and give our children and grandchildren a future, or will we choose, as our predecessors did in 1928, to believe the propaganda that all is well in Zion?

As a reminder, in the five years preceding the stock market crash of 1929, the market had increased some 400 percent, which was unprecedented.[30] Between September and November 1929, when the bough broke, the stock market crashed 89 percent, equally unprecedented.[31]

In 2008, in the blink of an eye, the house of cards came tumbling down.

It is my opinion that allowing the current administration to implement the AI program into Nixon's failed affordable housing experiment, without proper oversight, would be a monstrous betrayal to American taxpayers and homeowners alike. The members of HUD's AI implementation team have shown their utter, blatant discrimination against people of color and minorities; not only that, they have a propensity to abuse established rules.

Like King Solomon of old, the time has come to choose, but how do we choose between the beliefs which we hold most dear?

"Choose you this day whom ye will serve," the Bible says (Joshua 24:15, KJV). We always have a choice. Nevertheless, the window of opportunity is fading quickly. The special interests have run amok for far too long.

Occam's razor reminds us that the simplest explanation is usually correct.

Ferdinand Pecora warned us, "Men of might—not because of principle but because of economic power and wealth—have, by the waving of a hand and adoption of a resolution, taken millions and millions of the hard-earned pennies of the people [working class] and turned them into gold for themselves."[32]

The time has arrived for Americans to address AI technology. We must demand a set of rules for its use, as its control will ultimately define our nation; the use of this technology will be the ultimate test on our constitutional democracy.

The next time you vote, choose wisely.

NOTES

Chapter 1

1. Robert Fishman, "The American Metropolis at Century's End: Past and Future Influences," *Housing Policy Debate Volume 11, Issue 1*, personal. umich.edu /~mlassite/fishman.pdf.

2. "The State Of The Nation's Housing 2018," *Joint Center for Housing Studies of Harvard University*, http://www.jchs.harvard.edu/sites/default/files/Harvard_JCHS_State_of_the_Nations_Housing_2018.pdf.

3. "NLIHC Gap 2019 Report Calls for Significant Investments to Address Shortage of 7 Million Affordable and Available Homes for the Lowest-Income Households," *NLIHC.org*, March, 2019, nlihc.org/resource/nlihc-gap-2019-report-calls-significant-investments-address-shortage-7-million-affordable.

4. Michael Hobbs, "America's Housing Crisis Is A Ticking Time Bomb," *Huffpost.com*, June 2018, huffpost.com/entry/housing-crisis-inequality-harvard-report_n_5b27c1f1e4b056b2263c621e.

5. Mike Kingsella, "The First Step in Solving Washington's Housing Crisis Is Preserving Existing Affordable Housing Programs," Upforgrowth. org, March 2019, https://www.upforgrowth.org/news/first-step-solving-washingtons-housing-crisis-preserving-existing-affordable-housing-programs.

6. Buhayar and Deprez, "The Homeless Crisis Is Getting Worse in America's Richest Cities," Bloomberg BusinessWeek, November 2018.

7. "Housing Finance At a Glance: A Monthly Chartbook," *Urban Institute*, June, 2018, https://www.urban.org/sites/default/files/publication/98669/housing_finance_at_a_glance_a_monthly_chartbook_june_2018_0.pdf.

8. Charles J. Orlebeke, "The Evolution of Low-Income Housing Policy, 1949 to 1999," University of Illinois at Chicago, *Housing Policy Debate* Vol 11, Issue 2489 © Fannie Mae Foundation 2000.

9. "Press Release: Forbes 33rd Annual World's Billionaires Issue Reveals Number of Billionaires and Their Combined Wealth Have Decreased For the First Time Since 2016," Forbes.com, March 2019, forbes.com/sites/forbespr/2019/03/05/press-release-forbes-33rd-annual-worlds-billionaires-issue-reveals-number-of-billionaires-and-their-combined-wealth-have-decreased-for-for-first-time-since-2016/#670a16b245b9.

10. "Compendium of Open Recommendations," *Federal Housing Finance Agency OIG*, September, 2019, fhfaoig.gov/sites/default/files / CompendiumSeptember2019.pdf.

11. Neel Burton, M.D., "Our Hierarchy of Needs," *Psychology Today*, May, 2012, psychologytoday.com/us/blog/hide-and-seek/201205/our-hierarchy-needs.

12. Frederic C. Howe, Consumers' Counsel- (Speech) National Recovery Administration (NRA), *Washington Conference On Public Housing*, Willard Hotel, Washington D. C. January 27, 1934, National Public Housing Conference, New York, 728.1, W173, c.2.

13. "Major Legislation On Housing And Urban Development Enacted Since 1932," *U.S. Department of Housing and Urban Development*, hud.gov/sites/documents /LEGS_CHRON_JUNE2014.PDF.

14. "American Liberty League," *Encyclopedia.com*, encyclopedia.com/history/dictionaries-thesauruses-pictures-and-press-releases/american-liberty-league.

15. Paul F. Wendt, ""The Role of the Federal Government in Housing, 1956," American Enterprise Association, Inc. https://www.huduser.gov/portal/sites/default/files/pdf/Federal-Government-in-Housing.pdf

16. Everman, Henry Esli, "Herbert Hoover and the New Deal, 1933-1940," *LSU Historical Dissertations and Theses*, 1918 digitalcommons.lsu.edu/gradschool_disstheses/1918.

17. Gerhard Peters; "Executive Order 2594 - Creating Committee on Public Information." *University of California, Santa Barbara*, ipfsQmXoypizjW3WknFiJnKLwHCnL72vedxjQkDDP1mX Wo6uco/wiki/Committee_on_Public_Information.html.

18. "Lochner v. New York, 198 U.S. 45 (1905)," *Supreme.Justia.com*, https://supreme.justia.com/cases/federal/us/198/45/.

19. "Originalism: A Primer On Scalia's Constitutional Philosophy," NPR, February 2016, npr.org/2016/02/14/466744465/originalism-a-primer-on-scalias-constitutional-philosophy.

20. Everman, "Herbert Hoover and the New Deal," 1971.

21. David Moss, Cole Bolton, and Eugene Kintgen, "The Pecora Hearings." *Harvard Business School Case 711-046*, December 2010 (revised June 2018).

22. John C. Weicher, "The New Structure of the Housing Finance System," *Federal Reserve Bank of St. Louis*, stlouisfed.org/files/htdocs/publications/review/94/07 /Structure_Jul_Aug1994.pdf.

23. Wheelock, "The Federal Response to Home Mortgage Distress" *Federal Reserve Bank of St. Louis Review*, May/June, 2008.

24. Dr. Isadow Lubin, Commissioner Bureau Labor Statistics, *Washington Conference On Public Housing*, Willard Hotel, Washington D. C. January 27, 1934, National Public Housing Conference, New York, 728.1, W173, c.2. p. 15.

25. "Home Owners Loan Corporation," *Roosevelt Institute,* March, 2012, rooseveltinstitute.org/home-owners-loan-corporation/.

26. Robert E. Lang & Rebecca R. Sohmer, "Legacy of the Housing Act of 1949: The Past, Present, and Future of Federal Housing and Urban Policy," *Housing Policy Debate, 11:2, 291-298*, DOI: 10.1080/10511482.2000.9521369, (2000) https://doi.org/10.1080/1051148 2.2000.9521369

27. Weicher, "The New Structure of the Housing Finance System," *Federal Reserve Bank of St. Louis*, accessed January, 2020.

28. "A Chronology Of Housing Legislation And Selected Executive Actions, 1892-1992," Congressional Research Service Report, *The Committee On Banking, Finance And Urban Affairs,* huduser.gov/publications/pdf/HUD-11661.pdf.

29. *The US Department of Housing and Urban Development*, "Mission," hud.gov/about/mission.

30. "HOUSING ACT OF 1949 (Section 2 and Title V)," Office of the Legislative Counsel, enacted December, 2018, legcounsel.house.gov/Comps/81-171.pdf.

31. "Housing in the Seventies: A Report of the National Housing Policy Review HUD-0000968," *National Housing Policy Review (1974)*, huduser.gov/portal /Publications/pdf/HUD-968.pdf.

32. Aaron J. Howell, "The Federal Government Created Inner-City Ghettos With Racist Housing Regulations," *Timeline.com*, July, 2017, timeline.com/redlining-federal-housing-racist-14d7f48267e8.

33. "From One Voice to Many: Despite Setbacks and Opposition, How a Growing Chorus Paved the Way to Fair Housing," *National Association of Realtors*, March, 2018, www.nar.realtor/sites/default/files/documents/March-2018-Fair-Housing-3-9-2018.pdf.

34. "Federal Fair Lending Regulations and Statutes – Fair Housing Act," *Federal Reserve.gov*, federalreserve.gov/boarddocs/supmanual/cch/fair_lend_fhact.pdf.

35. Pedro da Costa, "Housing discrimination underpins the staggering wealth gap between blacks and whites," *Economic Policy Institute*, April, 2019,

epi.org/blog/housing-discrimination-underpins-the-staggering-wealth-gap-between-blacks-and-whites/.

36. Troy McMullen, Jason Henry and Natalia Jimenez , "The Heartbreaking Decrease in Black Homeownership," *The Washington Post*, February, 2019, washingtonpost.com /news/business/wp/2019/02/28/feature/the-heartbreaking-decrease-in-black-homeownership/.

37. "Go Deeper: Where Race Lives," *PBS.org*, pbs.org/race/000_About/002_06-godeeper.htm.

38. Florence Wagman Roisman, "George Romney, Richard Nixon, and the Fair Housing Act of 1968," *Poverty & Race Research Action Council*, prrac.org/pdf /RoismanHistoryExcerpt.pdf.

39. *The Department of Housing and Urban Development*, "HUD History," https://www.hud.gov/about/hud_history.

40. Nikole Hannah-Jones, "Living Apart: How the Government Betrayed a Landmark Civil Rights Law," *ProPublica.org*, June, 2015, propublica.org/article/living-apart-how-the-government-betrayed-a-landmark-civil-rights-law.

41. "The Evolution Of HUD's Public-Private Partnerships," *US Department of Housing and Urban Development*, October, 2015, huduser.gov/hud50th/HUD2-048-Public-Private_Partnership_508.pdf.

42. "Frederic C. Howe, Consumers' Counsel- (Speech)" *National Recovery Administration (NRA)*, Washington Conference On Public Housing.

43. "The 2018 Annual Homeless Assessment Report (AHAR) to Congress," *U.S. Department of Housing and Urban Development*, December, 2018, hudexchange.info/resources/documents/2018-AHAR-Part-1.pdf.

44. Buhayar and Deprez, "The Homeless Crisis is Getting Worse in America's Richest Cities," *Bloomberg BusinessWeek*, November, 2018 bloomberg.com/news/features/2018-11-20/the-homeless-crisis-is-getting-worse-in-america-s-richest-cities.

45. Mike Kingsella, "The First Step in Solving Washington's Housing Crisis is Preserving Existing Affordable Housing Programs," *Upforgrowth.org*, March, 2019, upforgrowth.org/news/first-step-solving-washingtons-housing-crisis-preserving-existing-affordable-housing-programs.

46. "Final Report and Recommendations for King County, WA," *Regional Affordable Housing Task Force*, March, 2019, kingcounty.gov/~/media/initiatives/affordablehousing /documents/report/RAH_Report_Final.ashx?la=en.

47. "Market Analytics," *Realpage.com*, accessed September, 2019, https://www.realpage.com/asset-optimization/market-analytics/

48. Dustin Dunham, "Innovations in 'Big Data' Are Impacting Real Estate Investment," *Cornell Real Estate Review*, March, 2018, realestate.cornell.edu/2018/03/22/innovations-in-big-data/

49. Troy Segal, "Conflict of Interest," *Investopedia.com*, updated April, 2019, investopedia.com/terms/c/conflict-of-interest.asp.

Chapter 2

1. "NLIHC Gap 2019 Report Calls for Significant Investments to Address Shortage of 7 Million Affordable and Available Homes for the Lowest-Income Households," *NLIHC.org*, March, 2019, nlihc.org/resource/nlihc-gap-2019-report-calls-significant-investments-address-shortage-7-million-affordable.

2. Michael Hobbs, "America's Housing Crisis Is a Ticking Time Bomb," *Huffpost.com*, June, 2018, huffpost.com/entry/housing-crisis-inequality-harvard-report_n_5b27c1f1e4b056b2263c621e.

3. Karen Weise, "Housing's 30-Percent-of-Income Rule Is Nearly Useless," *Bloomberg.com*, July, 2014, bloomberg.com/news/articles/2014-07-17/housings-30-percent-of-income-rule-is-near-useless.

4.   *The National Alliance to End Homelessness,* "Affordable Housing," endhomelessness.org/ending-homelessness/policy/affordable-housing/.
5.   *The Mobile Home Park Home Owners Allegiance*, "Mobile Home Owner News Sep 2019," *MHPHOA.com*, mhphoa.com/news/2019/09.
6.   Zachary Oren Smith, "National Trend Toward Consolidation of Mobile Home Park Ownership," *Iowa City Press-Citizen*, April, 2019, press-citizen. com/story/news/2019/04/09 /mobile-home-resident-advocates-worry-future-parks/3365446002/.
7.   "Working Hard but Struggling to Survive," *Alice*, accessed August, 2019, https://www.unitedforalice.org/home.
8.   Anna Bahney, "40 percent of Americans Can't Cover a $400 Emergency Expense," *CNNMoney*, May, 2018, money.cnn.com/2018/05/22/pf/ emergency-expenses-household-finances/index.html.
9.   "What is Affordable Housing v. Subsidized Housing v. Workforce Housing?" *HousingVirginia.org*, housingvirginia.org/housing-virginia-toolkit/what-is-affordable-housing-v-subsidized-housing-v-workforce-housing/.
10. Laura Sullivan and Meg Anderson, "Affordable Housing Program Costs More, Shelters Fewer," *NPR.org*, May, 2017, npr. org/2017/05/09/527046451/affordable-housing-program-costs-more-shelters-less
11. "Rental Burdens: Rethinking Affordability Measures," US *Department of HUD*, huduser.gov/portal/pdredge/pdr_edge_featd_article_092214.html.
12. Zack Freeman et al., "2019 Tax Preference Performance Reviews," *Washington JLARC*, July, 2019, leg.wa.gov/jlarc/AuditAndStudyReports/ Documents /TaxPrelimRepPres.pdf.
13. "Final Report and Recommendations for King County, WA," *Regional Affordable Housing Task Force*, revised March, 2019, kingcounty.gov/~/ media/initiatives/affordablehousing/documents /report/RAH_Report_Final. ashx?la=en.
14. "Income Level – Low Income Public Housing," *Seattle Housing Authority*, seattlehousing.org/housing/sha-housing/eligibility/income-level-low-income-public-housing.
15. Mike Kingsella, "The First Step in Solving Washington's Housing Crisis is Preserving Existing Affordable Housing Programs," *Upforgrowth. org*, March, 2019. https://www.upforgrowth.org/news/first-step-solving-washingtons-housing-crisis-preserving-existing-affordable-housing-programs.
16. "Final Report and Recommendations for King County, WA," *Regional Affordable Housing Task Force*, Revised March, 2019.
17. "The Gap: A Shortage of Affordable Homes," *NLIHC.org*, March, 2019, reports.nlihc.org/sites/default/files/gap/Gap-Report_2019.pdf.
18. Ibid.
19. Ibid.
20. Corianne Payton Scally, Amanda Gold and Nicole DuBois, "The Low-Income Housing Tax Credit: How It Works and Who It Serves," © July 2018. Urban Institute, https://www.urban.org/sites/default/files/ publication/98758/lithc_how_it_works_and_who_it_serves_final_2.pdf .
21. "American Housing Survey," *United State Census*, https://www.census.gov/ programs-surveys/ahs.html.
22. Gene Balk, "No Major City has Enough Affordable Housing to Meet Demand, but How does Seattle Stack up?," *The Seattle Times*, February, 2018, https://www.seattletimes.com/seattle-news/data/no-major-city-has-enough-affordable-housing-to-meet-demand-but-how-does-seattle-stack-up/
23. Zack Freeman et al., "2019 Tax Preference Performance Reviews," *Washington JLARC*, July, 2019. http://leg.wa.gov/jlarc/ AuditAndStudyReports/Documents/TaxPrelimRepPres.pdf
24. Ibid.
25. Ibid.

26. Scally, Gold, and DuBois, "The Low-Income Housing Tax Credit," © July 2018. Urban Institute, urban.org/sites/default/files/publication/98758 / lithc_how_it_works_and_who_it_serves_final_2.pdf.
27. "Regional Affordable Housing Task Force Five-year Action Plan," *KingCounty.gov*, updated November, 2018, kingcounty.gov/~/media/ initiatives/affordablehousing/documents/Meetings /1218/draft-action-plan-edited11-29-clean-with-amends.ashx?la=en.
28. "Final Report and Recommendations for King County, WA," *Regional Affordable Housing Task Force*, revised March, 2019.
29. "Mayor Durkan Unveils Biggest Low-Income Housing Increase in Seattle History," *MyNorthwest.com*, December, 2018. https://mynorthwest. com/1219167/mayor-jenny-durkan-low-income-housing-seattle/?
30. Mike Kingsella, "The First Step in Solving Washington's Housing Crisis is Preserving Existing Affordable Housing Programs," *Upforgrowth.org*, March, 2019.
31. "Mayor Durkan Unveils Biggest Low-Income Housing Increase in Seattle History," *MyNorthwest.com*, December, 2018. https://mynorthwest. com/1219167/mayor-jenny-durkan-low-income-housing-seattle/?
32. "Seattle's Comprehensive Plan Toward a Sustainable Seattle," *Seattle. gov*, January, 2005, seattle.gov/Documents/Departments/OPCD/ OngoingInitiatives/SeattlesComprehensivePlan/HousingAppendix.pdf.
33. Timothy Burgess, "Perspective on Multi-Family Tax Exemption Program," *City View*, June, 2011, timothyburgess.typepad.com/tim_burgess_city_ view_/2011/06/perspective-on-mfte.html.
34. "Comprehensive Housing Market Analysis (Seattle-Bellevue-Everett, Washington)," *US Dept. of HUD*, May, 2017, huduser.gov/portal/ publications/pdf/SeattleWA-comp-17.pdf
35. "Mayor Durkan Unveils Biggest Low-Income Housing Increase in Seattle History," *MyNorthwest.com*, December, 2018. https://mynorthwest. com/1219167/mayor-jenny-durkan-low-income-housing-seattle/?
36. Adina Marcut, "Multifamily Seattle Report – Winter 2019," *Multi-housing News*, multihousingnews.com/post/matrix-multifamily-seattle-report-winter-2019/.
37. "Multifamily Market Survey (MMS)," *National Association of Home Builders*, nahb.org/research/housing-economics/housing-indexes/ multifamily-market-survey.aspx
38. Jon Banister, "Greystar CEO Bob Faith On $4.6B EdR Acquisition And His Outlook For Multifamily," Bisnow.com, November 2018, https://www. bisnow.com/national/news/multifamily/greystar-ceo-bob-faith-on-46b-edr-acquisition-and-his-outlook-for-multifamily-95183.
39. Jen Stanley, "Seattle Mayor Pushes Tax Break Expansion for Affordable Housing," *Next City*, September, 2015, nextcity.org/daily/entry/seattle-mayor-tax-breaks-affordable-housing.
40. Ibid.
41. Doug Trumm, "Dissecting MFTE: 855 New Units Added in 2016 but Rent Limit Jumped 7 percent," *Theurbanist.org*, July, 2017, theurbanist. org/2017/07/19/mfte-provides-tons-affordable-apartments-use-tweaks/.
42. Ibid.
43. Ibid.
44. Government Accountability Office, "Federal Housing Assistance; Comparing the Characteristics and Costs of Housing Programs," GAO-02-76, January 2002, p. 18.
45. Jacqueline Rabe Thomas, "Separated by Design: Why Affordable Housing Is Built in Areas With High Crime, Few Jobs and Struggling Schools," *Propublica.org*, November, 2019, propublica.org/article/separated-by-design-why-affordable-housing-is-built-in-areas-with-high-crime-few-jobs-and-struggling-schools.
46. Ibid.
47. Gregory S. Burge, "Do Tenants Capture the Benefits from the Low-Income Housing Tax Credit Program?" *Real Estate Economics* (Blackwell Publishing Inc., December 2010), p. 95.

48. "Release of the 2014 California Affordable Housing Cost Study October 2014," *docplayer.net*, October, 2014, docplayer.net/14432676-Release-of-the-2014-california-affordable-housing-cost-study-october-2014.html.
49. Noah Buhayar and Esme E. Deprez, "The Homeless Crisis is Getting Worse in America's Richest Cities," *Bloomberg BusinessWeek*, November, 2018, https://www.bloomberg.com/news /features/2018-11-20/the-homeless-crisis-is-getting-worse-in-america-s-richest-cities.

Chapter 3

1. "Delivering Government Solutions in the 21st Century: Reform Plan and Reorganization Recommendations," *Performance.gov*, performance.gov/GovReform/Reform-and-Reorg-Plan-Final.pdf.
2. "Housing Finance: Prolonged Conservatorships of Fannie Mae and Freddie Mac Prompt Need for Reform," *United States Government Accountability Office*, GAO-19-239, January, 2019, gao.gov/assets/700/696529.pdf.
3. "History of Fannie Mae and Freddie Mac Conservatorships," *Federal Housing Finance Agency*, fhfa.gov/Conservatorship/Pages/History-of-Fannie-Mae—Freddie-Conservatorships.aspx.
4. Kelsey Ramírez, "Mark Calabria: New Director Changes Course for FHFA," *HousingWire*, September, 2019, housingwire.com/articles/49939-mark-calabria-new-director-changes-course-for-fhfa/.
5. "Semiannual Report to the Congress (October 1, 2011-March, 31, 2012)," *Federal Housing Finance Agency Office of Inspector General*, fhfaoig.gov/sites/default/files /ThirdSemiannualReport.pdf.
6. "Compendium of Open Recommendations," *Federal Housing Finance Agency OIG*, September, 2019, fhfaoig.gov/sites/default/files /CompendiumSeptember2019.pdf.
7. "Top Management Challenges Facing the U.S. Department of Housing and Urban Development in 2019 and Beyond," *U.S. Department of HUD OIG*, https://www.hudoig.gov/sites/default/files/2019-12/TMC%20-%20FY%20 2020.pdf.
8. "Testimony of Laura S. Wertheimer Inspector General, Federal Housing Finance Agency before the U.S. House Committee on Financial Services," September 27, 2018 https://financialservices.house.gov/uploadedfiles/09.27.2018_laura_s._wertheimer_testimony.pdf
9. "Corporate Governance: Review and Resolution of Conflicts of Interest Involving Fannie Mae's Senior Executive Officers Highlight the Need for Closer Attention to Governance Issues by FHFA," *Federal Housing Finance Agency OIG*, EVL-2018-001, January, 2018, oversight.gov/sites/default/files/oig-reports/EVL-2018-001 percent20 percent28Redacted percent29.pdf.
10. "Administrative Review of a Potential Conflict of Interest Matter Involving a Senior Executive Officer at an Enterprise (01G-2018-001)," *Office of Inspector General*, July, 2018, https://www.oversight.gov/sites/default/files/oig-reports/Management%20Alerts_OIG-2018-001_Redacted%20 %28with%20Redaction%20Codes%29.pdf
11. "Administrative Review of a Potential Conflict of Interest," *Office of Inspector General*, July, 2018.
12. "Ginnie Mae: Risk Management and Staffing-Related Challenges Need to be Addressed," *U.S. Government Accountability Office*, GAO-19-191, April, 2019, gao.gov/assets/700/698926.pdf.
13. Office of Audit, Financial Audits Division, Washington, DC. Audit Report Number: 2019-FO-0001, November 13, 2018 https://www.hudoig.gov/reports-publications/report/audit-government-national-mortgage-associations-financial-statements-1
14. "Housing Finance: Prolonged Conservatorships of Fannie Mae and Freddie Mac Prompt Need for Reform," *United States Government Accountability Office*, GAO-19-239, January, 2019.

15. "Top Management Challenges Facing the U.S. Department of Housing and Urban Development in 2019 and Beyond," *U.S. Department of HUD OIG*.

16. Joe Light, "Fannie, Freddie CEOs to Get $3.4 Million Raises," *The Wall Street Journal*, updated July, 2015, wsj.com/articles/fannie-freddie-ceos-to-get-big-pay-raises-1435760279.

17. Ibid

18. "FHFA's Approval of Senior Executive Succession Planning," https://www.fhfaoig.gov/sites/default/files/EVL-2019-001_0.pdf

19. "Compendium of Open Recommendations," *Federal Housing Finance Agency OIG*, September, 2019,

20. "Protection of HUD's Insurance Fund," *U.S. Department of HUD OIG*, hudoig.gov/priority-focus-areas/protection-huds-insurance.

21. Ibid.

22. "FHFA's Housing Finance Examiner Commissioning Program: $7.7 Million and Four Years into the Program, the Agency has Fewer Commissioned Examiners," *Federal Housing Finance Agency OIG*, COM-2018-006, September, 2018, fhfaoig.gov /Content/Files/Compliance percent20Review percent20COM-2018-006.pdf.

23. "FHFA's Targeted Examinations of Fannie Mae: Less than Half of the Targeted Examinations Planned for 2012 through 2015 Were Completed and No Examinations Planned for 2015 Were Completed Before the Report of Examination Issued," *Federal Housing Finance Agency Office of Inspector General*, AUD-2016-006, September, 2016, https://www.fhfaoig.gov/Content/Files/AUD-2016-006.pdf

24. "Internal Audit: Best Practices for Community Banks," *Clark Schaefer Hackett*, https://www.slideshare.net/ClarkSchaeferHackett/internal-audit-best-practices-for-community-banks.

25. "Standards for Internal Control in the Federal Government," *U.S. Government Accountability Office*, GAO-14-704G, September, 2014, https://www.gao.gov/assets/670/665712.pdf

26. "Chief Financial Officer Handbooks, HUD.com, https://www.hud.gov/program_offices/administration/hudclips/handbooks/cfo.

27. "Top Management Challenges Facing the U.S. Department of Housing and Urban Development in 2019 and Beyond," *U.S. Department of HUD Office of Inspector General*.

28. Ibid.

29. "FHFA's Housing Finance Examiner Commissioning Program: $7.7 Million and Four Years into the Program, the Agency has Fewer Commissioned Examiners," *Federal Housing Finance Agency OIG*, COM-2018-006, September, 2018

30. "FHFA Should Re-evaluate and Revise Fraud Reporting by the Enterprises to Enhance its Utility," *Federal Housing Finance Agency OIG*, EVL-2018-004, September, 2018.

31. "FHFA Should Address the Potential Disparity Between the Statutory Requirement for Fraud Reporting and its Implementing Regulation and Advisory Bulletin," *Federal Housing Finance Agency Office of Inspector General*, COM-2018-002, March 23, 2018, https://www.fhfaoig.gov/sites/default/files/2018_03_23%20Enterprise%20Fraud%20Reporting.FINAL_.pdf

32. Bill Grassano, "FinCEN Proposes Anti-Money Laundering/Suspicious Activity Reporting Rules for Fannie Mae, Freddie Mac, Federal Home Loan Banks," *Financial Crimes Enforcement Network*, November, 2011, https://www.fincen.gov/news/news-releases/fincen-proposes-anti-money-launderingsuspicious-activity-reporting-rules-fannie

33. Top Management Challenges Facing the U.S. Department of Housing and Urban Development in 2019 and Beyond," *U.S. Department of HUD OIG*

34. "Single Security Initiative and Common Securitization Platform," *Federal Housing Finance Agency*, accessed December, 2019, https://www.fhfa.gov/PolicyProgramsResearch/Policy/Pages/Securitization-Infrastructure.aspx.

35. *The Common Securitization Solutions*, "Our Work,"
     CommonSecuritization.com, http://www.commonsecuritization.com/our-
     work.
36. Ibid.
37. Ibid.
38. "FHFA Did Not Complete All Planned Supervisory Activities Related to
     Cybersecurity Risks at Freddie Mac for the 2016 Examination Cycle ,"
     Federal Housing Finance Agency OIG, AUD-2017-011, September, 2017,
     https://www.fhfaoig.gov/sites/default/files/AUD-2017-011%20FRE%20
     Cyber%20Examinations%20%28redacted%29.pdf.
39. Wertheimer, "Fiscal Year 2019 Management and Performance Challenges,"
     memo from *Office of Inspector General*, October, 2018.
40. "Top Management Challenges Facing the U.S. Department of Housing and
     Urban Development," *U.S. Department of HUD OIG*.
41. Laura S. Wertheimer, "Fiscal Year 2019 Management and Performance
     Challenges," memo from *Office of Inspector General*, October, 2018,
     fhfaoig.gov/Content/Files /FY2019 percent20Management percent20and
     percent20Performance percent20Challenges percent20Facing
     percent20FHFA_0.pdf
42. "Top Management Challenges Facing the U.S. Department of Housing and
     Urban Development," *U.S. Department of HUD OIG*.
43. Ibid.
44. "Ginnie Mae 2018 Annual Report," *Ginnie Mae*, ginniemae.gov/about_us/
     what_we_do/Annual_Reports/annual_report18.pdf.
45. David Kocieniewski and Caleb Melby, "Kushner Cos. Gets $800
     Million Federally-Backed Apartment Loan," *Bloomberg*, May, 2019,
     bnnbloomberg.ca/kushner-cos-gets-800-million-federally-backed-apartment-
     loan-1.1263563.
46. Ramírez, "Mark Calabria: New Director Changes Course for FHFA,"
     HousingWire, September, 2019.
47. "Press Release: Treasury Department and FHFA Modify Terms of Preferred
     Stock Purchase Agreements for Fannie Mae and Freddie Mac," *U,S,
     Department of the Treasury*, September, 2019, home.treasury.gov/news/
     press-releases/sm786.
48. David Wharton, "Industry Impact: President Trump's Call to End GSE
     Conservatorship," *DSNews.com*, March, 2019, dsnews.com/daily-
     dose/03-27-2019/fannie-mae-names-hugh-r-frater-as-ceo.
49. "Corporate Overview," *The PNC*, pnc.com/en/about-pnc/company-profile/
     corporate-overview.html?lnksrc=topnav.
50. "Board of Directors," *FannieMae.com*, revised August, 2019, fanniemae.
     com/portal/about-fm/governance/bd-frater.html.
51. Greg McFarlane, "How BlackRock Makes Money," *Investopedia*,
     September, 2019, investopedia.com/articles/markets/012616/how-blackrock-
     makes-money.asp.
52. Mark Ames, "Independent and Principled? Behind the Cato Myth," *The
     Nation*, April, 2012, thenation.com/article/independent-and-principled-
     behind-cato-myth/.
53. FHFA's Response to OIG's Alert and Recommendations, dated August 31,
     2018, OIG • OIG-2018-004 • September, 2018, oversight.gov/sites/default/
     files/oig-reports/Management%20Alert%20OIG-2018-004.pdf.
54. "Special Report on the Common Securitization Platform: FHFA Lacked
     Transparency and Exercised Inadequate Oversight over a $2.13 Billion,
     Seven-Year Project," *Federal Housing Finance Agency OIG*, OIG-2019-005,
     March, 2019.
55. Charles R. Pierce, "Mick Mulvaney is not the Sharpest Knife in the
     Drawer," *Esquire*, August, 2019, esquire.com/news-politics/politics/
     a28662186/mick-mulvaney-agriculture-department/.
56. Ibid.
57. Dave Jamieson, "White House Violated Law with Plan to Move Hundreds
     of USDA Workers: Inspector General," *Huffpost*, August, 2019, https://

www.huffpost.com/entry /mick-mulvaney-usda-relocation_n_5d4ae71ee4b0
9e72973fab05.

58. "Quarterly Financial Supplement Q3 2019," *Fannie Mae*, October, 2019,
fanniemae.com /resources/file/ir/pdf/quarterly-annual-results/2019/q32019_
financial_supplement.pdf.

59. "Freddie Mac Reports Net Income of $1.7 Billion and Comprehensive
Income of $1.8 Billion for Third Quarter 2019," *Freddie Mac*, October,
2019, freddiemac.com/investors/financials/pdf/2019er-3q19_release.pdf.

60. "FHFA's Targeted Examinations of Fannie Mae: Less than Half of the
Targeted Examinations Planned for 2012 through 2015 Were Completed
and No Examinations Planned for 2015 Were Completed Before the Report
of Examination Issued," *Federal Housing Finance Agency OIG*, AUD-2016-
006, September, 2016, fhfaoig.gov/Content/Files/AUD-2016-006.pdf.

61. "FHA Loans to Delinquent Debtors," *U.S. Department of Housing and
Urban Development, Office of Single Family Housing*, 2018-KC-0001,
hudoig.gov/sites/default/files/documents/2018-KC-0001.pdf.

62. "Top Management Challenges Facing the U.S. Department of Housing and
Urban Development in 2019 and Beyond," *U.S. Department of HUD OIG*.

63. "FHFA Should Re-evaluate and Revise Fraud Reporting by the Enterprises
to Enhance its Utility," *Federal Housing Finance Agency OIG*, EVL-2018-
004, September, 2018.

64. "Top Management Challenges Facing the U.S. Department of Housing and
Urban Development in 2019 and Beyond," *U.S. Department of HUD OIG*.

65. "HTF Endorsers (memo)," *The National Housing Trust Fund*, December,
2018, https://nlihc.org/sites/default/files/HTF%20Endorsers%20
12.18.2018.pdf.

Chapter 4

1. "FHFA's Housing Finance Examiner Commissioning Program: $7.7 Million
and Four Years into the Program, the Agency has Fewer Commissioned
Examiners," *Federal Housing Finance Agency OIG Compliance Review*,
September, 2018, https://www.fhfaoig.gov/Content/Files/Compliance%20
Review%20COM-2018-006.pdf.

2. Charles J. Orlebeke, "The Evolution of Low-Income Housing Policy, 1949
to 1999," University of Illinois at Chicago, *Housing Policy Debate* Vol 11,
Issue 2489 © Fannie Mae Foundation 2000.

3. "The Financial Crisis Inquiry Report: Final Report of the National
Commission on the Causes of the Financial and Economic Crisis in the
United States," *Discover Economic History, Federal Reserve*, January,
2011, fraser.stlouisfed.org/title/5034.

4. Ibid.

5. Ibid.

6. John Taylor, interview by FCIC, September 23, 2010, *Financial Crisis
Inquiry Commission (2011)*. The Financial Crisis Inquiry Report.
Washington D.C.: US Government Printing Office, govinfo.gov/content/pkg/
GPO-FCIC/pdf/GPO-FCIC.pdf

7. Robert Lenzner, "You Better Read This if You Don't Know Anything
About the Shadow Banking System," *Forbes.com*, June, 2014, forbes.com/
sites/robertlenzner/2014/06/30 /the-unregulated-shadow-banking-system-
triggered-the-2008-financial-crisis/#7d02b9e49637.

8. "The Financial Crisis Inquiry Report," *The Financial Crisis Inquiry
Commission*, February, 2011.

9. Ibid.

10. Ibid.

11. "Ten Years After The Financial Crisis, Global Securitization Lending
Transformed By Regulation And Economic Growth," S & P Global Ratings,
July, 2017, spratings.com /documents/20184/1393097/SF10Years/b0f1300a-
5ed5-407d-8d3b-77fdc3b1f20c

12. "The Financial Crisis Inquiry Report," *The Financial Crisis Inquiry Commission*, February, 2011.

13. Dom Beveridge, "The Multifamily Technology Projects that Dominated 2018," *Multifamily Insiders Demand Solutions Blog*, March, 2019, multifamilyinsiders.com /multifamily-blogs/the-multifamily-technology-projects-that-dominated-2018.

14. "Apartment Preliminary Trends, Q4 2018 Preliminary Trends Announcement: National Apartment Market," *Real Estate Solutions*, January, 2019, reis.com/apartment-preliminary-trends-q4-2018/.

15. "2019 Multifamily Midyear Outlook," Freddiemac.com, August, 2019. https://mf.freddiemac.com/docs/multifamily_2019_midyear_outlook.pdf

16. Ibid.

17. "The State Of The Nation's Housing 2018," *Joint Center for Housing Studies of Harvard University*, jchs.harvard.edu/sites/default/files /Harvard_JCHS_State_of_the_Nations_Housing_2018.pdf.

18. "Housing Finance at a Glance, a Monthly Chartbook," *Housing Finance Policy Center*, June, 2018, urban.org/sites/default/files/publication/98669/housing_finance_at_a_glance_a_monthly_chartbook_june_2018_0.pdf.

19. "Multifamily Market Commentary – July 2019 Multifamily Supply and Demand Varies by Metropolitan Areas," *Fanniemae.com*, multifamily. fanniemae.com/sites/g/files /koqyhd161/files/2019-07/MF_Market_Commentary_071619_0.pdf.

20. Ibid.

21. "The State Of The Nation's Housing 2018," *Joint Center for Housing Studies of Harvard University*.

22. Ibid.

23. Locked Out? Are Rising Housing Costs Barring Young Adults from Buying their First Homes?" *Freddiemac.com*, June, 2018, freddiemac.com/research/insight /20180628_rising_housing_costs.page.

24. "Final Report and Recommendations for King County, WA," *Regional Affordable Housing Task Force*, revised March, 2019, https://www.kingcounty.gov/~/media/initiatives/affordablehousing/documents/report/RAH_Report_Final.ashx?la=en.

25. "Housing Finance at a Glance, a Monthly Chartbook," *Housing Finance Policy Center*, June, 2018, urban.org/sites/default/files/publication/98669/housing_finance_at_a_glance_a_monthly_chartbook_june_2018_0.pdf.

26. "Prolonged Conservatorships of Fannie Mae and Freddie Mac Prompt Need for Reform," *GAO.gov Housing Finance*, January, 2019, gao.gov/assets/700/696517.pdf.

27. Jonathan Stempel, "Big banks settle Fannie Mae, Freddie Mac bond rigging litigation in U.S," Reuters.com, December, 2019, reuters.com/article/us-fannie-mae-freddie-mac-bonds-lawsuit/big-banks-settle-fannie-mae-freddie-mac-bond-rigging-litigation-in-u-s-idUSKBN1YL1RK.

28. "Top Management Challenges Facing the U.S. Department of Housing and Urban Development in 2019 and Beyond," *HUD OIG*, October, 2018, hudoig.gov/sites/default/files/2018-11/TMC%20-%20FY%202019.pdf.

29. "Freddie Mac Multifamily Seller/Servicer GuideChapter 60 –Appraisals," *Freddie Mac Multifamily*, mf.freddiemac.com/docs/freddie_mac_guide%20-%20chapter_60.pdf.

30. "The State Of The Nation's Housing 2018," *Joint Center for Housing Studies of Harvard University*.

31. "Housing Market Indicators Overall Showed Some Progress in the Second Quarter," *HUD PD&R National Housing Market Summary*, September, 2019, huduser.gov/portal/sites/default/files/pdf/NationalSummary_2Q19.pdf

32. Jeremiah Johnson, "Greystar Initiates Funding For $500 Million Debt Fund," *Housingwire.com*, June, 2018, housingwire.com/articles/43623-greystar-initiates-funding-for-500-million-debt-fund/.

Chapter 5

1. "The Financial Crisis Inquiry Report: Final Report Of The National Commission On The Causes Of The Financial And Economic Crisis In The United States," The Financial Crisis Inquiry Commission, February 2011, govinfo.gov/content/pkg/GPO-FCIC/pdf/GPO-FCIC.pdf.
2. Julie Segal, "Large Investors Will Be the Most At Risk in the Next Bond Sell-Off," *Institutional Investor*, November 2018, institutionalinvestor.com/article /b1c0x7kq08z5fs/Large-Investors-Will-Be-the-Most-At-Risk-in-the-Next-Bond-Sell-Off.
3. "NMHC Top 50 Apartment Owners," Multifamily Executive, April 2016, https://www.multifamilyexecutive.com/news/nmhc-2016-top-50-largest-apartment-owners_o
4. Jon Banister, "Greystar CEO Bob Faith On $4.6B EdR Acquisition And His Outlook For Multifamily," Bisnow.com, November 2018, https://www.bisnow.com/national/news/multifamily/greystar-ceo-bob-faith-on-46b-edr-acquisition-and-his-outlook-for-multifamily-95183.
5. James Pilcher, Liz Dufour, Sarah Taddeo and Matthew Prensky, "Dream home nightmares: Ryan Homes buyers face delays, hassles as repairs lag," *USA Today* Network, updated November 2019, https://www.cincinnati.com/in-depth/news/2019/10/31/ryan-homes-construction-building-warranty-claims/3929496002/
6. Ibid.
7. Dustin Dunham, "Innovations in 'Big Data' Are Impacting Real Estate Investment," Cornell Real Estate Review, March 2018, https://blog.realestate.cornell.edu/2018/03/22/innovations-in-big-data/
8. "The Age of Analytics: Competing in a Data-Driven World," *McKinsey Global Institute*, December, 2016, https://www.slideshare.net/MichielNoij/mgi-theageofanalyticsfullreport-80712672.
9. "Algorithm," *Lexico.com,* https://www.lexico.com/en/definition/algorithm.
10. "The Age of Analytics: Competing in a Data-Driven World," McKinsey Global Institute, December 2016.
11. Realpage.com, accessed September, 2019, https://www.realpage.com/.
12. BH Management Services, LLC, accessed November 2019, https://bhmanagement.com/marketing/
13. Rentlytics.com, accessed November 2019, https://rentlytics.com/products/business-intelligence/
14. "Culture," Alliance Residential Company, accessed November, 2019, http://www.allresco.com/culture/people-systems
15. "Unlock the Power of Rental Payment Data," Experian.com, accessed November, 2019, http://www.experian.com/rentbureau/rental-history.html
16. Michael Delgado, ed., "Experian RentBureau to Receive Rental Payment History from Riverstone Residential Group," Experian.com, May 2012, https://www.experian.com/blogs/news/2012/05/30/riverstone/.
17. "Unlock the Power of Rental Payment Data," Experian.com, accessed November 2019, http://www.experian.com/rentbureau/rental-history.html
18. "Artificial Intelligence Screening," https://www.realpage.com/apartment-marketing/ai-screening/.
19. Michael Delgado, ed., "Experian RentBureau to Receive Rental Payment History from Riverstone Residential Group," Experian, May, 2012, https://www.experian.com/blogs/news/2012/05/30/riverstone/
20. "Unlock the Power of Rental Payment Data," Experian.com, accessed November 2019, http://www.experian.com/rentbureau/rental-history.html
21. Rachel Davidson, "It's Time to Make the Change to Automated Renter Screening," Multifamily Executive, January 2019, https://www.multifamilyexecutive.com/property-management/its-time-to-make-the-change-to-automated-renter-screening_o
22. "Unlock the Power of Rental Payment Data," Experian.com, accessed November 2019, http://www.experian.com/rentbureau/rental-history.html
23. Michael Delgado, ed., "Experian RentBureau to Receive Rental Payment History from Riverstone Residential Group," Experian.com, May 2012.

24. Ibid.
25. Ibid.
26. We Are Apartment Management Consultants," Apartment Management Consultants, LLC, https://www.amcllc.net/amcrfp.pdf
27. Steve Auger, "RealPage Has a New Secret Weapon," *Seeking Alpha*, July, 2019, https://seekingalpha.com/article/4276343-realpage-new-secret-weapon
28. "Case Study: Bad-debt recovery," Experian.com, http://www.experian.com/rentbureau/experian-rentbureau-testimonial-casestudies-debt.html
29. Ibid.
30. Ibid.
31. Rentlytics.com, Business Intelligence 2.0 page, accessed November 2019, https://rentlytics.com/products/business-intelligence/
32. "Marketing," BH Management Services, LLC, accessed November, 2019, https://bhmanagement.com/marketing/
33. "2018 Pere Awards: North America," Perenews.com, March 2019, https://www.perenews.com/2018-pere-awards-north-america/
34. James Pilcher, Liz Dufour, Sarah Taddeo, and Matthew Prensky, "Dream home nightmares: Ryan Homes buyers face delays, hassles as repairs lag," *USA Today* Network, updated November 2019, https://www.cincinnati.com/in-depth/news/2019/10/31/ryan-homes-construction-building-warranty-claims/3929496002/
35. "Financing," NVR, accessed January 2020, http://www.nvrinc.com/financing/
36. NVR, Inc. Annual Report Pursuant To Section 13 or 15(d) of the Securities Exchange Act of 1934 for the Fiscal Year Ended December 31, 2018," U.S. Securities and Exchange Commission, https://nvri.gcs-web.com/static-files/31ce4d1f-277e-4bf5-b372-eb9a896de16c
37. Ibid.
38. "2019 Builder 100," Builderonline.com, accessed January 2020, https://www.builderonline.com/firms/nvr
39. Jacqueline Salmon, "Hard Times For a Builder," *The Washington Post*, August 1990, https://www.washingtonpost.com/archive/business/1990/08/27/hard-times-for-a-builder/2a9f81ac-e039-45dd-8c90-4c8a081a6b24/
40. Derek Mearns, "Greystar's $1.5 Billion Deal With Equity: A Closer Look, Multifamily Executive, March 2013, https://www.multifamilyexecutive.com/business-finance/business-trends/greystars-15-billion-deal-with-equity-a-closer-look_o
41. Ibid.
42. Jeremiah Jensen, "Greystar initiates funding for $500 million debt fund," Housingwire.com, June 2018, https://www.housingwire.com/articles/43623-greystar-initiates-funding-for-500-million-debt-fund/.
43. Jon Banister, "Greystar CEO Bob Faith On $4.6B EdR Acquisition And His Outlook For Multifamily ," *Bisnow.com*, November, 2018, https://www.bisnow.com/national/news/multifamily/greystar-ceo-bob-faith-on-46b-edr-acquisition-and-his-outlook-for-multifamily-95183
44. Ibid
45. Kayla Devon, "NMHC 50: Managers Follow the Opportunity," Multifamily Executive, April 2016, https://www.multifamilyexecutive.com/business-finance/top-50/nmhc-50-managers-follow-the-opportunity_o.
46. Dr. Adnan Özyilmaz, "Vertical Trust In Organizations: A Review Of Empirical Studies Over The Last Decade," *Mustafa Kemal University Journal of Social Sciences Institute* Issue 13, Vol. 7, p. 1-28 (2010), https://pdfs.semanticscholar.org/649a/014bb63418144cec96cb76b4c32f1d51247a.pdf
47. "What Are Vertical Restraints," Anti-trust laws, December 2019, https://anti-trust.laws.com/vertical-restraints/vertical-restraints
48. Crow Holdings, "Kim Hallet, Chief Accounting Officer," accessed January 2020, https://www.crowholdings.com/team/kim-hallett

49. Bill Maddux—Executive Managing Director," Greystar, accessed November 2019, https://www.greystar.com/-/media/pdf-files/press-kit/bill-maddux-bio-sept-2016.ashx

50. "Leadership," Greystar, accessed November 2019, https://www.greystar.com/about-greystar/leadership.

51. Cathy Cunningham, "Greystar's Bob Faith on Building a Global Multifamily Empire," Commercial Observer, June 2018, https://commercialobserver.com/2018/06/greystars-bob-faith-talks-multifamily/.

52. Greg Buchak, Gregor Matvos, Tomasz Piskorski, and Amit Seru, "Fintech, Regulatory Arbitrage and the Rise of Shadow Banks," May 2017, https://www.fdic.gov/bank/analytical/cfr/bank-research-conference/annual-17th/papers/15-piskorski.pdf.

53. "Total Household Debt Climbs for 20th Straight Quarter as Mortgage Debt and Originations Rise," Federal Reserve Bank of New York, August 2019, https://www.newyorkfed.org/newsevents/news/research/2019/20190813.

54. "Federal Government and State Attorneys General Reach $25 Billion Agreement with Five Largest Mortgage Servicers to Address Mortgage Loan Servicing and Foreclosure Abuses," U.S. Department of Justice Office of Public Affairs, February 2012, https://www.justice.gov/opa/pr/federal-government-and-state-attorneys-general-reach-25-billion-agreement-five-largest.

55. "The Financial Crisis Inquiry Report: Final Report Of The National Commission On The Causes Of The Financial And Economic Crisis In The United States," The Financial Crisis Inquiry Commission, February 2011, govinfo.gov/content/pkg/GPO-FCIC/pdf/GPO-FCIC.pdf.

56. David Moss, Cole Bolton, and Eugene Kintgen, "Pecora Hearings," Harvard Business School Case 711-046, December 2010 (revised June 2018).

57. Tom Borgers, "Financial Crisis Inquiry Commission is Biggest Financial Investigation Since 1930s' Pecora Commission," ACFE (Association of Certified Fraud Examiners,) November/December 2009, https://www.acfe.com/article.aspx?id=184.

58. Larry Bumgardner, "A Brief History of the 1930s Securities Laws in the United States—and the Potential Lesson for Today," Pepperdine University, http://www.jgbm.org/page/5%20Larry%20Bumgardner.pdf.

59. "Banking Act of 1933," Federal Reserve History, June 1933.

Chapter 6

1. "Fiduciary Duties," Risk Management & License Law Forum, National Association of Realtors, May 15, 2013, https://www.nar.realtor/sites/default/files/handouts-and-brochures/2014/nar-fiduciary-duty-032213.pdf.

2. Ashley Mayrianne, "Winn Management Battles Tenant Concerns in Housing Court," Science and Environmental Journalism, http://blogs.bu.edu/ashjones/investigative/winn.

3. "Mid-America Apartment Faces Rent Late-Fee Practices Lawsuit," Zacks.com, September 2018, https://www.zacks.com/stock/news/324209/midamerica-apartment-faces-rent-latefee-practices-lawsuit

4. "Kohler v. Greystar Real Estate Partners, LLC," Case No. 15-cv-02195 JAH (KSC), Leagle.com, March 2017, https://www.leagle.com/decision/infdco20170403a62

5. Anne Bucher, "Texas Greystar Water Utility Class Action Settlement," Top Class Actions, August 2017, https://topclassactions.com/lawsuit-settlements/closed-settlements/815872-texas-greystar-water-utility-class-action-settlement/

6. Dan Kane and Ely Portillo, "'It Wasn't Fair.' How Renters Are Battling Landlords Over Eviction Fees," The Fayetteville Observer, May 2018, https://www.fayobserver.com/news/20180517/it-wasnt-fair-how-renters-are-battling-landlords-over-eviction-fees

7. Ibid

8.   Ibid.
9.   Joel Winston, "How Landlords Learn Your Secrets: Special Renter Reports," Credit.com, October 2015, https://blog.credit.com/2015/10/how-landlords-learn-your-secrets-special-credit-reports-125334/
10. Ibid.
11. "What Are Specialty Consumer Reporting Agencies and What Kind of Information do They Collect?" Consumer Financial Protection Bureau, updated March 2017, https://www.consumerfinance.gov/ask-cfpb/what-are-specialty-consumer-reporting-agencies-and-what-kind-of-information-do-they-collect-en-1813/
12. "What are specialty consumer reporting agencies?" Specialtycreditreports.com, September 2015, http://www.specialtycreditreports.com/what-are-specialty-consumer-reporting-agencies/
13. "Applicant Screening Criteria," Independence Capital Property Management, accessed November 2019, https://www.icpmrentsmart.com/applicant-screening-criteria
14. McNelly Torres, "Consumers Say Debt Collector Abuses Continue," Consumer Affairs, https://www.bbb.org/us/ut/holladay-ctwd/profile/property-management/amc-1166-22006015/complaints
15. Aaron Glantz, "America's Largest Private Landlord Faces Civil Rights Lawsuit," Revealnews.org, December 2017, https://www.revealnews.org/blog/americas-largest-landlord-faces-civil-rights-lawsuit/
16. "Texas Company Will Pay $3 Million to Settle FTC Charges That It Failed to Meet Accuracy Requirements for its Tenant Screening Reports," Federal Trade Commission, October 2018, https://www.ftc.gov/news-events/press-releases/2018/10/texas-company-will-pay-3-million-settle-ftc-charges-it-failed
17. "Texas Company Will Pay $3 million to Settle FTC Charges Federal Trade Commission," Federal Trade Commission, October 2018.
18. Ben Lane, "HUD proposes changes to fair housing rules," *Housingwire.com*, August 2019, https://www.housingwire.com/articles/49873-hud-proposes-changes-to-fair-housing-rules/
19. "Cartel," *Federal Trade Commission*, updated January 2018, https://www.ftc.gov/public-statements/2011/02/theoretical-and-practical-observations-cartel-and-merger-enforcement
20. "Price Fixing," *Federal Trade Commission*, https://www.ftc.gov/tips-advice/competition-guidance/guide-antitrust-laws/dealings-competitors/price-fixing
21. "Business Intelligence®," Realpage.com, accessed November, 2019, https://www.realpage.com/asset-optimization/business-intelligence/
22. Rachel Davidson, "It's Time to Make the Change to Automated Renter Screening," Multifamily Executive, January 2019, https://www.multifamilyexecutive.com/property-management/its-time-to-make-the-change-to-automated-renter-screening_o
23. Steve Auger, "RealPage Has a New Secret Weapon," Seeking Alpha, July, 2019, https://seekingalpha.com/article/4276343-realpage-new-secret-weapon
24. Market Analytics," *Realpage.com*, accessed September, 2019, https://www.realpage.com/asset-optimization/market-analytics/
25. Ibid
26. "How We Survey Apartment Rental Rates," Yardi® Matrix, accessed November, 2019, https://www.yardimatrix.com/About-Us/Our-Methods/How-We-Report-Rental-Market-Conditions/How-We-Survey-Rental-Rates
27. "Quarterly report pursuant to Section 13 or 15(d)," March, 2018, https://investor.realpage.com/sec-filings/all-sec-filings/xbrl_doc_only/1517
28. Jason Brownlee, "A Tour of The Most Popular Machine Learning Algorithms," Machine Learning Mastery, August 2019, https://machinelearningmastery.com/a-tour-of-machine-learning-algorithms/
29. Michael Hoffman's LinkedIn page, accessed November 2019, https://www.linkedin.com/in/michael-hoffman-5351474.
30. James Pilcher, Liz Dufour, Sarah Taddeo, and Matthew Prensky, "Dream home nightmares: Ryan Homes buyers face delays, hassles as repairs lag,"

USA Today Network, updated November 2019, https://www.cincinnati.com/in-depth/news/2019/10/31/ryan-homes-construction-building-warranty-claims/3929496002/

31. Apartment Management Consultants LLC, accessed November 2019, https://www.amcllc.net/

32. Exhibit D, Daley v. Greystar Real Estate Partners No. 2:18-cv-00381-SMJ, 2019 US Dist. LEXIS 72778 (E.D. Wash. April 30, 2019)

33. "We Are Apartment Management Consultants," Apartment Management Consultants, LLC, accessed September, 2019, https://www.amcllc.net/amcrfp.pdf

34. Anne Bucher, "Texas Greystar Water Utility Class Action Settlement," Top Class Actions, August 2017, https://topclassactions.com/lawsuit-settlements/closed-settlements/815872-texas-greystar-water-utility-class-action-settlement/

35. "Working Hard but Struggling to Survive," *Alice*, accessed August 2019, https://www.unitedforalice.org/home.

Chapter 7

1. "Why I need to save the Consumer Financial Protection Bureau," *The Conversation*, July 2017, https://theconversation.com/why-we-need-to-save-the-consumer-financial-protection-bureau-80353.

2. Anisha Sekar, "The Consumer Financial Protection Bureau Explained," Nerdwallet, accessed January 2020, https://www.nerdwallet.com/blog/banking/consumer-financial-protection-bureau-explained/.

3. Consumer Financial Protection Bureau, accessed January 2020, https://www.consumerfinance.gov.

4. "Summary of the Administrative Procedure Act," U.S. Environmental Protection Agency, accessed January 2020, https://www.epa.gov/laws-regulations/summary-administrative-procedure-act.

5. "Financial Stability Oversight Council," U.S. Department of Treasury, accessed January 2020, https://home.treasury.gov/policy-issues/financial-markets-financial-institutions-and-fiscal-service/fsoc.

6. "Warning Letters," *Consumer Financial Protection Bureau*, accessed January, 2020, https://www.consumerfinance.gov/policy-compliance/guidance/supervision-examinations/institutions/

7. Megan Slack, "Consumer Financial Protection Bureau 101: Why I Need a Consumer Watchdog," The White House–President Barack Obama, January 2012, https://obamawhitehouse.archives.gov/blog/2012/01/04/consumer-financial-protection-bureau-101-why-we-need-consumer-watchdog.

8. "Fact Sheet: Credit Reporting Market," Consumer Financial Protection Bureau, accessed January 2020, https://files.consumerfinance.gov/f/201207_cfpb_factsheet_credit-reporting-market.pdf.

9. Karen Turner, "The Equifax Hacks Are a Case Study in Why I Need Better Data Breach Laws," Vox updated September 2017, https://www.vox.com/policy-and-politics/2017/9/13/16292014/equifax-credit-breach-hack-report-security.

10. "Consumer Financial Protection Bureau Settles with Employment Background Screening Company," Consumer Financial Protection Bureau, November 2019, https://www.consumerfinance.gov/about-us/newsroom/bureau-settles-employment-background-screening-company/.

11. "Fair Debt Collection Practices Act," Consumer Financial Protection Bureau, March 2018, https://files.consumerfinance.gov/f/documents/cfpb_fdcpa_annual-report-congress_03-2018.pdf.

12. Ibid.

13. "Sector Profile: Finance, Insurance & Real Estate," OpenSecrets.org, accessed January 2020, https://www.opensecrets.org/lobby/background.php?id=F&year=2019.

14. "Wall Street Money in Washington," Americans for Financial Reform, April 2019.
15. Matt Taibbi, "How Wall Street Killed Financial Reform," *Rolling Stone*, May, 2012, https://www.rollingstone.com/politics/politics-news/how-wall-street-killed-financial-reform-190802/
16. "Book Trump? Interest Groups Press Case at His Properties," *CBS News*, February 22, 2018, https://www.cbsnews.com/news/book-trump-interest-groups-press-case-at-his-properties/.
17. Cecilia Kang and Kenneth P. Vogel, "Tech Giants Amass a Lobbying Army for an Epic Washington Battle," *The New York Times*, June 2019.
18. Daniel Fisher, "Trump Administration Switches Sides, Argues CFPB Structure Is Unconstitutional," *Forbes*, March, 2017, https://www.forbes.com/sites/danielfisher/2017/03/17/trump-administration-switches-sides-argues-cfpb-structure-is-unconstitutional/#6e4190be3105.
19. Patricia Ann McCoy, "Inside Job: The Assault on the Structure of the Consumer Financial Protection Bureau," (103 Minnesota Law Review 2543, Boston College Law School, June 13, 2019), last revised September 2019, https://papers.ssrn.com/sol3/papers.cfm?abstract_id=3285589.
20. Steve Quinlivan, "Justice Department Tells Court CFPB is Unconstitutional," *Dodd-Frank.com*, March, 2017, http://dodd-frank.com/2017/03/18/justice-department-tells-court-cfpb-is-unconstitutional/.
21. "The Bureau of Consumer Financial Protection's Unconstitutional Design: Hearing Before the Subcommittee on Oversight and Investigations of the Committee on Financial Services U.S. House of Representatives, 115th Congress, 1st session," Serial No. 115-6, U.S Government Publishing Office, March 2017, https://www.govinfo.gov/content/pkg/CHRG-115hhrg27247/pdf/CHRG-115hhrg27247.pdf.
22. Ibid.
23. Tristan North, "Ruling Stands in PHH v. CFPB Mortgage Case," *Worldwide ERC*, May, 2018, https://www.worldwideerc.org/news/ruling-stands-in-phh-v-cfpb-mortgage-case/.
24. "PHH Corp., et al. v. Consumer Financial Protection Bureau, No. 15-1177, (D.C. Cir. 2018) https://scholar.google.com/scholarcase?case=13735252432428480002&q=phh+corp+2018&hl=en&as_sdt=2006
25. Ben Lane, "CFPB names Mulvaney, Hensarling aide Brian Johnson Deputy Director," HousingWire, May 2019, https://www.housingwire.com/articles/49033-cfpb-names-mulvaney-hensarling-aide-brian-johnson-deputy-director/.
26. Yuka Hayashi, "CFPB Interim Chief Mulvaney Taps Hensarling Aide for Senior Role," *The Wall Street Journal*, December 2017, https://www.wsj.com/articles/cfpb-interim-chief-mulvaney-taps-hensarling-aide-for-senior-role-1512151374.
27. Chris Arnold, "Democratic Senators Slam Trump's Pick To Run Consumer Financial Protection Bureau," NPR, July 2018, https://www.npr.org/2018/07/19/630485854/senators-clash-over-trumps-pick-to-run-consumer-financial-protection-bureau.
28. Thomas Ahearn, "CFPB Called Far Too Powerful with Little Oversight of Activities in Report," ESR News Blog, April 2018, https://www.esrcheck.com/wordpress/2018/04/05/cfpb-called-far-powerful-little-oversight-activities-acting-director/.
29. Jim Puzzanghera, "CFPB's Mick Mulvaney gives Lobbying Advice to Bankers, Further Infuriating Consumer Advocates," *Los Angeles Times*, April 2018, https://www.latimes.com/business/la-fi-mulvaney-cfpb-lobbyists-20180425-story.html.
30. Ibid.
31. Allison Preiss, "Statement: CAP Experts Decry 'Shameful' Confirmation of Kathy Kraninger to Serve as Next CFPB Director," Center for American Progress, December 2018, https://www.americanprogress.org/press/statement/2018/12/06/461641/statement-cap-experts-decry-shameful-confirmation-kathy-kraninger-serve-next-cfpb-director/.

32. Ibid.
33. Chris Arnold, "Democratic Senators Slam Trump's Pick To Run Consumer Financial Protection Bureau," NPR, July 2018,
34. Elizabeth Warren, "New Report Reveals Kathy Kraninger's Disastrous Management Record at OMB," Warren.senate.gov, July 2018, https://www.warren.senate.gov/oversight/reports/new-report-reveals-kathy-kraningers-disastrous-management-record-at-omb.
35. Jim Saksa, "Democrats Seek Info on CFPB Official's Ties to Christian Group," *Roll Call*, August 2019, https://www.rollcall.com/news/congress/democrats-seek-info-cfpb-officials-ties-christian-group.
36. Barney Jopson, "Trump Eyes Low-Profile White House Staffer to Head Consumer Body," *Financial Times*, June 2018, https://www.ft.com/content/d4b097f4-71e7-11e8-b6ad-3823e4384287.
37. Kathleen L. Kraninger, "Speech at the Bipartisan Policy Center By Kathleen L. Kraninger, Director, Consumer Financial Protection Bureau," Consumer Financial Protection Bureau, April 2019, https://www.consumerfinance.gov/about-us/newsroom/kathleen-kraninger-director-consumer-financial-protection-bureau-bipartisan-policy-center-speech/.
38. Ibid.
39. Christopher L. Peterson, "Report: Dormant: The Consumer Financial Protection Bureau's Law Enforcement Program in Decline," Consumer Federation of America, March 2019, https://consumerfed.org/wp-content/uploads/2019/03/CFPB-Enforcement-in-Decline.pdf.
40. "Press Release: CFPB Law Enforcement Plummets Under Trump Administration," Consumer Federation of America, March 2019. https://consumerfed.org/press_release/16137/.
41. Christopher L. Peterson, "Report: Dormant: The Consumer Financial Protection Bureau's Law Enforcement Program in Decline," Consumer Federation of America, March 2019.
42. Alan S. Kaplinsky, "CFPB's Constitutionality Again Before D.C. Circuit in Morgan Drexen Appeal," Consumer Finance Monitor, November 2014, https://www.consumerfinancemonitor.com/2014/11/06/cfpbs-constitutionality-again-before-d-c-circuit-in-morgan-drexen-appeal/.
43. Phil Hall, "CFPB Lawsuit Against Ocwen Thrown Out," *National Mortgage Professional Magazine*, September 2019, https://nationalmortgageprofessional.com/news/72254/cfpb-lawsuit-against-ocwen-thrown.
44. "Ocwen Says CFPB Suit Must End After Constitutionality Pivot," Law360, October 2019, https://www.law360.com/articles/1206070/ocwen-says-cfpb-suit-must-end-after-constitutionality-pivot.
45. Federal Reserve System, "Truth in Lending; Final Rule," Federal Register 73, No. 147, July, 2008, 12 CFR Part 226, https://www.federalreserve.gov/reportforms/formsreview/RegZ_20080730_ffr.pdf.
46. Gillian B. White, "What's at Stake in the Fight Over the CFPB," *The Atlantic*, December 2017, https://www.theatlantic.com/business/archive/2017/12/cfpb-fight/547466/.
47. Richard Cordray, "Prepared Remarks of CFPB Director Richard Cordray at the Consumer Advisory Board Meeting," Consumer Financial Protection Bureau, June 2017, https://www.consumerfinance.gov/about-us/newsroom/prepared-remarks-cfpb-director-richard-cordray-consumer-advisory-board-meeting-june-2017/.
48. "Supervisory Highlights," Consumer Financial Protection Bureau, Spring 2014, https://files.consumerfinance.gov/f/201405_cfpb_supervisory-highlights-spring-2014.pdf.
49. Consumer Financial Protection Bureau, accessed January 2020, https://www.consumerfinance.gov/.
50. "AFR/CRL Poll: Early State Voters Support Continued Reform of Wall Street," Americans for Financial Reform, October 2019, http://ourfinancialsecurity.org/2019/10/afrcrl-poll-early-state-voters-support-continued-reform-wall-street/.

51. Herbert Bayard Swope, "The Government Accepts the Challenge of the Slums," First Washington Conference on Public Housing, January 1934, https://www.huduser.gov/portal/sites/default/files/pdf/Speeches-Delivered-at-Washington-Conference.pdf

52. Dan Kane and Ely Portillo, "'It Wasn't Fair.' How Renters Are Battling Landlords over Eviction Fees," *The News & Observer*, May 2018, https://www.newsobserver.com/latest-news/article211154479.html

53. "Working Hard but Struggling to Survive," *Alice*, accessed August, 2019, https://www.unitedforalice.org/home.

54. Aaron Glantz, "Class Action Lawsuit Against Landlord Giant Gets Go-Ahead," Revealnews.org, December 2017, https://www.revealnews.org/blog/class-action-suit-against-landlord-giant-gets-go-ahead/

55. "Mid-America Apartment Faces Rent Late-Fee Practices Lawsuit," Zacks.com, September 2018, https://www.zacks.com/stock/news/324209/midamerica-apartment-faces-rent-latefee-practices-lawsuit

56. *Kohler v. Greystar Real Estate Partners, LLC*, Case No. 15-cv-02195 JAH(KSC), Leagle.com, March 2017, accessed November 2019, https://www.leagle.com/decision/infdco20170403a62

57. Anne Bucher, "Texas Greystar Water Utility Class Action Settlement," Top Class Actions, August 2017, https://topclassactions.com/lawsuit-settlements/closed-settlements/815872-texas-greystar-water-utility-class-action-settlement/

58. McNelly Torres, "Consumers Say Debt Collector Abuses Continue," Consumer Affairs, accessed January 2020, https://www.consumeraffairs.com/news04/2010/04/debt_collection_abuses.html.

59. *Better Business Bureau Complaints Department, July, 2019,* https://www.bbb.org/us/ut/holladay-ctwd/profile/property-management/amc-1166-22006015/complaints

60. "Testimonial: Chris Jenkins, Vice President of Financial Planning, Equity Residential: The benefits of sharing and accessing rental payment data," Experian.com, accessed September 2019, http://www.experian.com/rentbureau/experian-rentbureau-testimonal-casestudies-jenkins.html

61. Michael Delgado, "Experian RentBureau to Receive Rental Payment History from Riverstone Residential Group," Experian.com, May 2012, http://www.experian.com/blogs/news/2012/05/30/riverstone/.

62. Joel Winston, "How Landlords Learn Your Secrets: Special Renter Reports," Credit.com, October 2015.

63. Dan Kane and Ely Portillo, "'It Wasn't Fair.' How Renters Are Battling Landlords over Eviction Fees," *The News and Observer*, May 2018. https://www.newsobserver.com/latest-news/article211154479.html.

64. Aaron Glantz, "America's Largest Private Landlord Faces Civil Lawsuit," Revealnews.org, December 2017, https://www.revealnews.org/blog/americas-largest-landlord-faces-civil-rights-lawsuit/

65. "Final Report and Recommendations for King County, WA," Regional Affordable Housing Task Force, March 2019, kingcounty.gov/~/media/initiatives/affordablehousing/documents/report/RAH_Report_Final.ashx?la=en.

66. Anna Patrick, "A Seattle youth homeless shelter faces its final days, and its young residents confront an uncertain future," *The Seattle Times*, January 2020, seattletimes.com/seattle-news/homeless/a-seattle-youth-homeless-shelter-faces-its-final-days-and-its-young-residents-confront-an-uncertain-future

67. David Kroman, "'Heartbreaking': Seattle's homeless are getting sicker and shelters are struggling to keep up," Crosscut.com, June 2019, https://crosscut.com/2019/06/heartbreaking-seattles-homeless-are-getting-sicker-and-shelters-are-struggling-keep

68. "We Are Apartment Management Consultants," Apartment Management Consultants, LLC, accessed September 2019, https://www.amcllc.net/amcrfp.pdf

69. "CFPB and the New York Attorney General Settle with Debt Collection Group," Consumer Financial Protection Bureau, July 2019, https://www.

consumerfinance.gov/about-us/newsroom/cfpb-and-new-york-attorney-general-settle-debt-collection-group/.

70. Steve Auger, "RealPage Has a New Secret Weapon," *Seeking Alpha*, July, 2019, https://seekingalpha.com/article/4276343-realpage-new-secret-weapon

71. McNelly Torres, "Consumers Say Debt Collector Abuses Continue," *Consumer Affairs,* accessed January 2020, https://www.consumeraffairs.com/news04/2010/04/debt_collection_abuses.html.

72. Ibid.

73. Jack Karp, "From Hospital To Jail: Debtors Face Growing Arrest Threat," Law360.com, February 2020, https://www.law360.com/articles/1241734/from-hospital-to-jail-debtors-face-growing-arrest-threat.

74. "We Are Apartment Management Consultants," Apartment Management Consultants, LLC, accessed September, 2019, https://www.amcllc.net/amcrfp.pdf

75. Ibid.

76. "Testimonial: Chris Jenkins, Vice President of Financial Planning, Equity Residential," Experian.com, accessed September 2019

77. "We Are Apartment Management Consultants," Apartment Management Consultants, LLC, accessed September 2019

78. "Winn Management Battles Tenant Concerns in Housing Court," Ashley Mayrianne Science and Environmental Journalism, accessed September 2019, http://blogs.bu.edu/ashjones/investigative/winn.

79. Ibid.

80. Marc Styles and Coral Garnick, "The Price of Homelessness: The Seattle area spends more than $1 billion a year on this humanitarian crisis," Bizjournals.com, November 2017, https://www.bizjournals.com/seattle/news/2017/11/16/price-of-homelessness-seattle-king-county-costs.html

81. Mike Kingsella, "The First Step in Solving Washington's Housing Crisis Is Preserving Existing Affordable Housing Programs," Upforgrowth.org, March 2019, https://www.upforgrowth.org/news/first-step-solving-washingtons-housing-crisis-preserving-existing-affordable-housing-programs

82. Buhayar and Deprez, "The Homeless Crisis Is Getting Worse in America's Richest Cities," Bloomberg BusinessWeek, November 2018

83. FTC Bulletin, "World's Largest Debt Collector Pays the Price for Harassing Consumers," https://www.consumer.ftc.gov/blog/2013/07/worlds-largest-debt-collector-pays-price-harassing-consumers

84. Everman, "Herbert Hoover and the New Deal, 1933-1940," LSU Historical Dissertations and Theses

85. Tom Borgers, "Financial Crisis Inquiry Commission Is Biggest Financial Investigation Since 1930s' Pecora Commission," ACFE (Association of Certified Fraud Examiners), November/December 2009, https://www.acfe.com/article.aspx?id=184.

Chapter 8

1. Office of Audit, Financial Audits Division, Washington, DC. Audit Report Number: 2019-FO-0001, November 13, 2018 https://www.hudoig.gov/reports-publications/report/audit-government-national-mortgage-associations-financial-statements-1

2. "Top Management Challenges Facing the US Department of Housing and Urban Development in 2019 and Beyond," *US Department of HUD OIG*, hudoig.gov/sites/default/files/2018-11/TMC percent20- percent20FY percent202019.pdf.

3. Office of Audit, Financial Audits Division, Washington, DC. Audit Report Number: 2019-FO-0001, November 13, 2018.

4. Donald J. Trump, "Executive Order on Maintaining American Leadership in Artificial Intelligence," *The White House*, February 2019, whitehouse.gov/presidential-actions/executive-order-maintaining-american-leadership-artificial-intelligence/.

5. "Accelerating America's Leadership in Artificial Intelligence," *The White House*, February 2019, whitehouse.gov/articles/accelerating-americas-leadership-in-artificial-intelligence/.

6. Darwin McDaniel, "New Law Sets Initiative, Funding Boosting Quantum Computing Research," *Executive.gov*, December, 2018, executivegov.com/2018/12/new-law-sets-initiatives-funding-boosting-quantum-computing-research/.

7. Nancy Scola, "What Jared's Office Actually Does," *The Agenda*, July 2017, politico.com/agenda/story/2017/07/01/jared-kushner-office-american-innovation-000470.

8. Ibid.

9. Ibid.

10. Brad Berton, "Kushner Comes Back," *Multifamily Executive*, October 2012, multifamilyexecutive.com/business-finance/transactions/kushner-comes-back_o.

11. Zachary Cohen, "Jared Kushner Arrives in Israel," *CNN*, June 2017, cnn.com/2017/06/21/politics/jared-kushner-israel-arrival/index.html.

12. Lily Katz, Caleb Melby, and Shahien Nasiripour, "Kushner Cos. Buys Portfolio of Apartments for $1.15 Billion," *Bloomberg*, February 2019, bloomberg.com/news/articles/2019-02-22/kushner-cos-buys-apartment-portfolio-for-1-1-billion-wsj-says.

13. Alec MacGillis, "Kushner Companies Loses a Key Motion in Class Action Filed by Baltimore Tenants," *ProPublica*, July 2018, propublica.org/article/kushner-companies-loses-a-key-motion-in-class-action-filed-by-baltimore-tenants.

14. David Kocieniewski and Caleb Melby, "Kushner Cos. Gets $800 Million Federally-Backed Apartment Loan," *BNN Bloomberg*, May 2019, bnnbloomberg.ca/kushner-cos-gets-800-million-federally-backed-apartment-loan-1.1263563.

15. David Wharton, "Industry Impact: President Trump's Call to End GSE Conservatorship," *DSNews.com*, March 2019, dsnews.com/daily-dose/03-27-2019/fannie-mae-names-hugh-r-frater-as-ceo.

16. Jeremiah Johnson, "Greystar Initiates Funding For $500 Million Debt Fund," *Housingwire.com*, June, 2018, housingwire.com/articles/43623-greystar-initiates-funding-for-500-million-debt-fund/.

17. Brian Slodysko and Kevin Freking, "President Trump Gets in a Few Digs at California During West Coast Fundraising Blitz," *NBC Los Angeles*, September 2019, nbclosangeles.com/news/local/President-Trump-California-Fundraising-Visit-Los-Angeles-Beverly-Hills-Politics-560568751.html.

18. *G.H. Palmer Associates*, ghpalmer.com/home/.

19. "Texas Public Policy Foundation," *Ballotpedia*, ballotpedia.org /Texas_Public_Policy_Foundation.

20. Jonathan O'Connell, "Trump tech adviser Reed Cordish is leaving the White House," *The Washington Post*, February 2018, washingtonpost.com/politics/trump-tech-adviser-reed-cordish-is-leaving-the-white-house/2018/02/16/2895303c-0870-11e8-8777-2a059f168dd2_story.html.

21. "Right on Crime," *Ballotpedia*, ballotpedia.org/Right_on_Crime.

22. Max Chafkin, "Trump Finally Names a US CTO," *Bloomberg Businessweek*, March 2019, bloomberg.com/articles/2019-03-21/donald-trump-to-name-michael-kratsios-as-white-house-cto.

23. Peter Thiel's profile, *Forbes*, forbes.com/profile/peter-thiel/#725a1df6533a.

24. Peter Waldman, Lizette Chapman, and Jordan Robertson, "Palantir Knows Everything About You," *Bloomberg Businessweek*, April 2018, bloomberg.com/features/2018-palantir-peter-thiel/.

25. "2018, a Pivotal Year in the Affordable Housing Industry," RealPage.com, July 2018, propertymanagementinsider.com/2018-pivotal-year-affordable-housing-industry.

26. Benjamin S. Carson, Sr., "Testimony before Senate Committee on Banking, Housing, and Urban Affairs," US Department of Housing and Urban Development, September 2019, banking.senate.gov/imo/media/doc/Carson%20Testimony%209-10-19.pdf.

27. "Top Management Challenges Facing the US Department of Housing and Urban Development in 2019 and Beyond," US Department of HUD OIG, hudoig.gov/sites/default/files/2018-11/TMC%20-%20FY%202019.pdf.
28. Jose A. DelReal, "Trump campaign announces national finance chairman with ties to Wall Street and Democrats," *The Washington Post*, May 2016, washingtonpost.com/news/post-politics/wp/2016/05/05/trump-campaign-announces-national-finance-chair-with-ties-to-wall-street-and-democrats/.
29. Andrew Prokop, "Steven Mnuchin: Trump's Treasury Secretary pick is a Banker with No Known Qualifications or Views," *Vox*, November 2016, vox.com/policy-and-politics/2016/11/29/13698804/steve-mnuchin-treasury-trump.
30. John Ydstie, "Trump Picks Steve Mnuchin To Lead Treasury Department," *NPR*, November 2016, npr.org/sections/thetwo-way/2016/11/30/503791602/reports-trump-picks-steve-mnuchin-to-lead-treasury-department.
31. Jacob Pramuk, "Trump to Nominate Mnuchin as Treasury Secretary, Ross as Commerce Secretary," *CNBC*, November 2016, cnbc.com/2016/11/30/donald-trump-nominates-steven-mnuchin-as-treasury-secretary-wilbur-ross-as-commerce-secrtary.html.
32. Donald J. Trump, "Executive Order Establishing the President's National Council for the American Worker," *The White House*, July 2018, whitehouse.gov/presidential-actions/executive-order-establishing-presidents-national-council-american-worker/.
33. Anupreeta Das and Rachel Louise Ensign, "Treasury Pick Steven Mnuchin Bet on Donald Trump and Won," *The Wall Street Journal*, November 2016, wsj.com/articles/trump-plans-to-name-steven-mnuchin-as-treasury-secretary-1480459950.
34. "President Trump Names Joseph M. Otting Acting Director of the Federal Housing Finance Agency," *Office of the Comptroller of the Currency*, News Release 2018-140, December 2018, occ.gov/news-issuances/news-releases/2018/nr-occ-2018-140.html.
35. David Kocieniewski and Caleb Melby, ""Kushner Cos. Gets $800 Million Federally-Backed Apartment Loan," *BNN Bloomberg*, May 2019.
36. Brian P. Brooks bio, *Stanford.edu*, cdn.law.stanford.edu/wp-content/uploads/2018/08/Brooks_Brian-bio.pdf.
37. "Dune Capital in Purchase of $1.5 Billion Xanadu Meadowlands Mall," *Cleary Gottlieb*, November 2006, clearygottlieb.com/news-and-insights/news-listing/dune-capital-in-purchase-of-%2415-billion-xanadu-meadowlands-mall9?search=.
38. Karey Wutkowski and Megan Davies, "Private Equity Group Buying IndyMac Assets," *Reuters*, January 2009, reuters.com/article/us-indymac-fdic/private-equity-group-buying-indymac-assets-idUSTRE5014DP20090103.
39. "Press Release: Federal Reserve Board Issues Consent Order Against IMB HoldCo LLC," *Board of Governors of the Federal Reserve System*, March 2014, federalreserve.gov /newsevents/pressreleases/enforcement20140321a.htm.
40. John Ydstie, "5 Questions about Donald Trump's Cabinet Picks and his Economic Plan," *NPR*, December 2016, npr.org/2016/12/01/504033606/5 questions-about-trumps-cabinet-picks-and-his-economic-plan.
41. Bryce Covert, "Government Will Investigate Treasury Secretary's Bank for Alleged Redlining," *ThinkProgress*, February 2017, https://thinkprogress.org/mnuchin-onewest-hud-redlining-662a836155ea/.
42. "HUD Approves Settlement Between California Reinvestment Coalition and CIT Bank dba OneWest Bank Resolving Allegations of Discriminatory Redlining," *HUD.gov*, HUD No. 19-113, July 2019, hud.gov/press/press_releases_media_advisories /HUD_No_19_113.
43. "Texas Company Will Pay $3 million to Settle FTC Charges That it Failed to Meet Accuracy Requirements for its Tenant Screening Reports," Federal Trade Commission, October 2018, ftc.gov/news-events/press-

releases/2018/10/texas-company-will-pay-3-million-settle-ftc-charges-it-failed.

44. Jeremy Stahl, "This is Still Happening: Steven Mnuchin," *Slate*, October 2019, slate.com /news-and-politics/2019/10/steven-mnuchin-trump-corruption-still-happening.html.

45. Michael J. De La Merced, "Goldman Sells Mortgage Servicing Unit to Ocwen," *The New York Times*, June 2011, dealbook.nytimes.com/2011/06/06/goldman-sells-mortgage-servicing-unit-to-ocwen/.

46. James O'Toole, "Goldman Sachs, Morgan Stanley in $557 Million Foreclosure Settlement," *CNN Business*, January 2013, money.cnn.com/2013/01/16/news /companies/goldman-morgan-stanley/.

47. Lynn Szymoniak, "The Latest Goldman Sachs Settlement," *THJF.org*, January 2016, thjf.org/2016/01/15/the-latest-goldman-sachs-settlement/.

48. Richard Cordray, "Prepared Remarks of CFPB Director Richard Cordray on the Ocwen Enforcement Action Press Call," *Consumer Financial Protection Bureau*, December 2013, dwt.com/files/paymentlawadvisor/2014/10/Cordrays-Remarks.pdf.

49. "CFPB, State Authorities Order Ocwen to Provide $2 Billion in Relief to Homeowners for Servicing Wrongs," *Consumer Financial Protection Bureau*, December 2013, consumerfinance.gov/about-us/newsroom/cfpb-state-authorities-order-ocwen-to-provide-2-billion-in-relief-to-homeowners-for-servicing-wrongs/.

50. Phil Hall, "CFPB Lawsuit Against Ocwen Thrown Out," *National Mortgage Professional Magazine*, September 2019, nationalmortgageprofessional.com/news/72254/cfpb-lawsuit-against-ocwen-thrown.

51. "Ocwen Says CFPB Suit Must End After Constitutionality Pivot," *Law360*, October 2019, law360.com/articles/1206070/ocwen-says-cfpb-suit-must-end-after-constitutionality-pivot.

52. Ibid.

Chapter 9

1. Ian Goldin and Chris Kutarna, "Risk and Complexity," *International Monetary Fund Finance & Development*, September 2017, Vol. 54, No. 3, imf.org/external/pubs/ft/fandd/2017/09/goldin.htm.

2. Ibid.

3. "The Financial Crisis Inquiry Report : Final Report of the National Commission on the Causes of the Financial and Economic Crisis in the United States," *Discover Economic History, Federal Reserve*, January, 2011, https://fraser.stlouisfed.org/title/5034.

4. Ibid.

5. "Large Financial Institutions," Board of Governors of the Federal Reserve System, updated March 2019, federalreserve.gov/supervisionreg/large-financial-institutions.htm.

6. "2019 Risk Review," *Federal Deposit Insurance Corporation*, accessed January 2020, fdic.gov/bank/analytical/risk-review/full.pdf.

7. Matthew Yglesias, "The Origins And Perils Of Bank Consolidation," October 2011, thinkprogress.org/the-origins-and-perils-of-bank-consolidation-b5e7957c89d4/.

8. "Ginnie Mae: Risk Management and Cost Modeling Require Continuing Attention," *U.S. Government Accountability Office*, December 2011, gao.gov/products/GAO-12-49.

9. "GINNIE MAE: Risk Management and Staffing-Related Challenges Need to Be Addressed," *U.S. Government Accountability Office, GAO-19-191 Report*, April, 2019, https://www.gao.gov/assets/700/698185.pdf.

10. "The Financial Crisis Inquiry Report," *Financial Crisis Inquiry Commission*, updated February 2011, govinfo.gov/content/pkg/GPO-FCIC/pdf/GPO-FCIC.pdf.

11. Michelle Price, "U.S. Fed signals lighter touch on bank supervision, foreign bank oversight," *Reuters*, January, 2020, reuters.com/article/us-usa-fed-quarles/u-s-fed-signals-lighter-touch-on-bank-supervision-foreign-bank-oversight-idUSKBN1ZG27J.

12. Sergey Chernenko, Isil Erel, and Robert Prilmeier, "Nonbank Lending," *FDIC*, July 2018, fdic.gov/bank/analytical/cfr/bank-research-conference/annual-18th/7-erel.pdf

13. "2019 Risk Review," *FDIC*, fdic.gov/bank/analytical/risk-review/full.pdf.

14. Damian Paletta, "Federal Government Has Dramatically Expanded Exposure to Risky Mortgages," *MSN.com* (originally printed in The Washington Post), October, 2019, https://www.msn.com/en-us/news/money/federal-government-has-dramatically-expanded-exposure-to-risky-mortgages/ar-AAIcp3f.

15. "Selling Guide," *Fannie Mae*, December 2019, fanniemae.com/content/guide/selling/b3/6/02.html.

16. "The Role of Nonbanks in Expanding Access to Credit," *Ginnie Mae*, January 2017, ginniemae.gov/newsroom/publications/Documents/expand_role_nonbanks.pdf.

17. "Prolonged Conservatorships of Fannie Mae and Freddie Mac Prompt Need for Reform," *GAO Housing Finance*, January 2019, gao.gov/assets/700/696517.pdf.

18. "Federal government has dramatically expanded exposure to risky mortgages," *The Washington Post*, October 2019, washingtonpost.com/business/economy/federal-government-has-dramatically-expanded-exposure-to-risky-mortgages/2019/10/02 /d862ab40-ce79-11e9-87fa-8501a456c003_story.html

19. Ibid.

20. Paletta, "Federal Government Has Dramatically Expanded Exposure to Risky Mortgages," MSN.com (originally printed in The Washington Post), October 2019.

21. "The Role of Nonbanks in Expanding Access to Credit," *Ginnie Mae*, January 2017.

22. "Subprime Mortgages: Enterprise and FHFA Reporting," *Federal Housing Finance Agency, OIG White Paper WPR-2019-001*, March 2019, fhfaoig.gov/Content/Files/WPR-2019-001.pdf.

23. "Semi-annual Report to Congress," *OIG*, March 2018, hudoig.gov/sites/default/files /documents/SAR_Spring_%202018.pdf.

24. Paletta, "Federal Government Has Dramatically Expanded Exposure to Risky Mortgages," *MSN.com*, October 2019.

25. "Departmental Management Control Program (1840.1)," *HUD.gov*, hud.gov/program_offices/administration/hudclips/handbooks/cfo/1840.1.

26. Paletta, "Federal Government Has Dramatically Expanded Exposure to Risky Mortgages," *MSN.com*, October 2019.

27. Yun Li, "This is now the longest US economic expansion in history," *CNBC.com*, July 2019, cnbc.com/2019/07/02/this-is-now-the-longest-us-economic-expansion-in-history.html.

28. "2019 Multifamily Housing Trends," *Realtymogul.com*, realtymogul.com/knowledge-center/article/2019-multifamily-housing-trends.

29. "Housing Finance at a Glance, a Monthly Chartbook," *Housing Finance Policy Center*, June 2018, urban.org/sites/default/files/publication/98669/housing_finance_at_a_glance_ a_monthly_chartbook_june_2018_0.pdf.

30. Robert Adams and John Driscoll, "How the Largest Bank Holding Companies Grew: Organic Growth or Acquisitions?" *Board of Governors of the Federal Reserve System*, December, 2018, https://www.federalreserve.gov/econres/notes/feds-notes/how-the-largest-bank-holding-companies-grew-organic-growth-or-acquisitions-20181221.htm.

31. Global Markets Analysis Report, *Ginnie Mae*, September, 2018, https://www.ginniemae.gov/data_and_reports/reporting/Documents/global_market_analysis_sep18.pdf

32. "GINNIE MAE: Risk Management and Staffing-Related Challenges Need to Be Addressed," *U.S. Government Accountability Office, GAO-19-191 Report*, April 2019.

33. Steven T. Mnuchin and Craig S. Phillips, "A Financial System That Creates Economic Opportunities Nonbank Financials, FinTech, and Innovation," *U.S. Department of the Treasury*, July, 2018, home.treasury.gov/sites/default/files/2018-07/A-Financial-System-that-Creates-Economic-Opportunities—Nonbank-Financi... pdf.

34. 2017 Annual Report," Ginnie Mae, accessed January, 2020, https://www.ginniemae.gov/about_us/what_we_do/Annual_Reports/annual_report17.pdf

35. Andrea Riquier, "An old fear returns as new mortgage market players rise," *Market Watch*, February 2016, marketwatch.com/story/an-old-fear-returns-as-new-mortgage-market-players-rise-2016-02-29.

36. "Prolonged Conservatorships of Fannie Mae and Freddie Mac Prompt Need for Reform," *GAO Housing Finance*, January 2019.

37. "2019 Risk Review," *FDIC*, accessed January, 2020, https://www.fdic.gov/bank/analytical/risk-review/full.pdf.

38. You Suk Kim et al, "Liquidity Crises in the Mortgage Market." *Brookings Papers on Economic Activity*, Spring 2018, brookings.edu/wp-content/uploads/2018/03 /KimEtAl_Text.pdf.

39. Max Bruche, Frédéric Malherbe, Ralf R Meisenzahl , "From credit risk to pipeline risk: Why loan syndication is a risky business," *Vox*, September 2017, voxeu.org/article/why-loan-syndication-risky-business.

40. "Recent Trends in the Enterprises' Purchases of Mortgages from Smaller Lenders and Nonbank Mortgage Companies," *Federal Housing Finance Agency, OIG, EVL-2014-010*, July, 2014, fhfaoig.gov/Content/Files/EVL-2014-010_0.pdf.

41. Kim, Laufer, Prence et al, "Mapping the boom in nonbank mortgage lending—and understanding the risks," *Brookings.edu*, September 2018.

42. Ibid.

43. "Nonbank Mortgage Servicer Existing Regulatory Oversight Could Be Strengthened," *United States Government Accountability Office Report Number GAO-16-278*, March 2016, gao.gov/assets/680/675747.pdf.

44. Chernenko, Erel, and Prilmeier , "Nonbank Lending," *FDIC*, July 2018. https://www.fdic.gov/bank/analytical/cfr/bank-research-conference/annual-18th/7-erel.pdf

45. 2019 Risk Review," *Federal Deposit Insurance Corporation*, accessed January, 2020, https://www.fdic.gov/bank/analytical/risk-review/full.pdf.

46. Alex Harris, "The Fed Is Entrenched in the Repo Market. How Does It Get Out?," *Bloomberg.com*, December 2019, bloomberg.com/news/articles/2019-12-21/the-fed-is-entrenched-in-the-repo-market-how-does-it-get-out?utm_campaign=news&utm_ medium=bd&utm_source=applenews.

47. Olga Cotaga, "U.S. banks' reluctance to lend cash may have caused repo shock: BIS," *Reuters*, December 2019, reuters.com/article/us-markets-bis-fx/u-s-banks-reluctance-to-lend-cash-may-have-caused-repo-shock-bis-idUSKBN1YC0IQ?utm_source=applenews.

48. "Ginnie Mae Did Not Adequately Respond to Changes in Its Issuer Base," *OIG Audit Report Number 2017-KC-0008*, September 2017, hudoig.gov/sites/default/files /documents/2017-KC-0008.pdf.

49. "2017 Annual Report," Ginnie Mae, ginniemae.gov/about_us /what_we_do /Annual_Reports/annual_report17.pdf

50. "Semi-annual Report to Congress," *OIG*, March 2018.

51. "Fiscal Year 2019 Management and Performance Challenges," *OIG Memorandum*, October 2018, https://www.fhfaoig.gov/sites/default/files/FY2019%20Management%20and%20Performance%20Challenges%20Facing%20FHFA_0.pdf.

52. "The Financial Crisis Inquiry Report - Vincent Reinhart Interview," *Financial Crisis Inquiry Commission*, updated February 2011. https://www.govinfo.gov/content/pkg/GPO-FCIC/pdf/GPO-FCIC.pdf.

53. Ibid.

54. "GINNIE MAE: Risk Management and Staffing-Related Challenges Need to Be Addressed," *U.S. Government Accountability Office, GAO-19-191 Report*, April 2019.

55. Knyazeva, Lin and Park, "Issuance Activity and Interconnectedness in the CMBS Market," U.S. Securities and Exchange Commission, August 2019.

56. Arleen Jacobius, "Investors embrace multifamily as demographic trends shift," Pensions & Investments, February 2018, pionline.com/article/20180205/PRINT/180209914 /investors-embrace-multifamily-as-demographic-trends-shift.

57. Julie Segal, "Large Investors Will Be the Most At Risk in the Next Bond Sell-Off," *Institutional Investor*, November 2018, institutionalinvestor.com/article /b1c0x7kq08z5fs/Large-Investors-Will-Be-the-Most-At-Risk-in-the-Next-Bond-Sell-Off.

58. Jacobius, "Investors embrace multifamily as demographic trends shift," *Pensions & Investments*, February 2018.

59. William D. Cohan, "How Wall Street's Bankers Stayed Out of Jail," *The Atlantic*, September 2015, theatlantic.com/magazine/archive/2015/09/how-wall-streets-bankers-stayed-out-of-jail/399368/.

60. Jon Hilsenrath, Serena Ng and Damian Paletta, "Worst Crisis Since '30s, With No End In Sight," The Wall Street Journal, September 2008, wsj.com/articles /SB122169431617549947.

61. Tommy Andres, "Divided Decade: How the Financial Crisis Changed Housing," *Marketplace*, December 2018, marketplace.org/2018/12/17/what-we-learned-housing/.

Chapter 10

1. Orwell, George, 1903-1950, *Animal Farm: A Fairy Story*. New York: The New American Library, 1946.

2. Martin Luther King, Jr., "I Have A Dream..." Archives.gov, copyright 1963, archives.gov/files/press/exhibits/dream-speech.pdf.

3. Nina Renata Aron, "In 1956, the Racist Governor of Mississippi started a Secretive Commission to Fight Integration," *Timeline*, September 2017, timeline.com/mississippi-state-sovereignty-commission-4450b7f056a3.

4. Maryanne Vollers, *Ghosts of Mississippi: The Murder of Medgar Evers, the Trials of Byron de la Beckwith, and the Haunting of the New South*. New York: Little, Brown & Company, 1995.

5. "Sovereignty Commission Records Show Owner of Black Newspaper Worked for Group," AP News, July 1989, apnews.com/2a4fd050a3da9757dd79536c94fe228f.

6. "The Mississippi State Sovereignty Commission," American RadioWorks, americanradioworks.publicradio.org/features/mississippi/d1.html.

7. Ibid.

8. N.R. Aron, "In 1956, the Racist Governor of Mississippi Started a Secretive Commission to Fight Integration," *Timeline*, September 2017.

9. Ibid.

10. "History of Fair Housing," HUD.gov, hud.gov/program_offices/fair_housing_equal_opp /aboutfheo/history.

11. Ibid.

12. Ibid.

13. "Go Deeper: Where Race Lives," PBS.org, pbs.org/race/000_About/002_06-godeeper.htm.

14. Ben Lane, "HUD Proposes Changes to Fair Housing Rules," HousingWire, August 2019, housingwire.com/articles/49873-hud-proposes-changes-to-fair-housing-rules/.

15. "Policy Statement on Discrimination in Lending," Federal Deposit Insurance Corporation, fdic.gov/regulations/laws/rules/5000-3860.html.

16. Chris Arnold, "A New Trump Rule Could Weaken A Civil Rights Era Housing Discrimination Law," *NPR*, July, 2019, https://www.npr.

org/2019/07/31/747006108/a-new-trump-rule-could-weaken-a-civil-rights-era-housing-discrimination-law.

17. "HUD's Implementation of the Fair Housing Act's Disparate Impact Standard," *Federal Register*, August 2019, federalregister.gov/documents/2019/08/19/2019-17542/huds-implementation-of-the-fair-housing-acts-disparate-impact-standard.

18. Kriston Capps, "How HUD Could Dismantle a Pillar of Civil Rights Law (CityLab)," Poverty and Race Research Action Council, August 2019, prrac.org/how-hud-could-dismantle-a-pillar-of-civil-rights-law-citylab/

19. Ibid.

20. Natalie Moore, "Federal Housing Agency Seeks to Raise the Bar in Discrimination Cases," NPR.org, October 2019, npr.org/local/309/2019/10/16/770611393/federal-housing-agency-seeks-to-raise-the-bar-in-discrimination-cases

21. Ibid.

22. "HUD's Implementation of the Fair Housing Act's Disparate Impact Standard," *Federal Register*, August 2019.

23. David Grusky and Clifton B. Parker, "Stanford Report Shows that the US Performs Poorly on Poverty and Inequality Measures," Stanford News, February 2016, stanford.edu/2016/02/02/poverty-report-grusky-020216/.

24. "The Case for Fair Housing 2017 Fair Housing Trends Report," National Fair Housing Alliance, April 2017, nationalfairhousing.org/wp-content/uploads/2017/04/TRENDS-REPORT-4-19-17-FINAL-2.pdf.

Chapter 11

1. Tom Borgers, "Financial Crisis Inquiry Commission is Biggest Financial Investigation Since 1930s' Pecora Commission," *ACFE (Association of Certified Fraud Examiners,)* November/December 2009, https://www.acfe.com/article.aspx?id=184.

2. "Face Dancer," *Dune Wiki*, accessed January 2020 https://dune.fandom.com/wiki/Face_Dancer

3. "PHH Corporation; PHH Mortgage Corporations; PHH Home Loans, LLC; Atrium Insurance Corporation; and Atrium Reinsurance Corporation v. Consumer Financial Protection Bureau," No. 15-1177, *AARP.org*, accessed January 2019, https://www.aarp.org/content/dam/aarp/aarp_foundation/litigation/pdf-beg-01-09-2013/PHH-v-CFPB.pdf.

4. "AG Paxton and 48 States Reach $45 Million Settlement with PHH Mortgage Corporation," *Texasattorneygeneral.gov*, January 2018, https://www.texasattorneygeneral.gov/news/releases/ag-paxton-and-48-states-reach-45-million-settlement-phh-mortgage-corporation.

5. "CFPB Director Cordray Issues Decision in PHH Administrative Enforcement Action," *Consumer Financial Protection Bureau*, June 2015, https://www.consumerfinance.gov/about-us/newsroom/cfpb-director-cordray-issues-decision-in-phh-administrative-enforcement-action/.

6. "CFPB Wins Final Judgment Against Morgan Drexen for Illegal Debt-Relief Scheme," *Consumer Financial Protection Bureau*, March 2016. https://www.consumerfinance.gov/about-us/newsroom/cfpb-wins-final-judgment-against-morgan-drexen-for-illegal-debt-relief-scheme/.

7. "Civil Minutes RE: Consumer Financial Protection Bureau v. Morgan Drexen, Inc. et al.," Case No. SACV 13-1267-JLS (JEMx), *US District Court Central District of California*, March, 2016, https://files.consumerfinance.gov/f/201603_cfpb_civil-minutes-regarding-the-final-judgment-against-defendant-morgan-drexen-inc.pdf.

8. "PHH Corporation v. Consumer Financial Protection Bureau," No. 15-1177, decided January, 31, 2018, (found on) *FindLaw.com*, accessed January 2020, https://caselaw.findlaw.com/us-dc-circuit/1887572.html.

9. Ibid.

10. Ibid

11. Tristan North, "Ruling Stands in PHH v. CFPB Mortgage Case," *Worldwide ERC*, May, 2018, https://www.worldwideerc.org/news/ruling-stands-in-phh-v-cfpb-mortgage-case/.

12. "*PHH Corp., et al. v. Consumer Financial Protection Bureau, No. 15-1177, (D.C. Cir. 2018) https://scholar.google.com/ scholarcase?case=13735252432428480002&q=phh+ corp+2018&hl=en&as_sdt=2006*

13. Kaplinsky, "CFPB's Constitutionality Again Before DC Circuit in Morgan Drexen Appeal," *Consumer Finance Monitor*, November 2014. https:// www.consumerfinancemonitor.com/2014/11/06/cfpbs-constitutionality-again-before-d-c-circuit-in-morgan-drexen-appeal/.

14. *John Doe Company v. Consumer Financial Protection Bureau and Richard Cordray, in his official capacity as Director of the Consumer Financial Protection Bureau*, (D.C. Cir. 2017), https://www.cadc.uscourts.gov/ internet/opinionsnsf/34AB1D4FFDC97DEF852580D80081FF4B/$file /17-5026-1664341.pdf.

15. Ibid.

16. Ibid.

17. *Seila Law LLC v. Consumer Financial Protection Bureau*, "On Petition for a Writ of Certiorari to the United States Court of Appeals for the Ninth Circuit," accessed January 2020, https://www.supremecourt. gov/DocketPDF/19/19-7/104482/20190628140628272_18-_ PetitionForAWritOfCertiorari.pdf.

18. "Kavanaugh Responses to Questions for the Record," *Committee on the Judiciary*, September 2018, https://www.judiciary.senate.gov/imo/media/doc/ Kavanaugh%20Responses%20to%20Questions%20for%20the%20Record. pdf.

19. Andrew Nolan and Caitlain Devereaux Lewis (coordinators), "Judge Brett M. Kavanaugh: His Jurisprudence and Potential Impact on the Supreme Court," *Congressional Research Service*, August, 2018, https://fas.org/sgp/ crs/misc/R45293.pdf.

20. Kirkland & Ellis, "About Kirkland," accessed January 2020, https://www. kirkland.com/content/about-kirkland.

21. Reis Thebault, "Trump nominee who is anti-IVF and surrogacy was deemed unqualified. She was just confirmed.," *The Washington Post*, December 2019, https://www.washingtonpost.com/politics/2019/12/04/trump-nominee-who-is-anti-ivf-surrogacy-was-deemed-unqualified-she-just-got-confirmed/.

22. Ian Millhiser, "What Trump has done to the courts, explained," *Vox*, updated December 2019, https://www.vox.com/policy-and-politics/2019/12/9/20962980/trump-supreme-court-federal-judges.

23. Jim Parker, "Nation's Largest Apartment Manager, based in Charleston, keeps Faith in Rental Industry," *The Post and Courier*, November 2016, https://www.postandcourier.com/business/real_estate/jim-parker/nation-s-largest-apartment-manager-based-in-charleston-keeps-faith/article_ b029213a-aeca-11e6-9e57-c7a5a12cea3b.html.

24. Paulina Dedaj, "Lindsey Graham certain Kavanaugh 'is going to be on the Supreme Court,' weighs in on status of Mueller probe," *Fox News*, September 2018, https://www.foxnews.com/politics/lindsey-graham-certain-kavanaugh-is-going-to-be-on-the-supreme-court-weighs-in-on-status-of-mueller-probe.

25. Jen Kirby, "Lindsey Graham rages in Kavanaugh hearing: "This is the most unethical sham,"" *Vox*, September 2018, https://www.vox. com/2018/9/27/17911604/kavanaugh-lindsey-graham-ford-hearings.

26. "American Liberty League," *Encyclopedia.com*, accessed August 2019, https://www.encyclopedia.com/history/dictionaries-thesauruses-pictures-and-press-releases/american-liberty-league.

27. Matt Taibbi, "How Wall Street Killed Financial Reform," *RollingStone*, May 2012, https://www.rollingstone.com/politics/politics-news/how-wall-street-killed-financial-reform-190802/.

28. American Bankers Association, "About Us," accessed January 2020, https://www.aba.com/about-us.
29. "Wall Street Money in Washington," *Americans for Financial Reform*, April 2019. https://ourfinancialsecurity.org/wp-content/uploads/2019/04/FINAL-Wall-Street-Money-in-Politics-2019.pdf.
30. Rob Nichols, "ABA Congratulates Kraninger on CFPB Nomination," American Bankers Association, June 2018, https://www.aba.com/about-us/press-room/press-releases/congratulates-kraninger-on-cfpb-nomination.
31. "Book Trump? Interest Groups Press Case at His Properties," *Voice of America*, February 2018. https://www.cbsnews.com/news/book-trump-interest-groups-press-case-at-his-properties/.
32. Ibid
33. "Bank's Non-Interest Income to Total Income for United States (DDEI03USA156NWDB)," Federal Reserve Bank of St. Louis Economic Research, updated October, 2019, https://fred.stlouisfed.org/series/DDEI03USA156NWDB.
34. "AG Paxton and 48 States Reach $45 Million Settlement with PHH Mortgage Corporation," *Texasattorneygeneral.gov*, January 2018.
35. The website for US Chamber of Commerce, "home page," accessed January 2020, https://www.uschamber.com.
36. Corynne Cirilli, "The US Chamber of Commerce Might Not Be What You Think," *Racked.com*, October 2017, https://www.racked.com/2017/10/2/16370014/us-chamber-commerce-explainer.
37. Ann Zimmerman, "Rival Chains Secretly Fund Opposition to Walmart," *The Wall Street Journal*, updated June 2010, https://www.wsj.com/articles/SB10001424052748704875604575280414218878150.
38. Josh Harkinson, "Fact-Checking the US Chamber of Commerce," *Mother Jones*, accessed January 2020, https://www.motherjones.com/politics/2010/01/fact-checking-chamber-commerce-tom-donohue/.
39. Corynne Cirilli, "The US Chamber of Commerce Might Not Be What You Think," *Racked.com*, October 2017, https://www.racked.com/2017/10/2/16370014/us-chamber-commerce-explainer.
40. Harkinson, "Fact-Checking the US Chamber of Commerce," *Mother Jones*, accessed January 2020.
41. Cirilli, "The US Chamber of Commerce Might Not Be What You Think," *Racked.com*, October 2017.
42. Tom Donohue entry on Polluter Watch, https://polluterwatch.org/tom-donohue.
43. Katrina vanden Heuvel, "Chamber of Commerce Backlash," *The Washington Post*, November 2010, https://www.washingtonpost.com/wp-dyn/content/article/2010/11/02/AR2010110203633.html.
44. "US Chamber of Commerce," found on *SourceWatch*, last edited December 2019, https://www.sourcewatch.org/index.php/U.S._Chamber_of_Commerce.
45. Alyssa Katz, *The Influence Machine: The US Chamber of Commerce and the Corporate Capture of American Life*, (New York: Spiegel & Grau, 2015, ISBN 9780812993288).
46. Dan Dudis, "The Chamber of Litigation, Part II," *Public* Citizen, March 2017, https://www.citizen.org/wp-content/uploads/chamber_litigation_report_part_ii.pdf.
47. National Association of Realtors, "About NAR," accessed January 2020, https://www.nar.realtor/about-nar.
48. "National Assn of Realtors," *OpenSecrets.org*, accessed January 2020, https://www.opensecrets.org/orgs/summary.php?id=d000000062&cycle=2012.
49. "The Meaning of Political Power," (modified from column by Richard Mendenhall, 2001 NAR President), *International Real Property Foundation*, accessed January 2020, https://www.nar.realtor/AMR.nsf/pages/Lobbying.
50. E.B. Solomont, "NAR vs. the Naysayers," *The Real Deal*, December 2018, https://therealdeal.com/issues_articles/nar-vs-the-naysayers/.
51. Alexandra Duszak, "Real Estate Influence Group Spends 'Mind Boggling' Amount in California House Race," *The Center for Public Integrity*,

updated May 2014, https://publicintegrity.org/federal-politics/real-estate-influence-group-spends-mind-boggling-amount-in-california-house-race/.

52. "From One Voice to Many: Despite Setbacks and Opposition, How a Growing Chorus Paved the Way to Fair Housing," *National Association of Realtors*, March 2018, https://www.nar.realtor/sites/default/files/documents/March-2018-Fair-Housing-3-9-2018.pdf.

53. Ibid.

54. Mary Szto, "Real Estate Agents as Agents of Social Change: Redlining, Reverse Redlining, and Greenlining," *Seattle Journal for Social Justice* Vol. 12: no. 1, Article 2 (2013): https://digitalcommons.law.seattleu.edu/cgi/viewcontent.cgi?article=1722&context=sjsj.

55. Ibid.

56. Charlotte Hill, "America's Lobbying System is Broken," Huffington Post, updated September 2017, https://www.huffpost.com/entry/americas-lobbying-system-is-broken_b_5938a0cfe4b014ae8c69dd90.

57. Taibbi, "How Wall Street Killed Financial Reform," *Rolling Stone*, May 2012.

Chapter 12

1. Author Charles J. Orlebeke is a Professor of Urban Planning and Public Affairs at the University of Illinois at Chicago. http://www.michaelcarliner.com/files/Orlebeke-HPD-2000-Evolution-of-LI-Housing-Policy.pdf

2. "Frederic C. Howe, Consumers' Counsel (Speech)," National Recovery Administration (NRA), Washington Conference On Public Housing, Willard Hotel, Washington D.C., January 27, 1934, New York, 728.1, W173, c.2.

3. David L. Bahnsen, "Did The Financial Crisis End?" *National Review*, March 2019, nationalreview.com/magazine/2019/03/25/did-the-financial-crisis-end/.

4. "NLIHC Gap 2019 Report Calls for Significant Investments to Address Shortage of 7 Million Affordable and Available Homes for the Lowest-Income Households," NLIHC.org, March 2019, nlihc.org/resource/nlihc-gap-2019-report-calls-significant-investments-address-shortage-7-million-affordable.

5. Michael Hobbs, "America's Housing Crisis Is A Ticking Time Bomb," Huffpost.com, June 2018, huffpost.com/entry/housing-crisis-inequality-harvard-report_n_5b27c1f1e4b056b2263c621e.

6. Buhayar and Deprez, "The Homeless Crisis Is Getting Worse in America's Richest Cities," Bloomberg BusinessWeek, November 2018

7. Dr. Isadow Lubin, Commissioner Bureau Labor Statistics, WASHINGTON CONFERENCE On PUBLIC HOUSING, Willard Hotel, Washington D. C. January 27, 1934, NATIONAL PUBLIC HOUSING CONFERENCE, 112 East 19th Street, New York, N.Y., 728.1, W173, c.2. Page 15)

8. Wheelock, "The Federal Response to Home Mortgage Distress" *Federal Reserve Bank of St. Louis Review*, May/June, 2008.

9. Peter Kaplan, "Press Release: FTC Chairman Joe Simons Announces the Planned Departure of Bureau of Competition Director Bruce Hoffman," Federal Trade Commission, October 2019, ftc.gov/news-events/press-releases/2019/10/ftc-chairman-joe-simons-announces-planned-departure-bureau.

10. "Originalism: A Primer On Scalia's Constitutional Philosophy," NPR, February 2016, npr.org/2016/02/14/466744465/originalism-a-primer-on-scalias-constitutional-philosophy.

11. Sophie McBain, "Who are the Federalist Society? Inside the right-wing group picking Trump's Supreme Court judges," *NewStatesman America*, September 2018, newstatesman.com/world/north-america/2018/09/who-are-federalist-society-inside-right-wing-group-picking-trump-s.

12. Hatch at Religious Freedom Symposium: "Religious Liberty Deserves Attention," Orrin G. Hatch Foundation, April 2019, orrinhatchfoundation. org/?s=federalist.

13. Gail Russell Chaddock, "A Judicial Think Tank—Or a Plot?," *The Christian Science Monitor*, August 2005, csmonitor.com/2005/0804/p01s01-uspo.html.

14. Amanda Hollis-Brusky and Calvin Terbeek, "The Federalist Society Says It's Not an Advocacy Organization. These Documents Show Otherwise," *Politico Magazine*, August 2019, politico.com/magazine/story/2019/08/31/ federalist-society-advocacy-group-227991?cid=apn.

15. "What Is The Federalist Society And How Does It Affect Supreme Court Picks?" NPR, June 2018, npr.org/2018/06/28/624416666/what-is-the-federalist-society-and-how-does-it-affect-supreme-court-picks.

16. Stone Washington, "Originalism: The Supreme Legacy of Judge Bork," Ellis Washington Report, December 2016, elliswashingtonreport. com/2016/12/21/originalism-the-supreme-legacy-of-judge-bork/

17. Dylan Matthews, " 'Antitrust was defined by Robert Bork. I cannot overstate his influence' " *Washington Post*, December 2012, washingtonpost.com/news/wonk /wp/2012/12/20/antitrust-was-defined-by-robert-bork-i-cannot-overstate-his-influence/.

18. Stone Washington, "Originalism: The Supreme Legacy of Judge Bork," Ellis Washington Report, December 2016.

19. Moss, Bolton and Kintgen, "The Pecora Hearings," December 2010.

20. Alan Brinkley, "When Washington Took On Wall Street," *Wall Street Financial Watch,* May 2010, wallstreetfinancialwatch.blogspot. com/2010/05/when-washington-took-on-wall-street-by.html.

21. Gilbert King, "The Man Who Busted the Banksters," Smithsonian.com, November 2011.

22. Moss, Bolton and Kintgen, "The Pecora Hearings," December 2010.

23. Gilbert King, "The Man Who Busted the Banksters," Smithsonian.com, November 2011.

24. Willie Francois, "More than 3.6 Million US Children Don't Have Affordable Health Care," Truthout.com, October 2018, truthout.org/ articles/more-than-3-6-million-us-children-dont-have-affordable-health-care/.

25. Bradley Sawyer and Cynthia Cox, "How Does Health Spending in the U.S. Compare to Other Countries," Petersen-Kaiser Health System Tracker, December 2018, healthsystemtracker.org/chart-collection/health-spending-u-s-compare-countries/#item-start.

26. Zack Friedman, "Student Loan Statistics in 2019: A $1.5 Trillion Crisis," Forbes.com, February 2019, forbes.com/sites/zackfriedman/2019/02/25/ student-loan-debt-statistics-2019/#d2096f5133fb.

27. Riley Griffin, "The Student Loan Debt Crisis is About to Get Worse," *Bloomberg Personal Finance*, October 2018, bloomberg.com/news/ articles/2018-10-17/the-student-loan-debt-crisis-is-about-to-get-worse

28. Nancy LeTourneau, "McConnell's Plan: Stack the Courts and Legislate From the Bench," *Washington Monthly*, July 2019, washingtonmonthly. com/2019/07/15 /mcconnells-plan-stack-the-courts-and-legislate-from-the-bench/.

29. "Press Release: Forbes 33rd Annual World's Billionaires Issue Reveals Number of Billionaires and Their Combined Wealth Have Decreased For the First Time Since 2016," Forbes.com, March 2019, forbes.com/sites/ forbespr/2019/03/05/press-release-forbes-33rd-annual-worlds-billionaires-issue-reveals-number-of-billionaires-and-their-combined-wealth-have-decreased-for-for-first-time-since-2016/#670a16b245b9.

30. Will Kenton, "Stock Market Crash of 1929," Investopedia.com, April 2018, investopedia.com/terms/s/stock-market-crash-1929.asp.

31. "The 1929 Stock Market Crash," EH.net, eh.net/encyclopedia/the-1929-stock-market-crash/

32. Tom Borgers, "Financial Crisis Inquiry Commission is Biggest Financial Investigation Since 1930s' Pecora Commission," *ACFE (Association of Certified Fraud Examiners,)* November/December 2009, https://www.acfe. com/article.aspx?id=184.

ACKNOWLEDGMENTS

Many thanks to Shanda, Chad, and my family and friends who inspired and assisted me. Also, to my agents and editors who helped me find my voice.

ABOUT THE AUTHOR

James Nelson is a former bank regulator and commercial real estate broker, and the author of the book *Stealing Home: How Artificial Intelligence Is Hijacking the American Dream*.

Employed in the US banking system for nearly 40 years, Mr. Nelson spent much his career financing Main Street America.

A Brigham Young University graduate with a degree in agricultural economics, Mr. Nelson began his career as a federal banking examiner, which led to valuable experience as Acting Chief Credit Officer while working on a project with the FDIC. He is currently a member of both the Nationwide Multistate Licensing System & Registry (NMLS) and the National Association of Realtors. He holds a 2012 National License to Issue Real Estate Broker Opinions of Value.

In the last decade, Mr. Nelson took his unmatched knowledge of commercial finance in nearly every industry and founded a boutique company specializing in commercial loan brokerage services, including the financing of large multifamily projects.

Nelson has worked and lived in many of the western states and is the father of four and grandfather of nine. In fact, his decision to author this work came out of his concern for their future.

Find more information at
WWW.JAMESMARTINNELSON.COM